ECONOMIC THEORY VS
ECONOMIC REALITY

ECONOMIC THEORY

VS

ECONOMIC REALITY

HELMUT ARNDT

Translated by
William A. Kirby

MICHIGAN STATE UNIVERSITY PRESS
1984

Copyright © 1984 Helmut Arndt

Library of Congress Cataloging in Publication Data

Arndt, Helmut, 1911–
   Economic theory vs economic reality.

   Translation of: Irrwege der politischen Ökonomie.
   1. Economics.   I. Title.
HB71.A7613   1984   330   83-60727
ISBN 0-87013-235-0

Manufactured in the United States of America

Published by Michigan State University Press,
East Lansing, Michigan

Produced and Distributed by Wayne State
University Press, Detroit, Michigan 48202

Contents

Preface to the American Edition   7
From the Preface to the German Edition   9
Introduction by Warren J. Samuels   11

Chapter 1   Exclusion of Scarcity from Economic Theory   17

Section 1: Dream of an Absolute Standard   17
Section 2: Use of Concepts Outside Economics   19
Section 3: Determining Supply and Demand by Cost
     and Utility   25
Section 4: Dogma of the Reproducibility of Economic
     Goods   35

Chapter 2   Abstraction from Space and Time   37

Section 1: Jevons's "Law of Indifference"   37
Section 2: "Perfect" and "Imperfect" Markets   38
Section 3: Market Structures Outside Space and
     Time   41
Section 4: Confusion of Models with Reality   46
Section 5: Transformation of Macroeconomic
     Processes   61

Chapter 3   Generalizations of Model Results   66

Section 1: Theory of Comparative Cost   66
Section 2: Wage Theories of Ricardo and Marx   68
Section 3: Theories of Malthus and Meadows   70
Section 4: John Maynard Keynes's General Theory   73

Chapter 4   Elimination of Human Beings from Economic Theory 85

Section 1: David Hume's Foreign Trade Mechanism   85
Section 2: Neoclassical Market Mechanisms   88
Section 3: Accelerator-Multiplier Mechanism   95
Section 4: Inflation-Employment Mechanism   104

Chapter 5   "Infinite" Values in Economic Theory   113

Section 1: Infinite Elasticity, Infinite Sales, and
     Unlimited Supply   113
Section 2: Influence of Sales and Output on "Market
     Structures"   119
Section 3: Infinity in Macroeconomics   129

6 • Contents

Chapter 6   The Elimination of Power   130

    Section 1. Market Power   131
    Section 2: Partner's Power   136
    Section 3: Other Types of Power   142
    Section 4: Temporary Power in Competition   145

Chapter 7   Interactions between the State and the Economy   148

    Section 1: Influence of the Economy on the State   148
    Section 2: Influence of the State on the Economy   149
    Section 3: Confusion of the Results of State
           Intervention with Natural Phenomena   150

Chapter 8   Logical Inconsistencies and Incorrect Observations   153

    Section 1: Logical Inconsistencies   153
    Section 2: Oversimplifications and Their
           Consequences   158
    Section 3: Transformation of Hypothetical
           Statements into "Absolute Truths"   163
    Section 4: Sham Proofs   167
    Section 5: Confusion of Concepts   170
    Section 6: Arbitrary Choice of Premises   175

Chapter 9   From Metaeconomics to Economic Science   180

    Section 1: Balance   180
    Section 2: Solution of the Dilemma   184

    Notes   188

    Index of Names   207

Preface to the American Edition

This American edition is based on a fully revised text of the original German edition of 1979. Publication of this edition would not have been possible without the help and advice of a number of individuals, including Gilles Y. Bertin, Mary A. Holman, Charles P. Kindleberger, Alec Nove, François Perroux, Willis Peterson, Joan Robinson, G. L. S. Shackle, Clem Tisdell, and Melville J. Ulmer. In particular, I thank Walter Adams and Joe B. Dirlam for their suggestions, comments, and criticisms.

This book is primarily concerned with a critical discussion of the theorems presented in many textbooks, in both the West and the East, as unassailable truths, although such theorems may be based on oversimplifications or incorrect generalizations. It also aims to demonstrate approaches leading to a theory which is closer to reality and which would enable the creation of an economic policy more capable of adapting itself to changing historical conditions.

It is not the task of this analysis to provide a general survey of the current position of economic theory as it is presented in monographs or essays. This would be beyond the scope of the book, as would a history of the dogmas which treated all the various approaches equally, even though it will be necessary in certain cases to follow "false trails" back to their origins.

Helmut Arndt

Berlin, November 1983.

From the Preface to the German Edition

> The most widely-held opinions and the things which everyone considers to be certainties are often the things which most deserve investigation.
>
> G. Ch. Lichtenberg

This book asks the following questions: Does economic theory as presented in most textbooks and treatises, correspond to the reality which it is supposed to explain? Or have generalizations, oversimplifications, and the search for absolutes turned political economy into a metaeconomy, comparable to metaphysic, which has become independent of real problems?

Has the tendency of economists to generalize the conclusions which they have drawn from the models or from the experience of their time not repeatedly led to serious errors, errors which also effect the present? Has the tendency to oversimplify not bypassed the problems of the real economy and led to the emergence of unreal model worlds, in which "pleasure machines" instead of human beings and "mechanisms" instead of economic activity are the most important features? And, finally, has the inclination to express everything in absolute terms not favored the emergence of scientifically untenable ideologies which to this day enjoy an undeserved worldwide political currency?

If a theory prefers to use models in which the economy moves from equilibrium to equilibrium, if competition is defined as "perfect," if customers cannot influence either the prices or the qualities of products, if the demand and the sales of a firm are confused with each other, and if—to take a final example—the problems of employment are primarily considered from the viewpoint of a static closed economy, even though both economic development and foreign trade are of fundamental importance, it becomes necessary to take a long, hard look at the theoretical structure which claims to be universally valid.

This book is an attempt to bring about a reconsideration of the analysis of real economic problems. Sometimes it is necessary to question the very things which the experts—to use Lichtenberg's expression—consider to be "certainties".

Helmut Arndt

Berlin, October 1978

Introduction

Warren J. Samuels

From the beginnings of its self-conscious existence as an intellectual discipline in the late eighteenth and early nineteenth centuries, economics has been full of controversy. There has been disagreement, often heated, in every field of economic thought. Economists who agreed thoroughly on certain points conflicted, often deeply and irreconcilably, on others. Heterogeneity of belief and practice, both between and within schools of thought, long has characterized the discipline. To some this is a strength, a sign of viable inquiry; to others, a lamentable malady.

In recent decades there have been critiques of the neoclassical mainstream by post-Keynesian, neo-Ricardian (Cambridge, England), Marxist, and (neo-)institutionalist economists. There also have been numerous wide-ranging and powerful criticisms of mainstream theory and practice emanating from within the ranks of leading, hitherto quite orthodox, economists, often theorists themselves. These critiques have addressed the practices of theory and of empiricism, the professional socialization process and the products of graduate programs, and the application of economic analysis to policy.

Professor Helmut Arndt's wide-ranging critique of theory and practice must be seen in this "traditional" context of criticism. This book *is* first and foremost a work of criticism. Although it has its author's prescription for remedying the ills which he diagnoses, the great bulk of the work is unabashedly critical. It is a critique of economics as the discipline is practiced not only by mainstream neoclassicists but also by most other schools of economic thought, especially classical, Marxian, and Keynesian (and post-Keynesian), including both Western and Eastern economists, albeit especially the former.

Not every reader will be equally receptive to each criticism. No one reader likely will accept all. I, for one, do not fully agree with every point or characterization drawn by Arndt. But most, if not all, criticisms convey insights and an overall reasonable approach or interpretation worthy of extended and effective consideration.

11

Some of his criticisms are not wholly new, but many of these are presented in striking and pointed fashion. Altogether, they comprise a powerful critique, in part because of the unquestionable analytic and methodological depth of the argument.

One can more or less readily find examples in the literature which seem to contradict Arndt at various points; practice is not always exactly as he portrays it. There are writers who do not (or do not fully or always) commit the errors of conceptualization or execution which Arndt identifies. There *are* sophisticated versions of ideas and techniques with which to attempt to rebut criticism of the vulgar forms of belief and practice. But that is largely (albeit not completely) beside the point, for two reasons. First, the unsophisticated, if not vulgar, practice of economics, in the manner shown or suggested by Arndt, is very much the general condition of the discipline. Second, even the sophisticated versions have severe substantive and methodological limits which are not fully, or widely, appreciated in the discipline. All in all, economic thought and practice would be very different, and would be taught very differently, if Arndt's criticisms were constructively and effectively met.

Arndt raises fundamental questions as to the meaningfulness, limits, and descriptive, explanatory, and heuristic value of certain ideas, models, theories, and chains of reasoning. Arndt suggests qualifications of standard usages. Many of these qualifications run significantly counter to analytical, conceptual, and interpretive conventions current in economics. Some economists will seek to defend status quo practice and to modify, if not fully to rebut, Arndt's proposed qualifications. Any such necessary modifications should not be allowed to obscure or finesse the significance of his criticisms of received theory and practice. Arndt is severe, but in response one ought not to discount too readily because of that severity. The issue should not be the consonance of his criticisms with the conventions of belief and practice but the descriptive and heuristic value of belief and practice. To the reply that the conventional is useful, the responses are that the conventional may be severely constrained if not wrong, and that there is no reason not also to have other practice, even if contradictory with convention. For the latter situation to exist, however, economists would have to overcome their very human propensity toward exclusivism and tolerate, if not relish, variety.

This latter point anticipates the gravamen of Arndt's prescription. The power of Arndt's critique lies in the details of his examples, which are from every major area of economic thought and which have to be read with an open mind to be fully understood and appreciated. Running through the individual examples and the book as a whole, however, is a powerful and complex argument. It is not easily summaried in a few words, but its principal themes can be identified.

First, economic theory is dominated by an absolutist and deterministic mode of analysis. Although fundamental concepts, such as scarcity, are seen as intrinsically relativist; although economic laws are widely understood to be statements of tendency and therefore relativist; and although economic reality is understood to be characterized by the mutual determination of a multiplicity of variables, nonetheless standard practice long has been unreflective of these conditions. Economists have sought absolutes: absolute values, absolute answers. They have been induced to do so for several reasons, not the least of which is the belief that "scientific" work involves, indeed requires, deterministic analysis and results. All this has been exacerbated by another form of absolutism, in the nature of exclusivism, which has ruled the unconventional out of analytic bounds.

Second, this has been a concentration on equilibrium conditions which has neglected several arguably more important features of economic life: the processes of determination and adjustment, especially those which provide the actual substance economists treat, often and largely only formally; the consequences of space and time differences; the actual processes of choice at work in the economy, including the factors governing preferences; the organization, operation, and evolution of markets; the people with respect to whom scarcity exists; and so on.

Third, there has been a narrowness and stylization of theory. (The usual phrase is stylized facts, but these are predicted upon, give effect to, and reinforce stylized theory.) Although causation often is acknowledged in passing to be complex, economic analysis typically has a narrow focus on monocausation and singledirection causation. Conclusions drawn from specialized assumptions or from the consideration of certain variables or relationships often are generalized to cover a topic as a whole. Single governing factors (often themselves actually determined variables) are identified with the results of analysis to the neglect if not complete disregard of other governing factors. Experience relating only to a temporary historical situation often is generalized as universal. Formal statements are treated as if they had uniquely deterministic content. All in all, theorizing tends to focus on a number of traditionally accepted and understood variables and to treat them in limited, conventional ways, which renders nugatory the breadth, diversity, and complexities of the real world.

Fourth, in addition to incorrect observations and oversimplifications, there are manifest logical inconsistencies and other dubious practices which severely restrict the putative value of analysis. For example, formalization reifies aspects of reality and transforms hypothetical statements into absolute truths functioning to obscure the substantive robustness and relativism of real life.

Fifth, through the elimination or demotion of the processes of adjustment and thereby of human beings from economic theory, economists have severely neglected human choice, expectations, experience, learning historical circumstances and opportunities, and power. Here Arndt stresses at least two things. The first is the profound influence of expectations, changing expectations, and the reassessments on which changing expectations are based on the so-called real economic causes and categories. By using absolutist, deterministic, formalistic and reified categories, the role of expectations, indeed the general problems of uncertainty and choice, is largely omitted. (It is not a conclusive rebuttal of this point that leading economists in many areas have been struggling to incorporate uncertainty into economic analysis; the main corpus of theory has been largely unaffected as yet.)

The second is that mechanistic determinism either eliminates or obscures the practice and the effects of power *qua* power. Here Arndt's analysis is manifold. Competition is traditionally defined in a manner which rules out competitive behavior (a point made by F. A. von Hayek, for example). The purely competitive firm is defined in such a way as to omit entrepreneurial managerial behavior. The decisional scope of entrepreneurs and managers under both competition and monopoly is neglected. The many sources and forms of power also are neglected. The assumption of given demand and supply curves both obscures the reality and precludes the analysis of the exercise of power entering into their determination. (Institutional economists, generally not treated by

Arndt, in particular have made this point.) Complex power relationships exist largely beyond the formal or substantive reach of neoclassical economics. Power within the market is neglected, as is power beyond the market, as within corporations and in social relationships.

To Arndt it is obvious that neglect of adjustment processes and of choice has meant the almost total disregard of the realities of power, power structure, and power play. Even models which attempt to incorporate elements of power do so in an antiseptic, unreal fashion, abetted by the deterministic mode of analysis in which the power player *qua* player tends to be absent. Correlative to this neglect of power, says Arndt, is a failure to take full and effective cognizance of the interactions between state and economy. The economy is analyzed as if it were a self-contained and self-governing system, with the positive and normative conclusions of analysis being tautological with that paradigm (and with the implicit selective normative premises which enable ostensible "optimal" solutions). But doing so neglects the influence of economy on state and of state on economy, and the power of the state and of those in a position to control the state in its influence on economic affairs; if this is recognized, it is treated as aberrational and economically unsound. This neglect of adjustment processes, choice, expectations, power, the state, and so on, reflects the dominance not only of an absolutist deterministic mode of theorizing but also the conduct of analysis in a discourse of commodities rather than of human beings with the capacity to choose, with expectations, living within social relations, and engaged in power play.

Arndt's critique amounts to much more than the charge of incompleteness and the limits of abstraction. He challenges many of the fundamental characteristics of the paradigm and practice of economics in *all* schools. His argument is congruent with efforts to reform economic theory (in all schools) along behavioral, expectational, uncertainty, and problematic (in contrast to deterministic) lines, efforts which he does not seem fully to acknowledge but which have not (yet) had a profound effect on established economic theory.

As is often the case with profound and powerful critiques, the accompanying prescription may not appear to be sufficient. In the case of Arndt's, however, the proposal is pregnant with remedial possibilities. Arndt calls for less metaeconomics, less intrusion of a particular paradigm and of particular implicit theorizing; less replication of the procedures of the physical sciences; and, especially, less use of stylized theory. Arndt's prescription suggests the possibility that the controversy, *pace* Milton Friedman, over predictive power versus realism of assumptions has finessed effective challenge to the stylized theorizing of mainstream economics so that certain problems, and not others, and certain models, and not others, have been maintained intact. Arndt argues that we ought not to adhere to one absolute, stylized, and oversimplified model; that we ought to vary our premises and our models; and, especially, that we ought to permit a larger number of problems and of variables to be analyzed, and to be analyzed in various ways, not only the conventional few in the conventional way.

Economists must recognize, as Tjalling C. Koopmans has acknowledged, that the traditional model of competitive equilibrium is only "a fully worked out special case" which has ignored "many aspects of reality," such that economics can and should support "new approaches embodying other aspects of reality," accompanied by a "general and critical discussion of the choice of problems to be examined in economic theory."[1] There is no reason why the conventions of the stylized theory(ies) of economics must be taken as surrogates for reality. "Rigor," as Koopmans says, "has no hold on this question."[2] Economics has dealt (however unsatisfactorily) with the *relatively* easy questions. Arndt is telling us that now it is time to deal with the harder ones, and the way to do that is to open up economic theory in such mattters as the choice of problem, choice of variables, choice of models, choice of methodology, and so on.

Economics should be more than neoclassicism (or Marxism, for that matter), *and* other schools should not be slavish followers of neoclassical practice. If I understand Koopmans correctly, he is suggesting that neoclassicism, and economics generally, will prosper by becoming more eclectic and open. Arndt's critique, specific examples, and prescription help point the way. Economics might lose some of its capacity to set minds at rest, and thereby its ideological quality (including certain "safe" implications of welfare economics), but it would be more robust, more truly scientific, and the truer product of the Enlightenment whence it originated.

CHAPTER 1

Exclusion of Scarcity from Economic Theory

> You are right to question the classical principles. All principles should be subjected to the closest examination with respect to both logic and factual relevance.
>
> Paul A. Samuelson

Scarcity is the Cinderella of economic theory. While there is not one school of economic thought that does not allude to scarcity as a basic element in economics, there is almost no economic theory which does not put scarcity aside as a disturbing factor, especially *scarcity which changes in space and time.*[1] This has been attempted in several ways:

1. through the assumption of absolute values, which are concealed behind real phenomena,
2. through the choice of concepts outside economics, which hide the real problems in economics,
3. through the assumption of equilibria, in which supply is determined by costs and demand by utility,
4. through a definition of the economic good, which declares that the only economically relevant goods are those which are not "rare" and "can be increased by the exertion of human industry."

SECTION 1: Dream of an Absolute Standard

> The purpose of this section is to go behind the market demand curve.
>
> Milton Friedman

> Have these prisoners . . . ever had anything else to see apart from the shadows thrown by the fire onto the wall in front of them?
>
> Plato

As prisoners in a cave only see shadows which penetrate into their prison from outside, man—according to Plato[2]—only sees shadowy and fleeting images of "real" things.

The longing for an absolute which is concealed behind the phenomena accessible to us alone is, in the sciences, particularly unique to economists and has lasted from Adam Smith right up to the present. To discover the principles which determine the true value of goods, Adam Smith posed two questions: (1) What is the true standard for economic values? (2) Why do market prices deviate from the "natural prices" which they gravitate toward?

Smith makes a distinction (surviving to this very day in economic theory) between the true value and market prices which fluctuate in space and time. The true value is concealed behind the market prices, which alone are visible.

For Smith,[3] as later for Ricardo[4] or Marx,[5] the absolute standard was analogous to labor. The "value of a commodity," according to Smith, "is precisely equal to the quantity of labor which it can enable them to purchase or command."[6]

However, the absolute standard for which Smith was searching does not exist in a world in which everything is made relative by changes occurring in space and time. In a developing world, neither the quantity nor the quality of the labor in a good remains constant. As labor productivity rises (and the quality of raw materials improves), the average quantity of labor required for the manufacture of a product falls. At the same time if laws which prohibit workers' associations are no longer in existence—the real hourly wage rises from one period to another due to the presence of strong, independent trade unions, and that wage can be increased if and when labor productivity rises due to the use of machinery.

Values and value relationships[7] do not remain constant in space and time, any more than the products and the markets on which they are exchanged:

1. The valuation of labor varies not only from country to country, but also over the course of time.
2. The valuation of goods varies according to their scarcity. Goods which have become scarce, such as oil, increase in value.
3. Goods change over time. Many goods and markets which

existed in Smith's and Ricardo's day have disappeared, to
be replaced by others.
4. Even when the goods have not changed, they are not produced in the same way today as in Smith's day.

Economic values independent of space and time do not exist,
just as the "thing in itself" which metaphysicists have searched
for outside the material world does not exist. There is no such
thing as Adam Smith's "natural price;" the market price of goods
or services is determined by *scarcity which varies in space and time,
and which is expressed in the relationship of supply and demand at any
given time*. Prices and wages, if they are not laid down by the state
as in the Soviet Union, for example, are the result of valuations by
society, which are continually changing in space and time. Every
new good, every improvement to an existing good, every appreciable change in the relationships of scarcity, and every change in
taste and fashion is inevitably bound up with changes in value
relationships and therefore with revaluations. There are no absolute values in economics, just as there are none in politics.[8]

The view "behind the market demand curve" (Milton Friedman) is closed to human understanding. The "thing in itself"
which is supposedly concealed behind the visible phenomena is,
as Immanuel Kant taught, a transcendental concept,[9] about which
it is "impossible"[10] to say anything.

The attempt to comprehend the incomprehensible, to create an
absolute standard in economics, and to look behind the market
prices, which are determined by the relationship between supply
and demand at any given time, was a false trail. The fact that
many economists—not only David Ricardo, Karl Marx, and their
followers—have largely compounded this error and are still doing so does not make this statement any less true.

SECTION 2:   Use of Concepts Outside Economics

> A unit of pleasure-intensity during a unit of time
> is to "count for one."
>
> F. Y. Edgeworth

Any scientific discipline that is aware of the individuality of its
object of analysis uses specific concepts that correspond to that
particular field. Chemists use chemical concepts, physicists use

physical, and lawyers use legal. Economists, however, are less sure of their object of analysis. Economic theory uses concepts that have their origins in other disciplines: "pleasure" as a measure of the satisfaction of physical needs, or "return," which measures production in units, kilograms, liters, or other physical quantities.[11]

§1 Natural pleasure: the confusing of physical and economic utility

> By utility is meant that property in any object, whereby it tends to produce benefit, advantage, pleasure, good, or happiness.
>
> Jeremy Bentham

Gossen, whose ludicrous ideas still form the basis of many economic textbooks, investigates the "pleasure" derived from the consumption of goods over a period of time. According to his "law of satiation," the pleasure obtained from a good decreases with increasing satiation. According to his "pleasure equilibrium law," the total pleasure of a man who does not have enough time (!) to satisfy all his needs completely is at its maximum when he divides up his time to obtain an equal amount of pleasure for each need.

None of Gossen's laws has an economic component, despite the significance given to those laws by the marginal utility school. Scarcity of time is not the same as scarcity of goods. Gossen's goods have (as yet) no price, and his consumers have (as yet) no income. It is only *time* which determines the extent of satisfaction of physical needs. It is of no importance whether the quantity of goods on the market is large or small. According to Gossen, neither the scarcity of goods nor the limits to financial means are important; goods are given; needs, which are assumed to be constant, and the time available to satisfy them are all that matter. His consumers are like children standing before a table loaded with gifts at Christmas, not like householders who have to manage with scarce finances.

Jevons, who refers to Gossen in the second edition of his *Theory of Political Economy*, draws on Bentham and defines *utility* as "the abstract quality" of a good to "produce pleasure or prevent pain," without taking into account that "utility" and "pain" in Bentham's sense are noneconomic concepts.[12] "Utility" or "pain" can also be caused by things such as air, wind, water, or fire.

The "want curves" which Walras uses in his equations are also physical rather than economic in origin. He also overlooks the fact (in the same way as Gossen, whom he refers to in later editions) that economic utility, unlike natural or physical utility, is determined by prices, and therefore even at this point represents a relationship between "pleasure" and scarcity: consumers, if they behave economically enjoy commodities in relation to the prices they have paid for them.[13] It is true, however, that Walras, as well as Marshall and his followers, have operated with prices and income, but none of them has worked out the decisive difference between (natural) pleasure and (economic) utility. "Utility" in the sense of the marginal utility school is an individual phenomenon. Scarcity, which is immanent in "economic utility," is a social phenomenon: *Scarcity is the result of the evaluation of goods by society.*

Edgeworth, who introduced "indifference curves" into economic theory, also values goods not according to their scarcity, but according to the pleasure which they afford to an individual (like Jevons, he calls this quality of a good "utility"). For him, it is not resources that determine the extent of "happiness," but the "capacity for pleasure." In his *Mathematical Psychics,* where he develops the "line of indifference," he writes on page 77: " . . . The privilege of man above brute, of civilized above savage, of birth, of talent, and of male sex has a ground of utilitarism in supposed differences of capacity for pleasure . . . the aristocracy of sex is similarly grounded upon the supposed superior capacity of the man for happiness."[14] Edgeworth's "capacity for pleasure" and his "curves of indifferent happiness" have nothing to do which economic problems. In his system, as in Gossen's or Bentham's world, different degrees of scarcity are nonexistent.

Pareto, like Gossen, assumes "given needs," given goods, and the "pleasure" produced by these goods: "Take a man who allows himself to be governed only by his tastes and who possesses 1 kilogram of bread and 1 kilogram of wine. His tastes being given, he is willing to obtain a little less bread and a little more wine, or vice versa. For example, he consents to having only 0.9 kilograms of bread provided he has 1.2 of wine. In other terms, this signifies that these two combinations, 1 kilogram of bread and 1 kilogram of wine or 0.9 kilograms of bread and 1.2 kilograms of wine, are equal for him; he does not prefer the second to the first, nor the first to the second; he would not know which to choose; possessing the one or the other of these combinations is indifferent to him."[15] Whether bread is more expensive than wine or wine more expensive than bread is irrelevant to this act of choice, "his tastes" being the only deciding factor. In Pareto's "acts of choice," prices and price relationships play no part, nor do incomes or other financial resources. In fact, this has not always been taken into account by his followers, as will be shown later on. Whether wine is scarcer than bread or bread scarcer than wine is totally irrelevant to this act of choice. It is determined purely and simply by the pleasure afforded by these goods, and this pleasure is not an economic but a physical quantity.

Pareto, like Gossen, Jevons, or Edgeworth, has thus implicitly assumed *free goods,* i.e., goods which are not scarce and therefore do not have a price. His individuals live in a world in which everyone, as in utopian socialism, can take as much of what is available as he wants. As in the model of a communist society in which there are neither prices nor different price relationships, it is purely needs—and therefore the physical pleasure which the consumption of a good affords—which determine consumption. Pareto's consumers, like Gossen's individuals, are like children before a table loaded with gifts. Like three or four-year-old children who cannot yet read, write, or add, they do not know what these gifts cost in the store, and like children they do not yet relate the pleasure afforded by goods to their prices. Like Thomas More's communist Utopia, the model world of Gossen, Jevons, Edgeworth, and Pareto is noneconomic in nature; *different degrees of scarcity have no place in it.*

The marginal utility school has confused the physical utility of a good with its economic utility. The concept of a utility which is purely and simply derived from needs and the economic concept of utility which is related to scarcity are two very different phenomena. The utility of free goods, which is in the mind of the marginal utility school, depends solely on needs. The economic utility of goods which are traded on markets is determined by scarcity. The terminology used by the marginal utility school therefore shows itself, despite the misleading use of the word "utility," to be unsuitable for determining economic facts.

§2 The "law of diminishing returns"

> This law is in accordance with common sense
> and has been known in at least a vague way
> since the beginning of recorded history.
> Paul A. Samuelson

The law of diminishing returns, which even today is seen by many economists as a "technological-economic relationship" (Samuelson), does not operate with economic quantities either. Turgot, in his law of diminishing returns, links natural output, which can be measured in units, kilograms, or liters, to other physical units, namely working hours.

If land, technology, and the quality of labor are constant (as Turgot assumes), the (physical) marginal return will decline beyond the so-called "operational optimum." Although natural total output, measured in units, kilograms, or liters, continues to increase in the area beyond optimum production, the (natural) marginal return, i.e., the increase in output in units, kilograms, or liters per additional working hour declines.

However, there are no economic quantities in Turgot's law of diminishing returns. Natural output as well as marginal returns are not evaluated by the market. Incomes and prices are still irrelevant. His law is therefore not a law of economics, even if it produces economic effects, but a technological law, although generations of economists have considered the law of diminishing returns to be a major constituent of economic theory, and still do so to this day.[16]

It is not physically measured output (which is Turgot's only concern), but revenue which is economically decisive and this revenue is dependent on two economic influences: (1) the quantity which can be sold on the market; (2) the value put upon the good by society and therefore its price. Even if output is high, the farmer's revenue is low if he can only obtain a low price and can only sell part of his crop. On the other hand, if output is low, the farmer receives a high revenue if he can sell his whole crop at a high price. *The extent to which revenue varies from output depends on the relationship between supply and demand at any given time, and therefore on scarcity.*

Because the law of diminishing returns is a noneconomic law, no cost curves can be derived from it. Costs cannot be calculated simply from the hours worked, without any knowledge of wages, prices, interest rates, taxes, depreciation, etc.[17]

Due to its purely technological nature, the law of diminishing returns cannot show whether a firm is making a profit or a loss, although there are not a few economists who appear to believe that it can. There are three reasons for this: (1) this law says nothing about the quantities which can be sold in the market. (2) It gives no indication of the prices obtainable for the quantities which can be sold on the market. (3) It has nothing to say about the level of costs, and therefore the scarcity of the production factors employed. This valuation process by underlying economic determinants is still not to be found in the law of diminishing returns.

§3   The so-called "paradox of value"

The same confusion of economic quantities with natural quantities becomes apparent with the contrast made by Adam Smith, as in later years by Proudhon and Marx, between the "value in use" of a commodity and its "value in exchange" (market value). For Proudhon, the confrontation of these two concepts resulted in a contradiction inherent in capitalism, because as the value in use increases (i.e., of goods which have a value in use), the value in exchange decreases. However, the concepts of value in use and value in exchange belong to different scientific disciplines.

The value in use of a good derives from its natural characteristics. The natural value in use of air or water is high, since no one can live without air or water.

The value in exchange of a good is a consequence of its economic evaluation on the market, its level being determined not by its natural qualities but by the relationship of supply and demand, and therefore by scarcity, which changes in space and time.

It is therefore no contradiction if the value put upon a good by the market is lower the less it is in demand or the more it is available. *It is not* (primarily) *the natural characteristics of a good which are economically relevant, but the value put upon it by society.*

The production of surplus "utility goods" creates no economic value, despite the costs involved in their production. If a country produces goods which no one wants, it is just a senseless waste of production factors. The wealth of a country is not increased (but decreased) if goods are produced for which there is no demand.

Economists such as Smith, Proudhon, or Marx, therefore, confuse things in two ways: (1) The manufacture of products is confused with the production of economic value. However useful a good may be in itself, if it is manufactured in surplus its value in exchange falls below its costs and approaches zero. This statement is fundamental to the understanding of real economic problems; it shows that it is not the costs of production that determine the economic value of a good, but scarcity. (2) Natural characteristics are confused with economic values. Whether a good has valuable physical or biological characteristics is irrelevant in economic terms if society considers these natural characteristics unimportant. *It is consumers, not physicists or biologists, who decide the economic value of a good through the market.*

SECTION 3. Determining Supply and Demand by Cost and Utility

> *The conception of Man as a pleasure machine* may justify and facilitate the employment of mechanical terms and mathematical reasoning in social science.
>
> F. Y. Edgeworth

Current economic textbooks mainly assume that supply is determined by the costs of firms and demand by the utility of households. For example, Samuelson discusses production costs mainly under "supply" and consumption under "demand," as though supply and production or demand and consumption were simply two sides of the same coin.[18] However, the identification of supply with production or demand with consumption is wrong. It not only simplifies the object of analysis, it falsifies it. Other factors apart from cost and pleasure (utility) are important in economics.

§1 Cost theory

The theory that supply is determined exclusively or mainly by production costs is found in almost all relevant textbooks. However, this only applies if the following arbitrary assumptions are made:

1. All suppliers produce their goods themselves. There are no traders (e.g., chain stores), nor are goods (e.g., used cars) offered for sale by households.
2. The supply of a firm is determined by its marginal costs (or, more accurately, by its rising marginal cost curve).
3. The quantity produced is identical with the quantity sold. The market can always absorb the quantity produced; there are no sales problems.
4. Experiences[19] and expectations, which influence the size of the inventory, the level of orders, etc., are irrelevant; therefore, the quantity produced is always identical with the quantity offered for sale.

However, these assumptions, some of which are made implicitly, do not apply in reality:

1. The equating of the supplier with the manufacturer

The identification of the supplier of a good with its manufacturer is a false simplification. No trading organizations, such as chain stores or supermarkets, produce goods they sell; they purchase the items from other firms. Every store sells the goods that are in demand at high scarcity prices, while it gets rid of slow-moving lines or fashions after the end of the season at prices well below the purchase price.

2. The identification of the marginal cost curve with the supply curve

The rising course of the supply curve can only be derived from marginal costs in the case of so-called "perfect competition," even for firms which produce their goods under equilibrium conditions. In this hypothetical equilibrium, in which suppliers are nothing more than "quantity-adjusters" (Erich Schneider), the quantity offered for sale by a firm is determined by marginal costs. However, this does not apply to any other equilibrium situation. In the case of Cournot's monopoly, the supplier's price is located on its sales curve and this sales curve is falling. In the case of the "tangent solution," which according to Joan Robinson[20] and Edward H. Chamberlain[21] can occur in imperfect or monopolistic competition, the marginal costs are no longer relevant at all, because the sales curve has become a tangent to the average total cost curve, which in this area of diminishing individual costs also has a falling, not a rising, course.

Therefore, the rising course of the supply curve cannot be derived from costs even under equilibrium conditions, except in the case of so-called "perfect competition."

3. The influence of customers

In microeconomic equilibrium theory, the quantities produced are always identical with the quantities sold. This assumption however, is contradicted by reality. If customers and customers' preferences are involved, production and sales no longer necessarily coincide.

A firm produces more than it sells when it has to put a part of its output into inventory because of insufficient demand, perhaps due to the existence of a buyers' market or a recession.

On the other hand, a firms sells more than it produces if it can sell its total expected production for the next two years in the current year, as occurs, for example, in the automobile or engineering industry. In this case, the quantity offered for sale fluctuates largely independently of production and production costs.

The cause of this phenomenon is free consumer choice and the existence of customer preferences. Only when buyers have to buy what the supplier offers them do sales depend exclusively on the supplier.

4. Expectations

In an economy which operates in space and time, supply in economic terms is also influenced by expectations.

If firms expect prices and sales to rise appreciably in the near future, they hold back a portion of their goods in the hope that they will find a more favorable market for their goods in the future. (At the same time, buyers in this situation advance their purchases.)

If, on the other hand, firms expect prices and sales to fall appreciably in the near future, they push out goods which they would normally have kept in inventory. Buyers, on the other hand, postpone their purchases.

In both cases, supply is not determined by production, but by the expectations of entrepreneurs or managers. Prices in both cases do not depend principally on costs, but on the expected relationship of supply and demand, and therefore on scarcity. In both cases, the quantities sold on the market have nothing to do with cost curves, and are therefore not determined either by marginal costs or by average total costs.

5. The influence of scarcity on supply

Under conditions of competition, the shape of (short-term) supply curves is not primarily determined by costs, but by scarcity. Supply curves do not slope upward to the right because they coincide with the rising part of the marginal cost curve, which in reality is not the case. Firms raise their prices when demand rises and their sales curves shift to the right. On the other hand, firms lower their prices when demand falls, and their sales curves shift to the left.

In the first case the degree of scarcity in the market rises; in the second case it falls.

The economists' centuries-old dream of reading off market prices from cost curves has therefore turned out to be cloud-cuckoo land. In reality, competitive prices are not solely determined by costs, but by scarcity at any given time. Neither in buyers' or sellers' markets is scarcity determined by costs.

§2   *Utility theory*

> To maximise comfort and pleasure, is the problem of Economy.
>
> W. Stanley Jevons

Almost all textbooks of economic theory equate the demand curve for products with the marginal utility curve of households. For this reason, the authors assume that:

1. Only households have a demand for products. Demand emanating from firms (if it is mentioned at all) is limited to factors of production (e.g., labor).[22]
2. Household demand is determined solely by the "pleasure" (Gossen) or "marginal utility" (Walras, Pareto, Jevons, Menger) which the consumption of a good affords. Pleasure is not related to the price to be paid for it either by Gossen or in the examples given by the founders of the marginal utility school. (The introduction of "budget lines" by later economists will be discussed in Chapter 8 in connection with logical inconsistencies).

3. Demand and consumption are identical. Demand for a good ends when the consumption of another good offers a higher degree of pleasure (Gossen's law of pleasure equalization).

However, none of these assumptions, some of which are made overtly and others implicitly, is borne out by reality:

1. "Marginal pleasure" and firms' demand

The assumption that only households have a demand for goods is in stark contrast to reality. In fact, firms buy more products than households do. Manufacturers need raw materials and semifinished products to manufacture their own products such as automobiles or TV sets. Retail firms, such as chain stores or supermarkets, buy finished products to sell to households. However, firms do not "enjoy" the goods; they are not consumers. An automobile manufacturer who buys tools and components (panels, spark plugs, tires) for his vehicles from 10-30,000 different suppliers is not guided by his "marginal pleasure" (or by the "marginal productivity" of his goods). Nor is a chain store that buys household goods from its suppliers. Neither Pareto's "act of choice theory" nor Gossen's laws are applicable to firms which have a demand for products. This reason alone makes the derivation of the demand for goods from utility and the identification of the marginal utility curve with the demand curve false. Firms, as well as households, have demand curves for commodities. Any enterprise buys and sells goods.

The erroneous identification of households' demand with demand for goods pure and simple is responsible for economists speaking of the "demand curve of a firm" when they in fact mean its *sales curve*. In reality, every firm buys products (raw materials, semifinished and finished goods) from its suppliers and sell its products to its customers. The equating of the demand curve of a household with the demand curve of a firm is a false simplification which has led to wrong conclusions, as will be shown later.

2. (Natural) pleasure and households' (economic) demand

Even households do not determine their demand according to their (natural) pleasure, in contrast to the assumptions of Gossen and the founders of the marginal utility school. Goods are not "given" to them; they must be *demanded on the market* before they can be "enjoyed," and the items and quantities demanded are determined by the prices of the goods and the financial resources of the households.

The demand curve of every household is related to the prices of the goods it wishes to buy and the extent of the financial resources available.[23] *Curves which relate to the (natural) pleasure afforded by the consumption of the last unit (marginal utility curves) and curves which measure the demand on markets (demand curves) are not identical,* although economists have failed to recognize this right up to the present day.

The (natural) pleasure afforded by consuming a Porsche, a large Mercedes, a Cadillac, or a Rolls-Royce is high. In economic reality, however, it is not just pleasure or the kind and the extent of needs which are relevant. Any kind of demand is also related to economic quantities: buyers estimate goods according to prices and income. The economic demand curve D for superior goods such as Porsches or champagne therefore lies well to the left of the (natural) marginal utility curve MU for these goods (Figures 1 and 2). On the other hand, the economic demand curve D for inferior goods such as small cars or cheap sparkling wine lies well to the right of the non-economic marginal utility curve MU, which is determined solely by "needs" (Figures 3 and 4). In both cases, the difference is determined by the different degree of economic scarcity, which both Gossen and the utility theorists have omitted from their laws. The consumption of free goods is determined by pleasure: in this case, everyone can be guided solely by his needs. *Demand for economic goods, on the other hand, is regulated by economic scarcity, and scarcity is not an individual but a social phenomenon.*

The fact that demand for economic goods and the pleasure afforded by them are not identical shows that indifference curve analysis is on the wrong track. Economic demand curves cannot be derived (solely) from physical utility. *The marginal utility school has mistakenly investigated the consumption of free goods instead of the demand for economic goods,* and most textbooks are still teaching this mistake today.

3. Consumption and demand

Consumption and demand are not identical because products are not only demanded by households but also by firms, and also

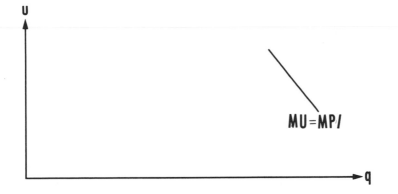

Fig. 1. MP*l* (marginal pleasure) = MU (marginal utility) of a superior good.

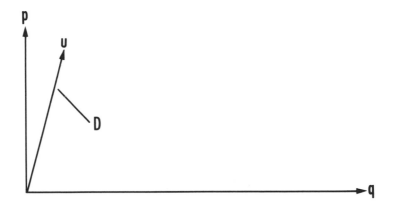

Fig. 2. Economic demand for a superior good (here "pleasure" is related to price and therefore to scarcity).[24] If people could choose the commodities which they consume solely on the basis of their needs and therefore on the basis of marginal pleasure (marginal utility), demand for large Porsches would be high (Figure 1). In fact, people have to act in acordance with prices and with their incomes, which means that relatively few people can demand a large Porsche. The physical marginal utility curve MU is replaced by the economic demand curve D, which lies well to the left of the marginal pleasure curve, because physical utility u is related to prices p (and therefore to scarcity), as Figure 2 shows. Needs are an individual phenomenon, and scarcity is a social phenomenon.

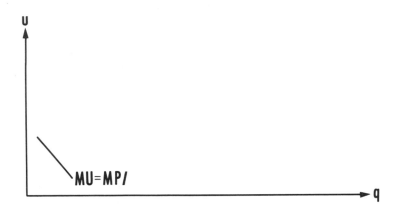

Fig. 3. MP*l* (marginal pleasure) = MU (marginal utility) of an inferior good.

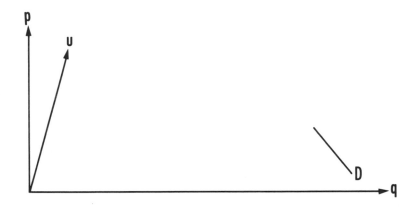

Fig. 4. Economic demand for an inferior good (here "pleasure" is related to price and therefore to scarcity). Inferior goods would only be consumed infrequently, or not even consumed at all, if pleasure were the only important factor. However, economic demand for inferior goods (e.g., small or used cars) depends not only on their pleasure, but on the prices to be paid and the incomes available. In place of the physical utility curve MU, shown in Figure 3, it is therefore the economic demand curve D which is important. It is economic scarcity which forces people to demand inferior goods, as shown in Figure 4, in which physical utility (pleasure) u is related to price p. The price indicates the social valuation of a good.

because even the households' demand develops, at least in many cases, independently of the actual rate of consumption. There are two main reasons for this: (1) the durability of manufactured goods, and (2) expectations, which influence the households' demand independently of the rate of consumption.

A tradition which dates back to the marginal utility school is to take as examples only those goods which can be consumed immediately and whose consumption can be stopped at any time (wine, bread, etc.). However, consumer durables such as autos, washing machines, dishwashers, color TVs, which are demanded in the present and consumed in the future, are far more important in a developed economy. Demand and consumption of these commodities take place at completely different times: an auto is bought in an hour but is consumed over several years.

The households' demand is, like firms' demand, not independent of expectations. Households bring forward their purchases, i.e., from the future to the present, when they expect prices to rise, and postpone their demand when they expect prices to fall. Employment security of workers plays a similar role for households as the expected sales developments for the purchasing decisions of firms. When expectations are negative, both the quantity and the quality of the goods demanded falls. It is not just a case of less goods being demanded; the type of goods demanded changes as well. Demand for inferior goods increases. The reverse happens when expectations are positive; the quantity of goods demanded increases, and demand shifts to superior goods. Neither the quantity nor the quality of demand is therefore independent of expectations.

If costs do not solely or even mainly determine supply, pleasure (utility) does not solely, or even mainly, determine demand: The theory of demand and the theory of consumption are not identical.

4. Real demand curves of households and firms

In contrast to the consumption of free goods, the demand for economic goods (commodities) is determined by scarcity.[25]

Households make their purchases in accordance with their limited financial resources. They have to budget (usually, at any rate) because the money they have available for making purchases is scarce. As a result of their scarce financial resources, they buy less or more of a good according to whether its price is high or low respectively.

Firms do not consume the goods which they demand, but process them or sell them elsewhere. Their demand, then, is determined by their sales, and therefore by the demand of their customers. The demand curves of firms slope downward to the right, because firms sell more of their products the cheaper they are, and their products can be cheaper the lower their purchase prices are.

Therefore, the description of the slope of supply and demand curves given by the marginal utility school and its supporters is correct, but the explanation is wrong. Their slope is not determined by costs or "utility," but by economic scarcity.

§3 Distortion of the facts by oversimplification.

The normal representation of supply and demand oversimplifies and also falsifies the facts:

1. Neither supply and production nor demand and consumption are identical.
2. Supply curves are not determined by marginal costs. Supply curves slope upward toward the right because suppliers raise their prices when scarcity increases and lower them when scarcity decreases. In reality, there is not a single supplier who acts in accordance with his marginal costs.
3. The normal equating of production with sales is just as wrong as the identification of production with supply. At times, firms sell more than they produce, and at other times produce more than they sell. Supply and sales are only identical if there is no consumer freedom and consumers have to buy what is on sale.
4. Products are not only demanded by households, but also, and to a much larger extent, by manufacturers and traders. Every auto demanded by a household incorporates the demand for thousands of primary products.
5. Demand for economic goods cannot be derived from Gossen's laws or from Edgeworth's indifference curves. Firms have no "marginal utility curves," and households do not act in accordance with them. *Only in the case of free goods can people act exclusively in accordance with their needs.*

6. Households' demand curves slope downward because households have only scarce financial resources, and therefore (assuming evaluations to be given) buy more of a good when it is cheaper and less when it is more expensive.
7. Firms' demand curves slope downward because the more of their own products they sell, the more products they need for their production (or their trading); the cheaper they can buy these products, the cheaper they can sell their own products.
8. A firm's demand and sales are two different things. Confusing them leads to wrong conclusions. Every firm has both demand *and* sales curves. It buys and sells products.
9. The economic value put upon a good is not a naturally fixed quantity; economic values are put upon goods by society and change in space and time.

SECTION 4: *Dogma of the Reproducibility of Economic Goods*

David Ricardo begins the first chapter of his *Principles* with the statement that "scarcity goods" such as "rare statues and pictures, scarce books and coins form a very small part of the mass of commodities daily exchanged in the market."[26] From this he concludes that they can be ignored, and defines as economic goods, like Marx in later years, only those goods which are not rare and which can be increased in quantity "by the exertion of human industry." However, a good becomes economically relevant not because it is reproducible, but because it is scarce. Antiques are also commodities and are traded on markets.

The theory of the reproducibility of economic goods reduces the problems of economics to a minimum. If all economic goods were reproducible at any time and in any place, trade loses its productivity (as Marx also logically concluded), and international trade largely loses its function of increasing the wealth of the nations. Not only foodstuffs such as bread and meat, but also raw materials such as oil and gasoline or chromium and manganese ores would be infinitely reproducible. According to this definition, goods such as oil, coal, or wood cannot become so scarce that they have to be replaced by other goods. Innovations would also be impossible, because both new consumer goods and new capital goods in the first period of their existence are by no means infinitely reproducible, but are in fact rare goods.

The rate of scarcity varies in space and time. Significant economic problems arise if essential goods become rare at certain times or in certain places. Just because valuable paintings and old coins are always scarcity goods does not mean that other goods, such as bread or meat, cannot temporarily become scarcity goods. If Ricardo's oversimplification were correct, there could be no shortages of rice from time to time in countries such as India or Pakistan, no shortages of winter gloves in Russia, and no shortages of meat or grain in South American countries.

The idea that economic goods are only those which can be increased in quantity by "the exertion of human industry" has led to numerous unproductive detours in economic theory, and also to disastrous mistakes in the real sociopolitical world.

In the real world in which we live, all economic goods without exception are governed by the law of scarcity which varies in space and time. *Goods become "commodities" in economic terms not because they are reproducible, but because they are scarce (and therefore relatively rare).* As a result, their economic value depends not on their cost of reproduction (Ricardo, Marx), but on their scarcity.[27]

CHAPTER **2**
Abstraction From Space and Time

It is untrue "that Pure Economy proves how facts follow in sequence; the opposite is true."
Vilfredo Pareto

Economic activity outside space and time is neither possible nor conceivable. Nevertheless, economists tend to work with models which operate outside space and time, although the use of such models in an empirical science inevitably leads to wrong conclusions.

SECTION 1: Jevons's "Law of Indifference"

The law of indifference . . . is but another name for the principle of competition which underlies the whole mechanism of society.
W. Stanley Jevons

It is quality which makes one existence different from another.
Georg Wilhelm Friedrich Hegel

In 1871 (the year in which the marginal utility school was born), William Stanley Jevons posed the question of what conditions prevail when only one price is applied to a market. When he answered this question by saying that this is the case "when a commodity is perfectly uniform or homogeneous in quality,"[1] he ignored space and time. The usual view today is that goods can be considered as "perfectly uniform or homogeneous" when there are no temporal, spatial, personal, or material differences between them.[2] (This definition is of course an overdefinition, because the absence of temporal or spatial differences already implies that no personal or qualitative difference exist.)

When goods are perfectly homogeneous, each purchaser is completely "indifferent" to the goods on sale on the market. The

37

market to which this law of indifference applies is called a "perfect market".[3]

However, the exclusion of space and time which occurs when a good is perfectly homogeneous also eliminates all economic problems resulting from scarcity. In a model world outside space and time there are not only no differences in goods or people but also (strictly speaking) no goods or people at all. Finally, in a world outside space and time there are no differences in prices for the simple reason that prices do not exist.

Even if it is assumed, however, as Jevons and other supporters of the marginal utility school do, that on a homogeneous "perfect market" a good is traded at a uniform price, (which is only possible if the assumption of "homogeneity" is not taken quite so seriously) the economic problems of our human world still turn out to have disappeared. If every good which is produced can also be sold, since production and sales, like demand and consumption, take place simultaneously, the only economic problem which still persists is that of distribution, and then only in the simplified form which permits an analysis of models of market structure on a perfect market. By this assumption, the real economic problems resulting from the scarcity of goods are eliminated.

SECTION 2: "Perfect" and "Imperfect" Markets

> One rather striking feature about such markets is the complete absence . . . of quality differences, quality variations, and hence of quality comparisons.
>
> Lawrence Abbott

How economic problems are eliminated by the analysis of such absolute equilibria becomes particularly clear when the theory of perfect and imperfect markets is considered.

§1 A uniform good at a uniform price

On a perfect market governed by the law of indifference there is according to Jevons, only one homogeneous product and one uniform price. Even ignoring the fact that in the absence of space and time there can be no goods and therefore no prices, it remains true that Jevons and his followers have not asked which functions a market has to fulfil in a society. *None of them has posed the question of what tasks a market has to perform in the interests of its users.* As to whether a market performs its economic functions in a society if a homogeneous product is traded on it at a uniform price, that question has been totally ignored by the supporters of the marginal utility school.

The concept of a *perfect market* had disastrous consequences for the future development of economic theory, for two reasons.

First, a market on which only a homogeneous good is offered for sale at a uniform price is useless from the point of view of the user. A weekly market on which only a single type of vegetable is offered for sale (and at only one point in time as well), or a market on which only one type of shoe can be purchased in only one color and in a single size can in no way satisfy the needs of society. A theory which considers this kind of market as perfect therefore fails in its task of analyzing the economic problems of the society.

Second, the model of a perfect market bears no relation to any kind of economic life. In such a "point market" (von Stackelberg) buyers' and sellers' markets on which prices are not determined by costs but by scarcity cannot exist. In a perfect market, neither overproduction nor underproduction is possible. Every good is produced and sold simultaneously. The definition of a perfect market also excludes the emergence of new markets (e.g., the automobile market around 1890 or the TV market around 1940/50) or the contraction of old markets (e.g., the movie theatre market and the movie production market between 1960 and 1970) and the disappearance of others (such as the market of horse-drawn carriages). In the unreal world of the perfect market, it is impossible to describe real economic problems resulting from variations and developments in supply and demand.

In reality, there is no market which is not fixed in space and time and to which differences are irrelevant. In the real world of economics which it is the economist's job to investigate, *every market is an imperfect market* in the sense of Jevons's law of indifference. On every real market, goods are traded which vary in size, design, and price, and thereby satisfy the different requirements of each customer.[4]

The perfect market which ignores all spatial and temporal differences is a transcendental concept. "Time," writes Immanuel Kant, "is a necessary concept on which all experience is based . . . It alone can reveal all the realities of the different phenomena."[5] The same, he adds, is true for space.[6]

§2 The "imperfect market": a meaningless concept

The concept of the imperfect market has been derived from the concept of the perfect market. Imperfect markets are therefore all those markets in which Jevons's law of indifference has been infringed in some way. Every market in which, as in the real world, spatial and temporal (and therefore qualitative and personal) differences play a part is imperfect. "It is now clear," writes von Stackelberg, "that every imperfect market can be thought of as being divided up into sub-markets in such a way that these sub-markets themselves must be considered as perfect markets. . . . Every imperfect market is composed of these sub-markets."[7] As the world of the Greeks was composed of atoms, so the microeconomic world is made up, as many economists see it, of perfect markets.

Nevertheless, this theory, however appealing it may seem on first sight, is untenable.

1. The concept of an imperfect market is only characterized by the negative quality of not being a perfect market. However, a real phenomenon cannot be defined in terms of the negation of a transcendental concept.

2. The concept of an imperfect market is just as meaningless as the unreal concept of a perfect market. There is not a single real market that is not imperfect for some reason or other. Imperfection is caused by every product variation and every customer preference as well as by any difference in space and time.

3. The concepts perfect and imperfect used by the marginal utility school have no economic connotation: they only suggest whether space and time exist or not.

4. The idea that perfect markets are the basic elements of which imperfect markets are composed is illogical. A perfect market exists outside space and time: it contains no temporal or spatial differences. Any imperfect market, however, like any real market, exists within space and time. *A phenomenon which exists in space and time cannot be composed of elements or atoms which are assumed to be found outside space and time.*

The idea that every imperfect market can be divided up into perfect markets is not only not clear (von Stackelberg); it is also simply wrong.

Although the marginal model of the perfect market cannot provide us with any economic knowledge, this has not deterred some economists from taking a further step into the realm of the unthinkable or, as Immanuel Kant says, the unimaginable. For example, Ott has postulated the theory that "given fixed quantities . . . the . . . solutions developed for oligopoly on a perfect market (Cournot, von Stackelberg, Bowley, etc.) can also be derived for oligopoly on an imperfect market."[8]

This is illogical for two reasons: (1) In reality there is not just one type of imperfect market. Every real market is imperfect. (2) The fact that there are no differences in space and time on a perfect market, while all imperfect markets are firmly fixed in space and time appears, according to this theory, to be of little relevance. By the same token, the proponents of Scholasticism could have postulated that the statement "an infinite number of angels can dance on the point of a pin" (because angels do not take up any space) could be applied to human beings without any further argument.

SECTION 3: Market Structures Outside Space and Time

> Greatest Happiness is the *end* of right action.
> Sidgewick

The market structures of the marginal utility school, with the addition of the equilibrium models of imperfect or monopolistic competition, still largely form the basis of textbooks on microeconomics, although the premises from which the results are derived are only rarely mentioned.

The authors can basically be divided into two groups. The first group at least mentions some of the premises from which the results are derived. The second group, which includes authors such as Samuelson and Erich Schneider, mostly state the results as absolute truths.

Only a few authors think it worth mentioning that these models of market structures are based, at least as far as their origins are concerned, on markets outside space and time. They are equilibria in an absolute sense.

§1 Perfect competition

Perfect competion, despite its misleading name, has nothing to do with competition. It is an absolute equilibrium on a perfect market, on which neither suppliers nor demanders can influence the price. The price is not only uniform, as required by Jevons's law of indifference, but is also a datum which suppliers and demanders must adjust to the quantities they supply or demand.

The firms of this model are "quantity-adjusters" (Erich Schneider)[9] whose only remaining entrepreneurial function is to vary the quantity (which is produced and sold simultaneously). As price and quality are "given," a supplier can practice neither price nor quality competition. There are no differences in payment or delivery terms, trustworthiness, fair trading, or reliability. Advertising is by definition impossible. New or improved products and new or cheaper production processes cannot be used as a means of competition. No firm can influence its situation by its policy. The amazing result of this is that the supporters of the marginal utility school give the name "perfect competition" to a situation in which any kind of competition is, as Friedrich A. Hayek has put it, "virtually impossible."[10]

§2 Homogeneous and absolute "monopoly"

Until the famous books by Joan Robinson and Edward H. Chamberlin appeared, economic theorists identified monopoly with Cournot's absolute, homogeneous monopoly, for which space and time are irrelevant. First of all, Cournot's monopoly is an (absolute) equilibrium: there is neither past nor future. Second, it is homogeneous: a uniform good is sold at a uniform price. Third, it is absolute: the monopolist has no substitution effect to take into account.

As Cournot's model world[11] is outside space and time, the monopoly's ability to act—or, more accurately, its ability to *react*— is limited. Like a perfect competitor, it cannot pursue any entrepreneurial policies. It cannot reduce its cost curves by using inferior raw materials, nor can it increase its sales by reducing the durability of its products. Its cost curves, as well as its demand

and marginal revenue curves, cannot be influenced and are "given." As the monopoly is also assumed to be attempting to maximize its profits, it is forced to charge the price at which the quantity which is produced and sold simultaneously corresponds to the equation "marginal cost (MC) = marginal revenue (MR)."

Cournot's homogeneous and absolute monopoly is therefore almost as powerless as a "quantity-adjuster," even if it is making a "monopoly profit." Like the perfect competitor, the homogeneous monopoly is unable to influence even its costs or its sales, let alone the price which it is mathematically forced to accept.

Entrepreneurial functions have no place in these models. Cournot's monopoly does not act, but only reacts like a computer, to programmed impulses. It has no "freedom" apart from mechanically responding to the impulse already given by the equation MC = MR.[12] To this extent, there is no difference between the monopoly model and the model of perfect competition.

§3 "Homogeneous" duopolies (oligopolies)

If Jevons's law of indifference is applied to all models of market structure, duopolists and oligopolists also always have the same price on a perfect market. Cournot, without knowledge of Jevons's law of indifference, has already assumed that this uniform price applied to a duopoly. "Now," writes Cournot, "take two owners and two wells, whose qualities are the same and who, due to the similarity of their location, are supplying the same competitive market. As a result, the price for both owners is the same."[13] If one dupolist changes his price, he automatically changes, at the same time, the price of the other duopolist "who sees himself forced to accept . . . this price."[14]

The first thing to note here is that Cournot considers changes in price (and also changes in quantity) to be possible, although he allows them to take place at infinite speed. Thus, time plays only an illusory role in his model.

The second thing to note is that Cournot assumes that when a duopolist changes his own price, he automatically changes the other's price, too. Why should the other duopolist be forced "to accept . . . this price"?

In the case of perfect competition, the individual suppliers are too weak to influence the price, and in the case of homogeneous monopoly there is only one supplier. What happens, however, if in an homogeneous duopoly, in which demanders act only in accordance with the price level, one supplier lowers his price below the other's price? As Rober Triffin[15] has shown, he gains all the customers and thus a (homogeneous) monopoly. And what happens if he raises his price above that of his competitor? He loses all his customers and his competitor gains the monopoly, which he loses again if the first duopolist lowers his price again. Time also plays an illusory role in this model: the customers transfer simultaneously, i.e., immediately or at infinite speed.

A third solution, the so-called "Bowley's duopoly," is incompatible with the neoclassical condition of equilibrium. The "independent supply" which a duopolist can sell "at any price he wants" until the first duopolist "gives up the struggle"[16] is, like the "power struggle with losses" (von Stackelberg) incompatible with Jevons's law of indifference. If the good is completely homogeneous, there can only be one price on a market, and never a price war. Price wars assume customer preferences, and therefore heterogeneous products, and are not possible outside space and time.

However, Cournot's and Triffin's solutions also contradict each other, because the former assumes that both suppliers change their price simultaneously, and the latter assumes that any price change by one side will lead to a simultaneous concentration of demand in favor of the cheaper supplier. This contradiction is of course inherent in the model, because for man, and therefore also for economists, concepts outside space and time, and therefore with no differences in product quality and no differences in the personalities of firms and their customers, are impossible. In reality, customers also do not act solely, or even mainly, according to prices. In fact, profit maximization through quantity or price variations is not the only task of an entrepreneur (or top manager). In reality, there are only a few customers to whom product quality is unimportant and no firms which neither change their products nor their workers. In fact, the customers in these models outside space and time bear no relation to real customers and their suppliers bear no relation to entrepreneurs (or top managers). In a model world in which the only economic dimensions left are price and quantity, and in which space and time do not influence the results, it is impossible to find conclusions that make sense.

§4 *Models of imperfect or monopolistic competition.*

The theory of imperfect or monopolistic competition, which is less well entrenched in current German textbooks than in English and American textbooks, originates mainly with Piero Sraffa.

When Sraffa discovered in the nineteen-twenties that the model of perfect competition did not agree with reality,[17] he looked for the cause of this discrepancy not in the fact that economic problems are determined by space and time, but in the existence of monopoly-like situations, as Knut Wicksell[18] did before him.

Sraffa was led to write his famous essay "The Laws of Returns under Competitive Conditions," which inspired Joan Robinson to write her *Economics of Imperfect Competition* and Edward H. Chamberlin his *Theory of Monopolistic Competition*,[19] by the observation that competing firms often work "under conditions of individual diminishing costs" (Sraffa) and still make a profit, although this is incompatible with the equilibrium conditions of perfect competition. In the model of perfect competition it is impossible that firms produce "under conditions of individual diminishing costs," because it is assumed that every supplier can sell as much as he wants; his "sale curve" runs horizontally and is "unlimited" or "infinite."

For the economists of the marginal utility school, however, there is one market structure in which a firm can make a profit "under conditions of individual diminishing costs"—monopoly.[20] From the point of view of traditional theory, therefore, Sraffa only had to find a reason to change competitors into monopolies in order to bring the theory back into line with reality.

Sraffa, like Wicksell before him, found this reason in customer preferences: "within its own market and under the protection of its own barrier each enjoys a privileged position whereby it obtains advantages which—if not in extent, at least in their nature—are equal to those enjoyed by the ordinary monopolist."[21]

However, Sraffa's line of argument, which Joan Robinson and Edward H. Chamberlin[22] took for granted, contains four errors in logic:

1. The model of so-called perfect competition, which is outside space and time, has not in the least bit to do with the competition to be found in economic reality. The application of any conclusion

drawn from this marginal concept outside space and time to reality is illogical, even though many economists believed (and still believe) that perfect competition exists in reality.

2. No conclusion about the market position of a firm can be drawn from the existence of customers and customer preferences. In reality, there is no enterprise which does not have customer preferences.

3. Jevons's law of indifference refers to the homogeneity of a *good* and not to the homogeneity of a *firm*. If every infringement of Jevons's law were sufficient to justify a monopoly, the monopoly would not lie with every firm, but with every good. A shoe company which markets different shoes in different sizes, colors, and styles at different times through various salesmen or saleswomen and perhaps in various branches would have as many monopolies as it has shoes, which is obviously absurd.

4. The confusion of product differences with the monopolies of firms transforms the concept of monopoly into a totally meaningless model. If every firm, including every grocery store and every hot-dog stand has a monopoly, it becomes impossible to explain the special characteristics of market-dominating firms and international cartels.

Sraffa (and Wicksell), like Robinson and Chamberlin, have failed to recognize that a theory which operates outside space and time can have no relevance to phenomena which occur within space and time. It is not possible to jump from perfect markets to the imperfect markets on which Sraffa's or Chamberlin's monopolies compete.[23] Any attempt to explain real economic phenomena with the aid of models which operate outside space and time inevitably leads to errors.[24]

SECTION 4:   Confusion of Models with Reality

> That it reached conclusions quite different from what the ordinary uninstructed person would expect, added, I suppose, to its intellectual prestige.
>
> John Maynard Keynes

By failing to recognize the model nature of perfect competition, many economists up to the present day have taken this equilibrium to be a real phenomenon (e.g., Wicksell, Eucken, or Samuelson) or at least considered it as an ideal to be copied in reality (e.g., Franz Böhm, Otto Lenel). This kind of confusion has led to dangerous errors. There has been a failure not only to realize that perfect competition is an absolute equilibrium, but there has also been a failure to recognize the basic differences between competition and monopoly. Attempts have even been made to explain oscillatory processes as a sequence of such equilibria (Leontief, Lange, etc.).

§1 Failure to recognize the equilibrium nature of perfect competition

> If we were to attempt an explanation of market behavior, we would need to take note of all the things, other than prices and quantities, which changed from period to period and have some influence on the market.
>
> Kelvin Lancaster

The confusion of the equilibrium model which the marginal utility school calls "perfect competition" with the competitive processes which occur in reality has led economists such as Erich Preiser to label every price which is a datum for the entrepreneur as a "competitive price." On the other hand, it has induced Wicksell, Eucken, and Samuelson to define the "datum" that a price represents under perfect competition in such a way that it becomes compatible with price changes.

1. Preiser's "administered price"
From the idea that in the equilibrium of perfect competition price is a datum, Erich Preiser[25] concluded that every price which a supplier has to accept as a datum is a competitive price. The competitive price, writes Preiser, "may have been formed by the free interplay of market forces; or it can just as easily be imposed by the government." An administered price based on average total costs is then also a competitive price "for it must be accepted by the individual supplier . . . "[26]

2. Wicksell's subjective datum
Wicksell, and later Eucken, posed the paradoxical question of how the competitive price could change if it were a datum. Without taking into acount that prices do not change in equilibrium, but only during economic processes, Wicksell found the answer. He argued that the competitive price is not an objective but only a

"subjective datum." This means that although no change could be brought about by the individual supplier, a change could be produced by the *sum* of the suppliers.[27]

Eucken, who also confuses the model with reality, even comes to the conclusion that it is wrong "to consider competition as a form of supply or demand in which no change in the relevant price is *actually* brought about by a supplier or a buyer by changing his supply or demand. This type of supply or demand does not exist in reality, nor it is conceivable."[28]

The model of perfect competition is indeed not "conceivable," as Eucken correctly remarks, because man cannot conceive of anything outside space and time. Nevertheless, the neoclassical economists work with markets outside time and space, in which price changes and price differences are by definition impossible. Real competition has nothing in common with this unreal model.

3. Samuelson's "personal influence"

Samuelson, who only rarely acquaints his readers with the premises on which his models are based, recognizes only partially the model character of perfect competition. For him, as for Wicksell and for Eucken, competition is perfect "where no farmer, business, or laborer is a big enough part of the total market to have any personal influence on market price."[29] In the equilibrium of perfect competition, however, prices cannot be influenced at all. The perfect market on which this (absolute) equilibrium is to be found is governed by Jevons's law of indifference and therefore lies beyond space and time.

Nevertheless, this has not prevented Samuelson from considering perfect competition as a "bench mark to appraise the efficiency of an economic system": "Russians, Chinese, Indians, as well as Swiss, need to study its analytical principles."[30] This in fact makes the confusion perfect. Compared with an equilibrium in which a uniform good is traded at a uniform price, even the Russian, Chinese, or Indian economic systems work excellently, at least from the point of view of the consumer. For they nevertheless still offer their consumers a certain freedom of choice. Obviously, Samuelson does not take into consideration the implications which a model such as perfect competition has for the society.

Changes in prices, qualities, preferences, evaluations, etc. do not occur in equilibrium, but only in processes which take place in space and time. Therefore, anyone who wishes to investigate changes in price, quality, capacity, and production technology, must leave aside equilibrium analysis and start analyzing economic processes, in which experiences, expectations, reevaluations and innovations play a decisive role.

§2 Failure to recognize the degree of abstraction

Not all the writers who work with concepts as the perfect market or perfect competition are fully aware of how far the premises on which their models are based diverge from reality. For example, the significance of Jevons's law of indifference for the neoclassical theory of market structures is misunderstood when Erich Schneider[31], Artur Woll,[32] and others use real examples (railway tickets, etc.) to explain price differentiation as "the sale of the same good at different prices" (Woll). Either the good in Jevons's sense is no longer the same, in which case there are different prices, or the good is homogeneous, in which case there is only one price. These authors distinguish between spatial, personal, or material price differentiation, without explaining to their readers what they mean by "the same good" and how far this concept diverges from the concept of a "homogeneous good," which by definition excludes any personal, material, spatial, and temporal differences, and which is also fundamental to the concept of the perfect market used by these authors.[33]

§3 Elimination of qualitative differences between competition and monopoly*

> ". . . as the monopolist has no competition to
> fear in his country, he does not make his goods
> as perfect as would otherwise be the case."
> Johann Georg Büsch (1799)

The transformation of market structures into equilibria eliminates the qualitative differences between competition and monopoly which exist in reality.

In perfect markets, competition and monopoly differ only in price and

---

*In this context monopoly means the permanent monopoly. The "process related monopoly" which occurs in the course of competitive processes and which is only temporary is discussed later.

quantity. Heinrich von Stackelberg therefore believes that these two market structures can be shown on the same graph. He assumes not only that the same marginal cost curve MC and the same sales curve V apply to both cases, but also that the same product quality is being offered for sale (see Figure 5).

Monopoly price P_c is merely higher than competitive price P_k, and therefore "monopoly quantity" Q_c is lower than "competitive quantity" Q_k.[34] From the point of view of neoclassical equilibrium analysis, which assumes that everything apart from price and quantity is "given," this is a logical result; under these assumptions, monopoly and competition differ only in price and quantity. Due to the elimination of all other kinds of influences, the

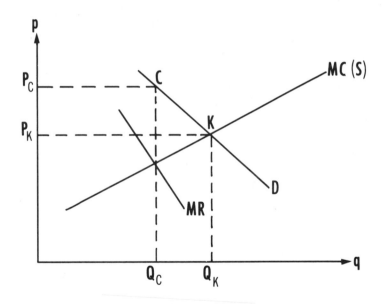

Fig. 5. If there are only the two variables, price P and quantity Q (and if the marginal cost curve MC(S) as well as the "demand curve" D are "given"), competition and monopoly can only differ, as von Stackelberg concludes, in price and quantity. Under competition, quantity Q_k is sold at price P_k, while monopoly requires the higher price P_c offering the smaller quantity Q_c. However, this assumption is arbitrary. Why should the sizes of firms, the production processes, the product quality, etc., be the same—regardless of whether firms are competitors or not?

only difference which is at all possible is a difference in price and quantity.

However, the decisive differences which exist in reality between competition and monopoly, are qualitative. Neither product quality nor production technology will be normally the same, because the influences generated by monopoly and competition differ in the course of time.

Competition is a process in space and time in which adjustments and developments take place.

Monopoly, because and insofar as it is not subject to competition, is much closer to being an equilibrium, and therefore to a market structure in the sense of the marginal utility theory, in which everything remains unchanged outside space and time.

The transformation of competition into an equilibrium eliminates therefore the basic difference between competition and monopoly: their differing readiness to adjust supply to changing demand and their differing appropriateness for developments of better and cheaper products. *Real competition adjusts supply to demand and develops new and better consumer and capital goods.*

First, competition is competition in adjustment (*adjustment competition*), which in a changing world causes buyers' and sellers' markets to disappear. In a buyers' market, competing firms are forced to adjust their supply by losses, and in a sellers' market they are induced to do so by profits. A monopoly, on the other hand, only adjusts its supply in exceptional cases. It tends to prevent buyers' markets by artificially restricting the supply and to perpetuate sellers' markets in order to make scarcity profits permanently.

Second, competition is competition in development (*development competition*), and is therefore the basic driving force behind economic development, which revolutionizes both production technology and the product range. Competing firms use new production methods so that they can produce more cheaply than other firms. Competing firms improve the quality of their products in order to increase their sales to the detriment of their competitors. Competing firms create entirely new products, in the hope that by this means they can escape the pressure of competition, at least temporarily. If they succeed, they establish a completely new market, on which they have a temporary monopoly (monopoly by efficiency) which enables them to make process-related monopoly profits until their imitators restore the competition. In all cases of this development competition, new or improved technology is used as a weapon in the battle of competition. Competition is therefore also the reason why we have achieved a high and still rising standard of living which far exceeds the wildest dreams of Adam Smith and the other fathers of the economic revolution.[35]

The (permanent) market monopoly, which secures its position by using its power against the emergence of outsiders, is in general sterile. It is not interested in innovations which mainly or even solely benefit its customers. It also takes little interest in innovations which could raise its profits. If high profits become permanent, profits lose the incentive function which is their particular role in competition. The risks and pains involved in developing and introducing innovations are not worth the trouble if the monopolist is already making so much profit that he hardly knows what to do with it all.

The qualitative difference which exists in reality between competition and monopoly is also shown by their completely different attitude to their customers. The pressure of competition forces competing firms to act in accordance with the varying and changing wishes of their customers. The monopolist, however, imposes his will on the buyers. He reduces the number of branches because the buyers have to come to him. He reduces his assortment and lowers the quality of his products because the buyers are forced to take what is offered. He does not even treat buyers like customers, because he knows that the purchasers have absolutely no choice on this market but to buy from him. Every buyer is dependent on him, but he is not dependent on every buyer.

If one starts out, however, like Chamberlin, from the perfect market, "product differentiation" appears to be a consequence of monopolistic influence on competition. Product differentiation, then, arises as a consequence of the "interplay of monopolistic and competitive forces."[36] If, as traditional theory assumes, there is only one uniform good under perfect competition, it therefore follows that a range of different products can only exist if monopolistic influences are at work. This conclusion is nevertheless wrong, because it is based on false premises. The equilibrium model of perfect competition, which assumes a market outside space and time, has nothing to do with real competition. Consequently, Chamberlin's theory contains two errors: (1) In reality, which economic theory ought to be dealing with, the pressure of competition forces suppliers to act in accordance with the individual wishes of their customers, which change over a period of time. (2) In reality, which an economic theorist ought to be acquainted with, a monopoly which dominates a demand market imposes its will on the buyers.

The more market monopolies there are and the less competition from substitutes there is from third markets, the less freedom of choice there is for consumers between products and producers, and the less they can use this choice to influence what is produced and the way it is produced.

The more intensive the competition, the more the quality and the differentiation of the products on sale are in accord with the individual and changing wishes of the customers.

Price and quantity are therefore by no means the only differences between monopoly and competition. The basic differences are qualitative. They become apparent when the perfect market governed by Jevons's law of indifference is put aside and competition is examined where it is effective, i.e., in space and time.

§4   The doctrine of losses in equilibrium

Anyone who attempts to transform economic processes into equilibria (which they are not) encounters difficulties in explaining empirical phenomena that are observable in the course of economic processes. There are two methods of analysis: Either the equilibrium theory can be put aside and processes can be analyzed instead (as it is in accordance with the object of analysis), or the results of the examination of equilibrium can be applied to economic processes by falsifying the object of analysis for this purpose. In the case of the temporary losses occurring in the course of economic processes, the supporters of the equilibrium theory have opted for the second approach.

Although losses are incompatible with an equilibrium outside space and time, economists such as Samuelson and von Stackelberg have applied the tools developed by the equilibrium theory to the analysis of process-related losses. A loss even equal to fixed costs then turns out, remarkably, to be compatible with equilibrium conditions. According to Erich Schneider, an enterprise is closed down "when the price falls below the minimum average variable costs."[37] Samuelson also deals with this "shutdown point" under equilibrium conditions, although he assumes "a period long enough for the firm to vary its output by hiring more or fewer variable factors of production." Above the "shutdown point" "the firm will be getting something toward covering its fixed cost; and either it will be getting maximized positive profits; or . . . at least the firm will be minimizing its losses."[38]

Although these or similar statements can be found in almost all textbooks,[39] they are wrong:

1. If a firm suffers permanent losses, it is not in equilibrium.

2. If the losses are only seen as temporary, as assumed by Samuelson and others, the equilibrium model outside space and time (within which the argument is presented) has been left behind. In a model (as the perfect market) in which there are no temporal differences (Jevons), there can by definition be no such thing as a "temporary" situation either.

3. An entrepreneur who shuts down his enterprise in a buyers' market, because the price temporarily falls below the variable average total costs in the "shutdown point" is not behaving rationally. Why should he dismiss his experienced work force and annoy his customers if he is only going through a short-run loss-making period and if he is confident of making profits again in the future? (The marginal utility school, however, assumes rational behavior.)

4. In the economic processes of the real world there is no bottom for losses which can be determined in terms of costs. In reality, firms act in accordance with their expectations provided they have enough liquid assets. If they expect the state of the market to change again in their favor in the foreseeable future, they will continue producing regardless of how much loss they are making, provided that they can hold out financially. If they expect their competitors to abandon the market or they expect a change from depression to prosperity, they will be prepared to use both their own assets as well as other means to pay for raw materials, semifinished products, or employees. The fact that firms also remain liable for "variable costs" is shown by bankruptcy when both the suppliers of materials and the employees lodge claims.

The "shutdown point" which is determined by the turning point of the

variable average total costs has no relevance for entrepreneurial decisions.
The so-called "shutdown point" is neither an equilibrium nor a
stage in a process taking place in space and time. The expression
"shutdown point" is therefore misleading. Variable costs are irrelevant to the question of whether and when a firm shuts down
its production, because a firm bases its decision not on its (mo-
mentary) costs and prices, but on its experiences and expectations. Its experiences originate in the past. Its expectations relate
to the future development of costs, prices, and sales. A static
analysis is therefore unable to explain the behavior of entrepreneurs and top managers—entirely apart from the fact that even in
neoclassical theory, the "shutdown point" only exists in the model of perfect competition.

§5 *Transformation of microeconomic processes into equilibria:*
the cobweb theorem

> Nothing is impossible in an inexact science like
> economics.
>
> Paul A. Samuelson

Even oscillatory processes have been explained as a succession
of equilibria. The "cobweb theorem"—so called because the resulting graph resembles a spider's web—originates from Wassily
W. Leontief's essay "Delayed Adjustment of Supply and Partial
Equilibrium".[40] He assumes, as did Oskar Lange after him, that
marginal costs determine supply in both oscillatory processes as
well as in equilibrium.

There is, says Samuelson, "a famous economic case which
shows us that tools of supply and demand are not restricted to
handling static and unchanging situations, but can also be used
fruitfully to analyze dynamic situations of change."[41] However,
neither Samuelson nor the other followers of Leontief have explained why conclusions which have been drawn from a model
operating outside space and time can be transferred to "dynamic
situations of change."

According to Leontief, the problems which lead to the cobweb
theorem spring from "the fact that supply takes longer to adjust
to a given market situation than demand. . . . This curious combination of circumstances produces wavelike price and quantity
fluctuations, which can be represented by the well-known cobweb diagram."[42] For both Leontief and Lange, the "delayed ad-

justment" is a succession of (partial) equilibria, in which, as (supposedly) in any other state of equilibrium, firms act in accordance with their marginal costs.

If, deduces Leontief, "quantity q_0 . . . is offered for sale in a given period of time, the temporary adjustment of demand will produce the price P_0 (point m_0). Production is increased accordingly; and the supply, lagging behind demand, is raised over the following periods of time to q_1 (point m_1). Now the price falls to P_1 (point m_2) and the supply is correspondingly reduced to q_2 for the following period of time. Then there is a renewed increase in price, the supply is raised again, etc.etc."[43] Leontief's graph is shown in Figure 6.

The only part of this which is correct is that fluctuations occur in oscillatory processes. However, it is not correct that the cobweb theorem explains these fluctuations. Oscillatory processes are not

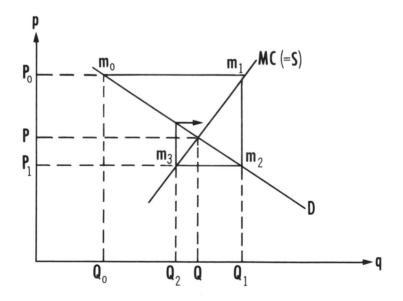

Fig. 6. Leontief and Lange explain oscillatory processes as a succession of (partial) equilibria. Because they assume that the supplier acts in accordance with his marginal costs both in equilibrium and during these processes (and that experiences, expectations, and re-evaluations are of no importance), the cobweb illustrated here results.

a succession of equilibria—and even under equilibrium conditions, firms only act in accordance with their marginal costs in the model of "perfect competition."

The assumption underlying this doctrine that a firm behaves in the same way in a process which takes place in space and time as it does in the (absolute) equilibrium of perfect competition has not been examined by any author. It does not stand up to examination:

1. There are no equilibria in oscillatory processes, although Leontief and Lange assume the contrary even in the titles of their essays; "Delayed Adjustment of Supply and Partial Equilibrium" and "Forms of Supply Adjustment and Economic Equilibrium," respectively;indeed, they logically have to do so if they apply the equilibrium theory to oscillations. As long as a process continues, there is no equilibrium.

2. The cobweb theorem is derived from the model of perfect competition in which the supply curve and the marginal cost curve are identical. Even in the neoclassical theory, however, neither monopolies, oligopolies, or competing monopolies (Chamberlin) behave according to the equation $P = MC$.

3. When producers reduce or expand their enterprises, their supply curves shift. It is therefore logically inconsistent for authors to deal first with shifts in supply curves and then show the consequences of net investment or disinvestment as points on the same supply curve. Samuelson, for example, discusses the one right after the other.[44]

4. Suppliers inevitably behave differently in a process which takes place in space and time than in an equilibrium outside space and time. The problems which a firm has to solve during an economic process either do not yet exist or have vanished in equilibrium. During an economic process firms do not act in accordance with their marginal costs but their process-related expectations; they calculate their net investment or their disinvestment, as well as their production, in accordance with the sales and the price changes which they expect. Supply and demand curves also shift with expectations: any firm which expects a price rise tends to restrict its supply and to increase its demand.

5. During processes, firms are induced to make revaluations. When business is good, they put a higher value on their assets of their own accord, while in a period of losses, they are forced to make write-offs which are not based on consumption. The profit

value and the capital value of a firm, and therefore its cost curves as well, vary with its profitability.

6. In a timeless equilibrium analysis, there are neither "temporal delays" or "next" and "next but one" periods of time. The distinction between short-run and long-run marginal costs, which has now become standard practice, also goes against Jevons's law of indifference. In a model world in which there are no temporal differences, it is logically impossible to make a distinction between short run and long run.

7. Equilibrium theory assumes "complete knowledge of the market," while oscillatory processes depend on the very fact that entrepreneurs are deceived in their expectations, because they have wrongly forecasted future developments in sales and prices. Without wrong forecasts, and therefore without errors, there can be no oscillatory processes.

Leontief and Lange, and all authors who draw on the cobweb theorem (such as Samuelson or Klein), apply results which have been deduced from a market model outside space and time to economic processes which take place within space and time. This is an error of logic.

Oscillatory processes are nothing else but alternating sellers' and buyers' markets, in which expectations, experiences, and revaluations play a decisive role. Prices are not determined by costs in either sellers' or buyers' markets. Sellers' markets change to buyers' markets when net investment has become too high as a result of excessive expectations. On the other hand, buyers' markets change to sellers' markets when disinvestment has been too high as a result of underestimation of future sales.

When analyzing oscillatory processes, as when analyzing sellers' and buyers' markets, three things must be taken into account:

First, Investment in expansion causes the supply curve to shift to the right; as a result of increased capacity, a greater quantity can be offered for sale at any price. Disinvestment prompted by a buyers' market, on the other hand, leads to a shift of the supply curve to the left.

Samuelson, who draws on the cobweb theorem without further examination, writes, "by an 'increase' in demand or supply is meant a *shift* of the whole curve in question to the right."[45] The cobweb theorem, however, does not show these shifts in the supply curve which result from positive or negative investment.

Second, important factors in economic processes are experiences, which originate in the past, and expectations, which are related to the future. If expectations are excessive, investment in expansion will be too high in a sellers' market and disinvestment will be too high in a buyers' market. A sellers' market changes to a buyers' market when future sales are overestimated. A buyers' market changes to a sellers' market when future sales are underestimated. Oscillatory processes are therefore the result of wrong forecasts, which have various causes, including the accelerator.[46]

Third, there are no oscillatory processes without re-evaluations. The value of goods falls during a buyers' market. In extreme cases, the factors used in their manufacture have become valueless. In a sellers' market, on the other hand, the price of goods rises, and production costs have therefore again become irrelevant. There is no cost-determined bottom to these re-evaluations. Moreover, neither do cost curves remain constant in the course of adjustment processes; they shift not only as a result of net investment and disinvestment, but also with profit-related changes in "calculatory costs", and therefore with the re-evaluation of fixed and current assets.

§6 Inappropriateness of models outside time and space as objects of economic analysis

In a model world which ignores temporal and spatial differences, the imagination of the authors knows no bounds. If the models of the marginal utility school, which still influence textbooks, are compared with the real problems, the following become apparent:

1. Adjustment of supply to changes in demand and adjustment of demand to changes in supply are only analyzed by the marginal utility school on a comparative, static basis not as a process. No attention is paid to changes which take place over time; comparisons are made only between situations or states of affairs which are assumed to be "given" at different "times." It is wrongly assumed that an economy moves from equilibrium to equilibrium. This falsifies the object of analysis; economic processes do not consist of a succession of equilibria.

2. In the traditional model world, markets are assumed to be given: the emergence and the disappearance of markets, like the

problems of developing or declining economies, lie outside this model world.

3. In a model world in which all economically important products are reproducible, the absence of scarcity also eliminates the problems resulting from the exhaustion of resources.

4. In such a model world, there are also no changes in productivity; competition in rationalization which leads to increases in real income as a result of increased productivity does not exist.

5. In a model world, in which the same products are manufactured all the time, there is no development competition which improves the quality of products and is constantly producing new products.

6. In a world in which there is no time and no space (or in which everything takes place at infinite speed, as other economists have assumed), there can be no disharmony between supply and demand resulting in sellers' and buyers' markets; shortages and surpluses cannot ocur on the same markets at different times, nor in different places at the same time. In a model world of this kind, circulation is not yet a problem and trade is unnecessary.

7. In a model world outside space and time, people's needs are also constant; there are neither new products which give rise to new needs, nor increases in average real incomes which enable superior needs to be satisfied. New methods of production do not increase the supply nor do new goods or better qualities create new demand.

8. In a world in which there are not temporal and spatial differences, there are neither experiences, which originate in the past, nor expectations, which relate to an uncertain future. In this world, economic values are by definition not only measurable, but also constant. Revaluations are by definition impossible.

In reality, we live in a world in which everything is transitory and subject to change. Experiences and expectations as well as evaluations change in space and time and can also be manipulated by those who have the power to do so. The problem of economic power gains its fundamental importance only in an economy in which values are parameters of action. In reality, new methods of production do increase the supply and new goods or better products do increase the demand.

An economic theory which works with equilibria outside space and time fails to deal with its object of analysis. It has as little to do with economics as metaphysics has to do with physics. It is "metaeconomics."[47]

SECTION 5: Transformation of Macroeconomic Processes

The tendency to change economic processes into absolute equilibria by ignoring space and time is not limited to microeconomics. It is also to be found in macroeconomic theory. This is shown by two examples: Say's theorem and Keynes's general theory.

§1 Say's theorem

The French economist Jean-Baptiste Say taught us that there can be no total (or overall) depression in an economy, only partial disturbances. He justified this surprising claim with the sentence that "supply creates its own demand." He maintains: "every product, from the moment it is produced, opens up a market for other products to the full extent of its value."[48]

Although experiences apparently show the opposite, even Keynes has grappled with this theory. In fact, Say has done only what other economists writing before or after have done: he has assumed an economy in equilibrium. An equilibrium of this kind, which is constant outside space and time, is only possible if supply creates its own demand, because otherwise a process-related development would occur. If sellers' markets are not equated by buyers' markets a macroeconomic equilibrium is not more existent and a macroeconomic process occurs within space and time. In equilibrium, a disequilibrium is impossible.[49]

For Keynes, the doctrine "that it was impossible for effective demand to be deficient" was "something of a curiosity and a mystery."[50] That "victory," wrote Keynes, "must have been due to a complex of suitabilities in the doctrine to the environment into which it was projected. That it reached conclusions quite different from what the ordinary uninstructed person would expect, added, I suppose, to its intellectual prestige. That its teaching, translated into practice, was austere and often unpalatable, lent it virtue. That it was adapted to carry a vast and consistent logical superstructure, gave it beauty. That it could explain much social injustice and apparent cruelty as an inevitable incident in the scheme of progress, and the attempt to change such things as likely on the whole to do more harm than good, commended it to authority."[51]

§2 Keynes's equilibrium with underemployment

Keynes does not accept the conclusions which Say and Ricardo have drawn from their equilibrium models, but even he does not investigate economic processes; he takes an economic equilibrium in which, as he again assumes, there is involuntary unemployment. He replaces the process-related business cycle theory, as promoted in particular by supporters of the Later Historical School, by an equilibrium theory of employment (or underemployment). Consequently, his general theory says that the sum of savings is always equal to the sum of investment:

"Income = value of output = consumption + investment.
Saving = income−consumption.
Therefore, saving = investment."[52]

The multiplier was developed by Keynes in a model of a closed economy in which there are no changes in technology; experiences and expectations[53] as well as innovations are irrelevant and the propensity to consume is constant. He did not take into account that public investment, if it has an appreciable effect, changes the marginal propensity to consume and also produces various effects, depending on past experiences and future expectations.

The marginal efficiency of capital, which according to Keynes determines the extent of induced investment, is defined as that discount rate which would make the profits expected "just equal to its supply price."[54]

Although expectations are mentioned by Keynes "for the sake of formal completeness," they are at the same time deprived of their process-related nature. Keynes speaks of the "state of expectation" and considers it "sensible for producers to base their expectations on the assumption that the most recently realised results will continue."[55] And in particular he assumes that "changes in expectations of the relation between the present and the future level of income" are "likely to average out for the community as a whole." In addition, he adds, there is "too much uncertainty for it to exert much influence."[56] However, if expectations are defined as states which are permanent or average out and uncertainty is not taken into account, the process-related element inherent in expectations is thus at the same time eliminated from the analysis.

Keynes works with the model of a closed, static economy in which there is "involuntary unemployment"; however, he does not discuss the question of how macroeconomic equilibrium can be compatible with the existence of involuntary unemployment, nor does he discuss the question of whether it is not necessary to distinguish several causes and types of underemployment, each requiring a different employment policy. The unemployment which, for example, existed after World War II in the emerging Federal Republic of Germany or in Great Britain had in any case different characteristics from the underemployment which Keynes had in mind and required a different treatment (cf. next chapter).

What is interesting here is that Keynes transforms the macro-economic process which is simplified and misleadingly termed a "Great Depression" into a macroeconomic equilibrium; in doing so he derives not only his concept of equilibrium but also his terms ("marginal propensity to consume," "marginal efficiency of capital") from the tools of marginal utility theory, which he trans-fers from microeconomic to macroeconomic theory. His definition of expectations as "states" and his failure to take changing experi-ences into account are also in keeping with this model world.

(a) Expectations are not "states," nor do they average out

Expectations, which influence households' propensity to con-sume and firms' investment and inventories, do not average out for "the community as a whole" either in a depression or a period of prosperity.[57] In a depression, pessimistic expectations predomi-nate; firms fear that prices and sales will fall, and households are afraid that short-time working will be introduced and that unem-ployment will increase. In a period of prosperity, optimistic ex-pectations predominate; firms hope that prices and sales will rise, and households believe that real incomes will increase and their jobs will be safe.

The "marginal propensity to consume" does not remain con-stant during a macroeconomic process. It rises "for the commu-nity as a whole" when unemployment is falling and goes down when underemployment is rising. If underemployment rises ap-preciably, many households postpone purchases of consumer durables such as refrigerators and autos in order to be better equipped for the emergencies of unemployment. The "liquidity preference"[58] of firms rise during this period, because they fear that in this situation their creditors will get tough and their debtors will become unable to pay their bills.

On the other hand, if employment increases and jobs appear to be safe, many households are prepared to buy on installments or to borrow money to a greater extent, especially if real income is rising as well. Firms also tend to stretch their liquidity to the limit when the economy is booming so that they can invest like their competitors. They invest not only to expand their enterprises (investment in expansion), but also, and in particular, to reduce their costs (investment in rationalization) and to bring out new or improved products (investment in development).

The assumptions that expectations remain constant and that households have the same propensity to consume and firms the same liquidity preference during periods of prosperity and during depression bear no relation to reality.

(b) Influence of experiences on macroeconomic processes

Keynes analyzed an "equilibrium with underemployment" but not economic processes and failed to take into account the influence of varying experiences on employment. Experiences which people have gained in the past are, however, by no means irrelevant to their economic behavior. The effects of price increases, for example, are influenced by the experiences which people have gained in the past.

People, who have become used to constantly rising prices behave differently from those who are experiencing inflation for the first time.[59] For example, if workers and unions have as yet no experience of inflation, wage increases will lag behind price rises. However, if workers and unions have learned of inflation from experience, the price increases which they expect to occur in the future will be compensated for in their wage agreements; in this case, wage increases no longer lag behind price rises, but precede them. This time-shift has a negative effect on employment.

According to Haberler, stagflation—i.e., the combination of inflation with high or rising unemployment—is "the predictable consequence of prolonged inflation."[60] Even if this is an unjustified generalization, it cannot be denied that past experience of price rises is *one* of the causes of the negative effect of inflation on employment. As it is impossible to live without experiences and expectations, it is impossible to find a household or a firm whose behavior is not influenced by experiences and expectations.

Keynes interpreted the macroeconomic process which took place during the Great Depression as an "equilibrium with under-employment" without asking to what extent an "equilibrium" can exist if, as during the Great Depression, workers become desti-tute, children starve, fields become steppe, mines flood, machin-ery rusts away, and factory buildings collapse. Nor has Keynes posed the question of whether the type of underemployment which is characterized by "poverty midst plenty" is the only type of underemployment or whether there are other types which are accompanied by other phenomena and have other consequences.

The post-Keynesians, like Keynes himself, have not really broken through the vicious circle which economic theory has got into. Domar, Harrod, Hicks, Samuelson, Solow, and Tobin have largely retained the basic premises of equilibrium theory, despite the misleading titles of their writings.[61] A comparison of equilibria at various times may be called "dynamic" (Ragnar Frisch), but cannot be called a theory of processes. The same is true for a theory which assumes important features such as evaluations, expectations, needs, markets, products, production processes, etc., to be constant. In economic processes, as we will see later on, evaluations, expectations, and experiences change, and mar-kets, products, and production processes do not remain constant.

CHAPTER 3

Generalizations of Model Results

That its teaching, translated into practice, was
austere and often unpalatable, lent it virtue. That
it was adapted to carry a vast and consistent
logical structure, gave it beauty.

John Maynard Keynes

The history of economic theory is characterized by the following tendencies: (1) the generalization of conclusions which have been drawn from specialized assumptions,[1] and (2) the generalization of experiences relating only to a temporary historical situation.

This tendency of economists to make premature generalizations will be illustrated in this chapter by four doctrines of economic theory:

1. theory of comparative cost,
2. wage theories of Ricardo and Marx,
3. theories of Malthus and Meadows,
4. Keynes's general theory.

SECTION 1: Theory of Comparative Cost

Ricardo has postulated that a country can still successfully engage in international trade even if every good costs more to produce in that country than in other countries. He derives this theory which is still found in textbooks on macroeconomics or international trade theory from a *two-country model,* in which there is no money and in which all goods are valued only in terms of the hours of labor used to produce them.

In such a two-country model the Ricardian theory of comparative cost is entirely correct. If there are only two countries and no money, trade can be carried on profitably even if this trade involves the exchange of a good which can be produced more cheaply in the country importing it.

Ricardo demonstrates his theory with the example of wine and cloth. Cunningly, he makes England the country in which it is more expensive to produce both goods—including cloth (!)—than in Portugal:

> England may be so circumstanced, that to produce the cloth may require the labour of 100 men for one year; and if she attempted to make the wine, it might require the labour of 120 men for the same time. England would therefore find it her interest to import wine, and to purchase it by the exportation of cloth.
>
> To produce the wine in Portugal, might require only the labour of 80 men for one year, and to produce the cloth in the same country, might require the labour of 90 men for the same time. It would therefore be advantageous for her to export wine in exchange for cloth.[2]

In Ricardo's example, a barter transaction which brings wine from Portugal to England therefore saves 40 hours (80 instead of 120 hours per year), while the export of cloth to Portugal results in a "loss" of only 10 hours (100 instead of 90 hours per year). The net surplus from this bilateral barter trade is therefore 30 hours (i.e., 40 minus 10 hours per year). It is therefore sensible to allocate resources in accordance with the principle of comparative cost if there are only two countries and goods are exchanged by barter.

However, Ricardo's theory ceases to apply if it is transferred, as he and his followers have done, to a world economy in which (a) international trade is no longer restricted to two countries, and (b) foreign exchange is available.[3] The barter transactions are now broken down into two exchanges on two different markets: (a) the exchange of wine for money, (b) the exchange of cloth for money. This eliminates the obligation to make a counter purchase on unfavorable terms. Portugal now receives foreign exchange for its wine. Why, in an international economy, should Portugal buy from England to satisfy its demand for cloth if it can now obtain the same product cheaper elsewhere?

In an international economy in which money is freely convertible, it no longer makes sense to allocate resources in accordance with the principle of "comparative cost," quite apart from the fact that it is no longer a question of cost differences but of price differences, and that productivity differences can be over compensated for by comparable differences in wages. Nor is it possible to restore the universal validity of Ricardo's theory, which wrongly equates hours of labor with costs, by converting "differences in comparative cost," as Taussig or Haberler[4] have done, into absolute price differences which take the different wage levels into account. First, wages are nothing more than costs, which ought to be already included in the "differences in cost"; second, it does not require a theory of comparative cost to confirm Adam Smith's theory that given an international division of labor, goods are purchased in the country in which they can be obtained more cheaply; and third, this kind of proof was not what Ricardo intended. Confirmation of the fact that in international trade with free convertibility, goods are bought where they are cheapest does not require a theory of comparative cost.

Although Ricardo's theory of comparative cost is only relevant in economic terms to bilateral barter transactions (where no other choice exists), it is even today proclaimed as a basic component of international trade theory.[5] Samuelson, for example, teaches his readers that Ricardo showed that even in the case "where American laborers (or resources generally) are more productive than Europe's in *both* food *and* clothing—trade is still likely to be mutually advantageous."[6] However, Ricardo showed nothing of the sort. Even during the period when productivity in the United States was (or would have been) higher in every respect, trade between the United States and Europe was not the result of Ricardo's law of comparative advantage, but of the lower wage rates in Europe, which compensated for the lower productivity. No American businessman imports from Europe goods that can be obtained more cheaply (assuming that the quality is the same) in his own country.

SECTION 2: Wage Theories of Ricardo and Marx

Ricardo conceived his wage theory, which is still the basis of the commonly made assumption of "given cost curves," for a static economy in which both population and technology remain constant and government anti-union legislation (which Ricardo does not mention) forces the unskilled worker to accept the wage dictates of his employer. According to these premises, the "natural price of labour" is that price "which is necessary to enable the labourers, one with another, to subsist and to perpetuate their race, without either increase or diminution."[7] Marx draws on this statement in his definition of the value of labor as "the value of the means of subsistence necessary for the maintenance of the labourer"[8]; he adds that "the sum of the means of subsistence necessary for the production of labour-power must include the means necessary for the labourer's substitutes, i.e. his children, in order that this race of peculiar commodity-owners may perpetuate its appearance in the market."[9]

According to Ricardo, the market price of labor can only temporarily rise above or fall below its natural price. Ricardo justifies this statement, which he considers to be a natural law, by saying that a higher wage causes an increase in "labour-power," while a lower wage reduces the number of laborers as a result of destitution. Wages therefore gravitate toward the natural price of labor (and therefore toward the necessary "means of subsistence" in all cases).

In his wage theory Ricardo has generalized an experience which applied specifically not only to his time (but also to Marx's time). The wage of the unqualified laborer, to the analysis of which Ricardo's and Marx's theories are limited, was then at (society's) subsistence level, because the government, which permitted firms to concentrate workers in the factory system, prohibited workers' associations. The wage of the laborer, who was not protected by a trade union and had no special skills to offer, could therefore be restricted to a minimumm and his working day extended to a maximum by his employer.

Government laws, however, whether they prohibit or facilitate the formation of workers' associations, are not natural laws. They are transitory, like the people who make them. Nor is it inevitable, as it was in Ricardo's and Marx's day, that the vast majority of workers will be employed on simple tasks. The level of skills of the work force in general and the proportion of skilled workers in particular are many times higher today than they were in the time of Ricardo or Marx.

In the parliamentary democracies of today, in which independent trade unions protect workers from exploitation, Ricardo's supposed "wage law" has ceased to apply. If a worker's real income rises by two to five percent per annum, as has been the case in Western countries in the past, the statement that a worker only earns, on average, "the means of existence necessary for the maintenance of himself and his substitutes" is untenable. The reality, that wages rise in accordance with labor productivity and that employers and unions renegotiate wages from year to year or from time to time, is incompatible with an "iron law of wages"[10] according to which the wage is only adequate for the "means of subsistence" required to maintain the work force. In a developing economy, in which the distribution of power on the labor market is no longer influenced by government to the detriment of the work force and real wages rise with productivity, it is not the poverty but the wealth of the population which increases.

SECTION 3. Theories of Malthus and Meadows

> We cannot predict the future course of human history.
>
> Karl R. Popper

> Commercialized . . . nature has not only restricted the world of human existence in an ecological sense, but also in a very existential sense.
>
> Herbert Marcuse

Under the dramatic title *The Limits to Growth*,[11] Dennis Meadows and his coauthors have proclaimed the dangers and limits of "exponential growth" in the Report for the Club of Rome's Project on the "Predicament of Mankind." This report, which contains the results of the research carried out at the Massachusetts Institute of Technology (MIT), bases its conclusions on three axioms:

1. If the present rate of development is maintained, "the limits to growth on this planet will be reached some time within the next one hundred years."[12]
2. It is possible "to alter these growth trends and to establish a condition of ecological and economic stability that is sustainable far into the future," a "state of global equilibrium."[13]
3. "The sooner the world's people begin working to attain this state of global equilibrium . . . the greater will be their chances of success."[14]

This respect is interesting in this context for two reasons: (1) because it considers the establishment of a "state of equilibrium" to be an ideal goal of economic policy, thus resembling to a certain extent the concepts of the classical and neoclassical economists, and (2) because, like Malthus, it expresses the danger of "exponential growth" in mathematical terms: "there is a simple mathematical relationship between the . . . rate of growth, and the time it will take a quantity to double in size."[15]

Thomas Robert Malthus, who is not mentioned in the "Report for the Club of Rome," expressed similar ideas more than 150 years ago.[16] In his *Essay on the Principle of Population* he postulated the theory that the human race multiplies in geometric progression, but the "means of subsistence" necessary for its maintenance only increases in arithematic progression, which means that humanity repeatedly comes up against the "limits to growth." "Supposing"—Malthus would have us believe—"the present population equal to a thousand millions, the human species would increase as the numbers 1,2,4,8,16,32,64,128, 256, and subsistence as 1,2,3,4,5,6,7,8,9."[17] Because "population has this constant tendency to increase beyond the means of subsistence,"[18] the consequence must therefore be poverty in its manifold forms if the human race does not voluntary restrict its growth (which according to Malthus and others curiously includes the abolition of any kind of welfare as well as unemployment payments).[19]

Malthus based his conclusions on two assumptions which on closer examination turn out to be generalizations of the experience of a particular (or limited) time: (1) that population increases not only at certain times and in certain areas, but constantly and universally, (2) that as a result of constant technology, the rates of increase in food production are always and everywhere decreasing.[20]

No one can doubt that Malthus observed an alarming increase in population in his day. In many countries, especially in less developed countries, population growth is at present also taking the form of an explosion. However, it is by no means inevitable that such an explosion will continue. In England, Malthus's prophecies were never fulfilled. In the Soviet Union, the population has remained constant for some time, and West Germany's population fell from 62 million to 60.1 million between 1974 and 1976. The birthrate of China fell from 4.4 to 2.2 percent (of Tawain to nil), of Indonesia from 4.6 to 3.6 percent, of India from 4.3 to 3.5 percent and of Brazil from 4.4 to 3.0 percent in the years between 1950 and 1975. There is no such thing as a "natural law" which causes population to increase constantly and universally in the same way. The poor and the exploited have high birthrates if child labor brings their parents additional income. An increase in wealth and the prohibition of child labor, on the other hand, has a negative effect on population growth. Technological developments such as television or medical discoveries such as the pill also influence population growth.

No one can dispute either that if technology remains constant, marginal returns in agriculture will fall. The economy, however, in which we live, is an economy in which—thanks to development competition—new and better goods, new kinds of raw materials, and new and cheaper production processes are developed. In such a developing economy, technology does not remain constant.[21] Since Malthus, the "means of subsistence" have increased not arithmetically but exponentially (or, as Malthus would have said, "geometrically"), for two reasons: (1) *the development of new or improved production techniques:* improved methods of cultivation, new types of fertilizer, more fertile seeds, more effective pest control, etc.; (2) *an increase in the "nature" available to support the human race:* by the replacement of draft animals by tractors, which do not require any feeding stuffs to be cultivated for them, but also by the extraction of nitrogen from the atmosphere, the manufacture of synthetics, plastics, etc.

In the first case the productivity of the soil has increased, and in the second case the production factor "nature" available to support the human race has itself increased.

The approach of Meadows and his coauthors is undoubtedly more comprehensive than that of Malthus. But even their analysis is comparatively static, because it concentrates on a "state of global equilibrium" and does not take into account the development which has repeatedly extended the "limits of growth." The absolute "limits of growth" postulated by the Club of Rome do not exist. However—and this makes the warning particularly important—the development which the people of the Western world have become used to over the past two hundred years is not inevitable either. It can not only slow down, it can also stop. This will certainly be the case if the development competition which so far has only eliminated bottlenecks but has also brought about an increase in wealth in many countries should cease to function.[22] Moreover, the maintenance of the ecological balance in the future requires the development not only of material resources, but also of the abilities which increasingly are needed to solve the problems for which the term "conservation" is only an imprecise definition.

SECTION 4: John Maynard Keynes's General Theory

> If Keynes had known the facts about the Great Depression as we know them, he could not have interpreted that period as he did.
>
> Milton Friedman

Keynes wanted to show "that the postulates of the classical theory are applicable to a special case only and not to the general case."[23] In fact, he himself generalized the events which could be observed during the thirties after the collapse of the international economy.

Keynes's general theory is limited to:

1. the case of underemployment of *all* factors of production;
2. the analysis of a *closed* economy and therefore (corresponding to the events of that time) to the analysis of nations which are largely separated from the international economy which previously existed;
3. the examination of economies in which *government intervention* (price controls, price freezes, price commissioners, etc.) had restricted or eliminated price (and wage) flexibility (as was then the case in countries such as Great Britain, the German Reich, etc.); and
4. the analysis of a *stationary* economy: investment in rationalization and development play no part in Keynes's system.

Keynes therefore excluded the following phenomena from his general theory:

1. the underemployment of some factors of production accompanied by shortages of others:
2. the influence of foreign trade on both employment and the effects of the employment policy;[24]
3. the significance of price increases for employment policy, in particular the simultaneous occurrence of underemployment and inflation; and
4. the significance of economic development for employment.

§1 The claim of being "general"

Keynes was aware of only one type of underemployment: that which occurs when the production apparatus is in full working order but is not operating at full capacity. In fact, in 1935, the year in which he wrote his book, there were not only millions of people unemployed but also machines at a standstill and piles of raw materials waiting to be (re-)incorporated into the production process. With this kind of "general underemployment," the measures proposed by Keynes (stimulation of private consumption, deficit spending and autonomous investment) made good economic sense under the circumstances of the closed economy which then existed. They get production going again and thereby eliminate underemployment of land, capital goods, and labor.

However, Keynes unjustifiably generalized this case. It is possible for only labor to be underemployed while there is a shortage of capital goods (and therefore of machines). At least two different cases must be distinguished here; in the first case there are sufficient raw materials (i.e., "nature") available, and in the second there is a shortage of raw materials (i.e., "nature") as well.[25]

When Lenin and Trotsky began rebuilding the Soviet Union, they not only had to reintegrate millions of soldiers into the economic production process but were also faced with the task of creating the "manufactured means of production" without which it was impossible to undertake any economically viable production. There were two reasons for this particular shortage of capital goods: (1) economic underdevelopment, which was a legacy from the tsar's regime, (2) World War I, which had destroyed a large proportion of the existing capital goods. Under these circumstances, the main task was to create "capital goods" by restricting consumption, so that as much of the gross national product as possible could be used for investment and therefore for building up an industrial potential.[26]

The underemployment which existed immediately after World War II in countries such as Great Britain, France, and (after elimination of the black market) West Germany was of a different kind. In this case there were specific shortages not only of capital goods but also of raw materials, i.e., of "nature." The countries which were at that time affected by involuntary unemployment were nations which before the war had been highly industrialized and which, due to insufficient reserves of raw materials in their own countries, had to import the "nature" which they lacked and these imports could only be paid for by exporting a corresponding quantity of manufactured goods. This situation also differs from the case of general underemployment, which was the only case that Keynes analyzed, in that the production apparatus is inadequate. Here, as in the case of the Soviet Union mentioned earlier, the main problem is not the revitalization of an existing production potential, but the expansion of an inadequate production apparatus.

Germany's postwar economic policy was aimed at stimulating saving and restricting consumption. It was the right solution under these circumstances, as it was in the Soviet Union at the time of its industrial development. On the other hand, Great Britain's use of Keynesian full employment policy at that time was wrong. In this situation, the stimulation of consumption and the granting of additional government aid restricted investment and prevented industrial recovery.

However, the problems of the emerging Federal Republic of Germany and those of the Soviet Union differed in one respect. Countries such as West Germany, France, or Great Britain are not self-sufficient in raw materials. They must export finished goods to pay for their imports of raw materials. A country such as the Soviet Union, which like the United States is largely self-sufficient in raw materials, is not faced with this problem. It is not forced, as West Germany is, to produce manufactured goods of a quality which is competitive on world markets.

There are therefore at least three different types of underemployment:

1. The *"general unemployment"* analyzed by Keynes, which affects all factors of production to the same extent and in which the only problem is the revitalization of the existing production apparatus by means of stimulation of consumption, deficit spending, etc.; this is possible to do in an economy which is isolated from other countries by exchange control or high tariff barriers without taking foreign trade into account.

2. *Involuntary underemployment of labor acompanied by a shortage of capital goods but adequate reserves of raw materials.* In this case "abstinence," and therefore a reduction in consumption, is necessary; at the same time, there is no obligation to export manufactured goods.

3. *Involuntary underemployment of labor with a shortage of both capital goods and raw materials.* In this case, abstinence of consumption alone is not enough. The quality of manufactured goods must become competitive on export markets so that imports of raw materials can be paid for.

§2 The neglect of foreign trade

In his *General Theory*, Keynes mainly analyzed a closed economy,[27] corresponding to the situation which prevailed in the thirties. Countries had shut themselves off from each other: some, like the United States, by means of high tariff barriers; some, like France, by means of import duties; and some, including most of the other industrialized countries, by means of exchange control. Keynes, in keeping with the neomercantilism of that time, relegated his comments on foreign trade to Chapter 23 of his *General Theory*, which characteristically carries the heading "Notes on Mercantilism, the Usury Laws, Stamped Money and Theories of Underconsumption."

However, an analysis of a closed economy cannot produce a "general theory." In an international economy such as that which again exists at the present time in the free world, the problems have changed in two respects: (1) Employment is no longer only a national problem but an international one. (2) The level of employment in each national economy depends on the growth or decline of exports and imports; it is by no means only the question of whether foreign trade balances are favorable or unfavorable, as Keynes and his followers believe, which is effective with regard to the level of employment.

1. The employment problem in the international economy

The establishment (or re-establishment) of the international economy turns national problems into international ones. This applies to employment in two respects: (1) Employment or underemployment in one country influences employment or underemployment in other countries. (2) Pursuing a national employment policy through deficit spending now increases employment internationally, but no longer necessarily in the country pursuing the policy.

In an international (or world) economy, the level of employment in one country (also) depends on the international level of employment. Underemployment in less developed countries influences employment in advanced industrial nations and vice versa. If there is underemployment in the international economy, national full employment will always be a temporary exception.

Since they have concentrated solely on a closed economy, neither Keynes nor his followers have posed the question of on what factors the level of international employment depends or what are the main causes of international underemployment; nor have they asked whether the uneven development of the countries involved in the international economy or the unequal distribution of power among them contributes to international unemployment. Keynes and his school have not discussed the problem of international unemployment at all.

Keynes's theory that an economy can raise its level of employment through national measures only applies without limitation to a closed economy. In an open economy, in which commodity prices are determined by supply and demand (i.e., are not regulated by price controls) its competitive position with regard to other countries worsens if it pursues an employment policy in isolation. If prices in a country rise as a result of deficit spending, exports fall and imports rise, with the result that employment does not increase but decreases. This at least is true with fixed exchange rates, as we will see later on.

2. The effect of foreign trade on employment

Keynes supported the theory, already put forward by the mercantilists, that only the balance and not the volume of foreign trade influences the level of employment in the economy. A favorable balance[28] "will prove extremely stimulating" and an unfavorable balance "may soon produce a state of persistent depression."[29] This means that a growth or a decline in foreign trade has no effect on the level of employment in an economy. This is a misconception.

An increase in foreign trade regularly has a favorable effect on employment, even if a country's balance of payments is in deficit. There are two main reasons for this: (1) A country which imports raw materials which it does not itself possess, and uses them to manufacture finished products thereby increases its level of employment. (2) A country which exports the finished products (steel tubes, machines, autos, etc.) which it has manufactured from the imported raw materials thus also exports the labor added to these products during their manufacture. In West Germany, approximately every fourth person is working for the export trade, but only about every hundredth person—and then only temporarily—is working to produce an export surplus.

A decline in foreign trade, even if the balance of trade becomes positive, has an unfavorable influence on a country's level of employment. Every fall in exports in real terms (all other things being equal) reduces a country's level of employment. This is still the case even if imports fall more than exports (at least if the goods previously imported are not now manufactured in the importing country, which in many cases is only possible with a time lag and in other cases not possible at all). In 1931/32, the steepest ever rise in unemployment happened in Germany at a time when the German balance of payments became positive.

Because Keynes and his followers assume an economy which is not only closed but also stationary, they also fail to recognize that in a growing economy employment will be unfavorably effected if foreign trade grows more slowly than labor productivity.

§3 The neglect of the effects of inflation

In his general theory, Keynes has only skimmed over the problem of inflation, as he assumes with the "given . . . degree of competition" that government price control common in the thirties is also a basic premise. Nevertheless, he does not leave the problem of inflation completely untouched. "The economic history of Spain in the latter part of the fifteenth and in the sixteenth centuries," writes Keynes, "provides an example of a country whose foreign trade was destroyed by the effect on the wage-unit of an excessive abundance of the precious metals."[30] He might have added that imported inflation (for that is what it was) has a detrimental effect on a country's level of employment. In fact, the development of Spain in the latter part of the fifteenth, and particularly in the sixteenth, century is an early example of the phenomenon which is now called *stagflation* and which German cameralists described as far back as the eighteenth century in connection with the controversy over the state treasury.

Keynes entirely omitted the detrimental effects of homemade inflation on foreign trade and employment from his analysis. He ignored homemade inflation (in contrast to the post-Keynesians) because he assumed that deficit spending does not cause price increases during a period of underemployment, provided that there are no bottlenecks.[31] However, this assumption is only correct if the government controls prices, as was indeed the case in many countries as a result of the Great Depression.[32]

If prices are not government controlled but flexible as is the case in a free economy, the policy of deficit spending causes inflationary price and wage increases even in a period of prevailing underemployment. This is shown by the experiences of the United States and Great Britain over the last couple of decades, and by the recent experience of West Germany as well. Despite—or, perhaps more accurately, because of—rising prices, underemployment has in this case increased and not decreased. If Keynes were correct, the phenomenon of stagflation could only occur in particular cases, namely, when imported inflation leads to an "excessive abundance" of money.

The effects of inflation on foreign trade and employment do not, of course, depend on whether the increase in the money supply is homemade or imported. The following are more important: (1) whether and in what form economies have trading relations with other countries; and (2) whether exchange rates are fixed, as was initially the case after Bretton Woods, or flexible, as is often the case today.

In a closed economy, the increase in employment brought about by an increase in the money supply must inevitably remain in that country; as there is no foreign trade, it cannot be "exported." The situation is different in an open economy with fixed exchange rates. In this case, an increase in the money supply which takes place in isolation has an unfavorable effect on domestic employment. If national deficit spending causes the country to become less competitive with other countries, exports will go down and imports up.[33] The domestic level of employment then falls below the previous level, while the additional employment is transferred to other countries via foreign trade. After World war II "Keynesian full employment policy" therefore increased underemployment in countries such as the United States and Great Britain while in West Germany and in other countries with below-average rates of inflation it created additional jobs. The effects of a national employment policy in an international economy are different from those in a closed economy.

The effect of foreign trade furthermore depends on whether exchange rates are fixed or flexible. If exchange rates are fixed, as under the Bretton Woods agreements, unfavorable international developments cannot be compensated for via exchange rates. This results in false exchange rates. In countries which are suffering from inflation (to a greater extent than others), the exchange rates are overvalued, while the exchange rates of countries which are keeping the value of money stable (or have less inflation than other countries) are undervalued. The first group of countries is suffering from underemployment with rising prices, i.e., from stagflation. The second group of countries is forced by fixed exchange rates to "currency dumping," which results in over-full employment and necessitates the employment of foreign workers, as has been the case in West Germany, Switzerland, or Austria, for example.

If, on the other hand, exchange rates are flexible, in keeping with a competitive international economy, changes in the competitive position of a country on the world market can more or less be compensated for by movements in exchange rates in the opposite direction. Exchange rates fall in a country with an unfavorable balance and rise in a country with a favorable balance. However, this stabilizing effect on a country's international competitive position occurs neither automatically nor without time lags, as shown by the rapid fluctuation of the rate of exchange of the dollar against the Deutschmark in the years 1976 to 1983. Even when exchange rates are in themselves flexible, an isolated increase in the money supply in the relevant country causes underemployment, at least until the adjustment process is complete.

§4   The role of government in Keynes's theory

Keynes, drawing on Kahn,[34] makes government the central feature of his multiplier theory.[35] According to Keynes, the task of government is to fill the gap in demand that has arisen due to the failure of private households and firms by means of additional public investment, and thereby to restore full employment. To this extent government is considered as a kind of "repair shop" for failures of private enterprises and private households.

At no point in his general theory, however, does Keynes examine the question of *whether and to what extent governments themselves cause unemployment.* For him, the responsibility for the lack of sufficient employment lies with private households due to their tendency toward "oversaving" and with private firms due to their liquidity preference. The unfavorable effects on the economy which can be produced by the activities of government (including regional and local government), have not been considered by Keynes in this context. In fact, a government does cause unemployment: (1) if it cuts public expenditures at the wrong time, or (2) if it enacts measures of economic policy which have an unfavorable effect on business.

1. Errors of "fiscal policy"

Keynes embarked upon his general theory with no mention of the performance of "fiscal policy" in the years preceding the Great Depression. If he had done so, he would have discovered the following:

1. In a number of countries, public expenditure had only formed a proportion of the revenue which had been taken by taxation. This applied both to defeated countries such as Austria and Germany, who used tax revenues for the payment of reparations, and to victorious countries such as Great Britain as well as to neutral countries such as Switzerland, who paid back loans dating back to World War I out of tax revenues.

2. Other countries, such as the United States or France, which had a favorable balance of payments, neutralized the inflow of money. They did this to prevent underemployment, and therefore the stagflation, which would otherwise be caused by imported inflation.

It is irrelevant to the consequences of such a policy that the gap in world demand which resulted from this monetary policy with its disastrous consequences for the international economy was temporarily filled (i.e., until the Black Friday of 1929) by means of private credit creation. The only important factor is that at that time, economically powerful nations were pursuing a fiscal policy which was in conflict with the aim of international full employment. *Governments whose domestic spending is lower than the income from taxation and governments which neutralize the money that they are receiving from the tax revenues of other countries influence the level of world employment negatively.*

In a growing and developing economy, underemployment also

occurs if deficit spending does not rise in step with the increase in productivity. In a growing and developing economy, an increase in borrowing at the same rate as the increase in productivity in the economy in both the private and the public sector is a prerequisite for full employment; both too much and too little borrowing have a harmful effect on employment policy.

Governments therefore contribute to underemployment in a world with increasing labor productivity when they: (1) Spend less at home than they receive from taxation. (2) Combat imported inflation (which is not caused by the deficit spending of other countries) by neutralizing the inflow of money. (3) Do not keep their fiscal policy in line with the development of productivity and foreign trade.

2. Errors of economic policy

Economic policy can have a favorable as well as a harmful effect on national and international levels of employment. This will be discussed elsewhere in this book; therefore, it is sufficient here to show by means of examples how economic policy causes unemployment.

Government subsidies to the construction market, regardless of whether they are in form of savings bonuses, special depreciation allowances, or low-cost loans, certainly increase employment at first, but distort the market. The higher such subsidies are and the longer they last, the greater is the danger that buildings will be put up for which there is no demand. Consequently, a construction boom which has been artificially stimulated in this way cannot be sustained in the long run. One day it turns out that the distortion of the market has resulted in mistakes being made in planning for actual demand. Then the construction boom changes into a slump, combined with underemployment of all factors of production in this sector. If subsidies are reduced in such a situation, as in West Germany in 1974, this only increases the difficulties of the construction market. The same negative results wil be found if the government regulates rents in such a way that construction of houses for rent becomes unprofitable.

Another example is the "currency dumping" mentioned above. An exchange rate which is too low first causes "overfull employment" and then, after it has been adjusted, underemployment.

In an international economy, a government also causes national underemployment when it pursues a Keynesian monetary policy without taking into account the consequences for foreign trade.

Governments cause world unemployment when they destroy free trade and diminish foreign trade through trade barriers and exchange control. If governments were again to separate their nations from other countries by trade barriers and exchange control, as they did in the thirties, a new Great Depression would be the result.

Governments do not only improve the rate of employment; they are also able to create unemployment.

§5 Oversimplifications of John Maynard Keynes

In his general theory, Keynes oversimplified the problems, at least to the following extent:

1. Keynes viewed the economic phenomena of the thirties as an equilibrium; but it is really a process, in which workers become destitute, machinery rusts away, and factory buildings collapse and in which varying experiences of the past and varying expectations of the future play an important part. Keynes's assumption that changes in income expectations average out in both booms and slumps is incorrect.

2. Keynes implicitly assumed that the only type of underemployment is that in which not only labor but also machines (capital goods) and raw materials (nature) are waiting to be reincorporated into the production process. However, there are other types of underemployment: involuntary unemployment may be combined with a shortage of capital goods or a shortage of raw materials. The treatment for these is not the same.

3. Keynes assumed that prices rise only when bottlenecks occur, which is incorrect; prices rise when they are free, i.e., not government controlled. Prices rise in industries affected by underemployment, as shown by the experiences of the United States, Great Britain, and the Federal Republic of Germany in the past few years.

4. Keynes assumed, as his example of Spain shows, that only an "excessive abundance" of money has a detrimental effect on economic life. However, the relationship between inflation and employment is more complicated, especially since there are not

only imported and homemade inflations, but also various causes of stagflation, as will be shown later.

5. Keynes analyzed the underemployment which prevailed during the Great Depression with reference to a model of a closed economy. The influence of a decline in foreign trade on employment (as a result of neomercantilism) is not included in his investigations.

6. Keynes saw the government only as a deus ex machina which reduces or eliminates the existing unemployment by means of its employment policy. He completely overlooked the fact that governments can also cause underemployment by their fiscal or economic policy.

7. Keynes restricted his theory to the analysis of a stationary economy. He has not treated the effects of new markets (for example, of the railroad, automobile, or computer industry) or of automation on employment. Neither rationalization investment nor investment in development (new or better goods, new and cheaper production processes) play a role in his theory (cf. section 2, Chapter 4).

Keynes, like many economists before and after him, oversimplified the problems and unjustifiably generalized the results which he discovered. *His theory is neither general, nor does it explain a world depression.* This is not particularly surprising. It is more surprising that even economic authors of today largely fail to recognize this fact.

Elimination of Human Beings from Economic Theory

> Man finds himself in the awkward and embarassing situation of being an animal who is also a self-conscious spiritual being.
>
> Arnold Toynbee

Under the influence of the natural sciences, economists have always shown a tendency to ignore the specific characteristics of human activity and to view economic phenomena as mechanisms which cannot be influenced by human beings. The resulting elimination of man from economic theory will be demonstrated by the following theorems:

1. David Hume's foreign trade mechanism,
2. neoclassical market mechanisms,
3. accelerator-multiplier mechanism,
4. inflation-employment mechanism.

SECTION 1: David Hume's Foreign Trade Mechanism

David Hume, whose theorem is still to be found in standard textbooks[1], saw the international economy as a pre-established harmony. Temporary deviations are indeed possible, but returns to natural equilibrium always follow automatically.

"Suppose," says Hume in his famous essay "Of the Balance of Trade"[2] "four-fifths of all the money in Great Britain to be annihilated in one night, and the nation reduced to the same condition, with regard to specie, as in the reigns of the HARRYS and EDWARDS, what would be the consequence? Must not the price of all labour and commodities sink in proportion, and everything be sold as cheap as they were in those ages? What nation could then dispute with us in any foreign market, or pretend to navigate or to sell manufactures at the same price, which to us would afford sufficient profit? In how little time, therefore, must this bring back the money which we had lost, and raise us to the level of all the neighbouring nations? Where, after we have arrived, we immediately lose the advantage of the cheapness of labour and commodities; and the farther flowing in of money is stopped by our fulness and repletion."[3]

On closer examination, David Hume's theorem can be seen to contain two—albeit linked—automatic mechanisms: (1) automatic equalization of "trade balances,"[4] and (2) automatic equalization of the money supply in the trading countries.

Because (according to Hume) a country which loses money automatically gains pre-eminence in international trade, it must automatically receive back the money it has lost. In the same way, Hume postulated, the country into which money is flowing is automatically at a disadvantage in international trade, so that it also has to automatically spend the accumulated money. As Hume considers these equalization effects to have the invitability of natural laws, he compares them with the automatic equalization of levels in communicating tubes: "All water, wherever it communicates, remains always at a level. Ask naturalists the reason; they tell you, that, were it to be raised in any one place, the superior gravity of that part not being balanced, must depress it, till it meet a counterpoise; and that the same cause, which redresses the inequality when it happens, must for ever prevent it, without some violent externed operation."[5]

However, the international economy is not a system of communicating tubes, and there are no automatic mechanisms in the international economy which have the inevitability of natural laws. An economy does not work by "superior gravity"; it is human activity, not least in the form of economic policy, which is the important factor. Whether and to what extent trade flows and international flows of money equalize in reality depends, among other things, on the following human decisions:

1. A country can set up a central bank[6] by Act of Parliament, the task of which is to regulate the national circulation of money. If, for example, the board of the Deutsche Bundesbank takes action to neutralize the money flowing in from abroad, the imported inflation is eliminated. The "mechanism" by which an inflow of money leads to price increases and a worsening of the country's competitive position with regard to other countries is thus put out of action. The same effect can be achieved, as the

German cameralists were already aware, by setting up a "state treasury." If, on the other hand, the central bank of a country suffering from a balance of payments deficit replaces the money which is flowing out by creating new money, the deflation which would otherwise be expected does not occur. The mechanism by which trade balances equalize and a deficit country becomes a surplus country and vice versa ceases to operate.

2. There is no inevitable connection between the quantity of money on the one hand and prices (and wages) on the other, as David Hume, drawing on Bodin's quantity theory of money, assumes. If people expect the value of money to fall, they spend their money more quickly. If, on the other hand, people expect the value of money to rise, they will delay certain purchases. In the first case the velocity of circulation of money rises; in the second case it falls. Why and to what extent such expectations occur again depends on past experiences and therefore on learning processes. People who already know from experience what inflation means react more quickly and more strongly than people who have not yet experienced this phenomenon. In the same way, wages do not mechanically adjust to prices. Wages may lag behind prices; but wage increases may, on the other hand, run ahead of price increases, insofar as union leaders have the power to compensate for future price increases in their wage negotiations.

3. The circulation of goods and money does not remain constant in a "developing economy." In each nation as well as in the whole world, economic development depends on human achievements. A country which stands out from other countries by introducing new goods and new production processes raises not only its competitive position with regard to other countries, but also its per capita income and therefore its wealth. A country whose inhabitants are lazy or whose economic system offers no incentives to introduce innovations suffers a decline of its competitive position; its per capita income and its wealth fall, at least in relative terms. New goods and better qualities create new demand by households and firms in the domestic market as well as in international trade.

4. Lastly, the development of a country is dependent upon its use of power.[7] Spain initially became rich by exploiting the South American Indians. This wealth was in its turn the cause of the impoverishment mentioned by Keynes,[8] which nevertheless con-

tinued for centuries. Ireland became poor because it was exploited by England (which, in contrast to Spain, invested its balance of payments surpluses overseas).

Hume's mechanisms did not operate in either case. The Spaniards became poor despite the inflow of money; and after the flow of money dried up, they did not become rich again. The Irish, as they became increasingly poor, also lost their competitive position, as Jonathan Swift had prophesied in 1726 in his *Short View of the State of Ireland*.

Hume observed trends and misunderstood them to be inevitable mechanisms. However, economic history, like all history, is written by human beings and is not produced by mechanisms.

SECTION 2: Neoclassical Market Mechanisms

> In more general terms, the neoclassical theory assigns to everyone the behavior attributes suggested by Jeremy Bentham. Humans are economic hedonists, pleasure machines.
> *Kalman Goldberg*

Neoclassical economists do not only largely ignore space and time, but also view people as resembling automatons which react to impulses like robots. They interpret the processes which take place on markets as mechanisms which cannot be influenced by human beings.

The neoclassical economists consider firms as suppliers whose sales are automatically determined by marginal cost or marginal revenue, and households as consumers whose purchases of goods result from marginal utility or marginal expenditure. The coordination of supply and demand in "perfect competition" or the coordination of price and quantity in "monopoly" is an automatic, even functional, relationship which is totally devoid of any human influence.

§1 The automatons of neoclassical economics

In neoclassical models of equilibrium, suppliers and consumers do not behave as human beings but as machines. They are "pleasure machines" or "profit machines." Consumers maximize their pleasure, and producers, their profit.

The "competing firms," "oligopolies" and "monopolies" of

this theory make no entrepreneurial decisions, nor do they carry out any of the functions which are in reality the responsibility of entrepreneurs or top managers. Their work force as well as their products are given. They cannot increase or decrease the quality of their products, nor can they take other products or entirely new products into their range. They do not improve the quality of their laborers. They are not faced with the questions of whether they should replace their out-of-date machinery with new, more efficient banks of machines or whether and how they can win new customers or persuade their existing customers to buy more. Their production processes, like their sales, are predetermined. Neither different experiences nor changing expectations nor varying evaluations play any role.

In the model world of this bleak theory, in which there are no sales problems and no place for either new technology or new or improved products, the only task left for suppliers is to maximize their profit. As it is assumed that the cost and sales curves of these pseudo-firms or pseudo-managers cannot be influenced, their profit is determined solely by the equation $MR = MC$.

The "competing firms" of this model world earn less than the "monopolies," but they have also less to do. Their price is predetermined by the market and is also identical to their marginal revenue. They only have to adjust their output, which is by definition equal to their sales, in such a way that the equation $MC = P$ applies to the last unit in each case. The entrepreneur or manager of the real world has degenerated into a mere "quantity-adjuster" (Erich Schneider) who is unable to pursue any kind or entrepreneurial policy. He cannot influence the success of his business. He can only take his "differential return" as a "residuum."

The "monopolies" of this model world also bear no resemblance to entrepreneurs; nevertheless, they are virtually able to vary prices and quantities because their (actual) sales curve no longer runs parallel to the horizontal axis but slopes toward it. However, as they are assumed to maximize their profit at all times, they actually have no choice either. They must produce (and simultaneously sell) the quantity at which their marginal revenue curve intersects their marginal cost curve. Even their profit is a kind of "residuum" because they have no way of influencing it through entrepreneurial decisions.

The automatons of this theory have as much in common with

the entrepreneurs and managers of the real world as parrots have with human beings. They take no decisions or action; they just react. And just as parrots do not understand the things they repeat, these automatons understand nothing of the tasks to be performed in their firms. They are spiritless and soulless creatures who only react to impulses and are incapable of making any human decisions.

§2 The market mechanism

It is almost unanimously agreed that in competition, supply and demand are subject to the market mechanism. If demand on a market rises, the price automatically increases; if, on the other hand, demand on a market falls, the price automatically decreases, without any need for any kind of entrepreneurial action by the competing firms, who have no choice but to accept the price which forms on the "market" as a "datum." Experiences, expectations, and revaluations play no part in this mechanism, in which there are neither learning processes nor entrepreneurial achievements, with the result that under these assumptions, the "competition in efficiency" (Leistungswettbewerb) appears somewhat nonsensical. Firms are not faced with the decision of whether to get out of a declining market, nor are they able to enter another market or to create a new market by launching an entirely new product. The coordination of supply and demand occurs largely without their aid, through the market mechanism which is steered by an "Invisible Hand." With given markets, given production technology, and without any sales problems, there is nothing left that requires any kind of human intervention.

In reality, of course, this kind of mechanism does not exist. The coordination of supply and demand which occurs in competition is the result of entrepreneurial decisions. If firms are subject to the pressure of competition, they must make their decisions in the interest of their customers; they must increase their supply when there is a sellers' market, and they must change the quality of their products in accordance with the wishes of their customers if they do not want to lose any of them to their competitors. On the other hand, they must reduce their output of goods for which demand is declining if they are not to be forced out of the market due to intolerable losses.

Profits are therefore not a residuum which entrepreneurs have to accept. Profits *and* losses are the result of entrepreneurial decisions and therefore of entrepreneurial policy, at least to a great extent.

§3 *The price-quantity functions of monopoly and monopsony*

The prevailing opinion is that there is a functional relationship between price and quantity in monopoly (supply monopoly) and monopsony (demand monopoly).

1. The functionalism of monopoly theory

A "monopoly" is, as Woll states, "in the happy position of being able to impose either the quantity or the price on the market as he wishes. If the monopolist chooses the price, he has to accept a certain sales volume; if he chooses the quantity, he has to accept the price."[9] Heinrich von Stackelberg expresses this automatic coordination by saying that an increase in sales volume "causes a fall in the selling price; an increase in the selling price causes a fall in sales volume."[10] Henderson and Quandt put it even more simply; according to them, the monopoly's sales volume is "a single-valued function of the price"

$$\text{"}q = \int(p)\text{"}$$

and the price is "a single-valued function of quantity"

$$\text{"}p = \int(q)\text{"}$$

where p = price and q = quantity.[11]

However, this kind of functional relationship between price and quantity does not exist. *If a monopoly raises its price, but makes no decision on the quantity it produces, it will continue to produce the same quantity as before.* The result is overproduction, because consumers purchase a smaller quantity at the higher price. If OPEC raises the price of oil, for example, this does not necessarily cause the quantity of oil produced to go down. Output may even rise. Similarly, the price for coal does not fall just because the "Coal Board" is producing so much coal that it is piling up at the mines. *If, on the other hand, a monopoly reduces the quantity without making a decision on price, the old price remains in force and the reduced production is no longer sufficient to fully satisfy demand.* The first case gives rise to unsalable inventory; in the second case there are queues outside the stores, as constantly occurs in Eastern bloc countries, for example.

Like all firms, therefore, a monopoly also has to make two entrepreneurial decisions if it wishes to coordinate supply and demand: a decision on the price which it charges *and* a decision on the quantity it produces.

If it restricts itself to only one of these decisions, the result for both private and state monopolies is either unsalable inventory or queues outside the stores or delivery times stretching into years or even decades, as in the case of automobiles in some Eastern bloc countries.

The fact that it is rational to reduce supply when raising the price (assuming that the state of the market remains unchanged) or to raise the price when less is being produced does not mean that the quantity determines the price or vice versa.

2. The mechanical reactions of monopsony

The functionalism which assumes that mechanical relationships exist when everything really depends on economic decisions is also found in the neoclassical theory of monopsony (demand monopoly).

In this theory, which is still almost universally recognized, monopsony is: (1) identified either with consumers whose actions are determined by marginal utility and marginal expenditure, or with firms which demand factors of production, for whom "marginal product" and "marginal cost" are decisive,[12] (2) deprived of all real tasks, with the result that like the (supply) monopoly his only remaining "parameter of action " is price "or" quantity, (3) subject to a mechanism by which the quantity available adjusts to the price or the price to be paid adjusts to the quantity, and finally, (4) buys less goods than a competing firm in the same situation; this means that a department store which buys goods to resell them or an industrial concern which buys raw materials and semifinished products for manufacturing its own products is subject to a kind of mechanism which is in stark contrast to its own interests (with the result that no neoclassical author has in fact attempted to deal with this normal case of a demand monopoly).

None of these four statements is borne out by reality:

(1) Demand monopolies are not consumers. They are either

firms, who demand not only resources (such as labor) but also (if not mainly) "commodities," and in doing so act in accordance not with "marginal utility" or "marginal product," but with their sales opportunities; or they are public authorities (states, communities), whose expenditure is determined by every possible economic, social, or political criterion, but certainly not by the "marginal pleasure" or "marginal utility" of national or local government.

(2) "Demand monopolies" do not only have a choice between price or quantity. They can stipulate the qualities they buy, lay down delivery dates and terms of payment; they are able to influence the production or the production processes of the products they will buy. They can even try to affect the valuations of their suppliers (the "calculatory costs," for example).

(3) In a monopsony, as in a monopoly, the quantity does not automatically adjust to the price (or vice versa); instead the firm must decide the quantity it will buy at a particular price or vice versa.

(4) A firm which has a demand monopoly on a market does not reduce its purchases if it can obtain products for its production or its trading more cheaply than before. The cheaper it gets its goods or raw materials, the more it can sell in its turn and the more semifinished products and raw materials it will buy.

The neoclassical theory of monopsony, therefore, does not coincide with the reality it is supposed to explain. If, as in this case, the theory does not correspond to reality, it is not the fault of the reality which is to be explained, but of the theory which is not providing this explanation. It is the theory and the premises underlying it which have to be changed. In fact, the assumptions and the results of this model world are in stark contrast to reality, because a factor which decides the fortunes of the economy is entirely absent: real people and therewith thinking and acting human beings.[13]

§4 *The distorted image of the entrepreneur in neoclassical economics*

The entrepreneur of neoclassical theory concentrates solely on maximizing his profit. He does not perform entrepreneurial tasks in the real sense; indeed he cannot perform them, because sales curves as well as technology, quality, etc. are assumed to be "given." The specific economic tasks for which the entrepreneur is in reality responsible are carried out automatically or are assumed to be nonexistent.

The neoclassical economists have thus reinforced Marx's dislike of capitalists. If entrepreneurs (or managers) really had nothing to do apart from maximizing their profit, they would in fact be superfluous to the economy. The "free nationalization" (*freie Vergesellschaftung*) which Karl Marx dreamed of would present no problems if cost and sales curves were constant, if supply and demand equalized automatically, if there were a functional relationship between price and quantity, and if product quality was economically irrelevant.

If the oversimplified models of the neoclassical economists were correct, however, the four basic problems of the Soviet economy would not existent:

1. The co-ordination of supply and demand, which is no problem if the firms produce and sell only the quantities which the households buy and consume. The production of too much of one good and too little of another is then impossible.
2. The transfer of factors of production from declining to growing markets, which is no problem if there are no declining or growing markets.
3. The achievement of technological process in the complex consumer goods sector, which prevents no problem if there is by definition no technological progress.
4. The manufacture of high-quality (or at least trouble free) products, which is not a problem if product qualities are given and the only economically relevant factors are price and quantity.

In reality, however, there are sales problems, changes in customers' tastes, the disappearance of old markets and the emergence of new ones, and technological development which is vital to the competitive position of both firms and countries; in addition, increasing wealth means that quality becomes more important than mere quantity. *In reality, therefore, entrepreneurs and top managers have quite different problems and parameters of action from those in neoclassical theory.*[14]

SECTION 3: Accelerator-Multiplier Mechanism

". . . the object of economics is the chain of unique events we call human history."
Jürg Niehans

Hicks,[15] Samuelson,[16] and others have further developed Keynes's general theory by combining the multiplier and the accelerator into a model of unstable growth.[17]

The multiplier describes the influence of additional investment on national income. According to Samuelson, the word *multiplier* "is used for the numerical coefficient showing how much above unity is the increase in income resulting from each increase in investment."[18]

The accelerator is based on the phenomenon observed in the nineteenth century, mainly in the primary industries, that a change in demand for consumer goods produces a far greater change in demand for investment goods.

Hicks, Samuelson, and others consider the accelerator, as Keynes did the multiplier, as a mechanical relationship unaffected by experiences, expectations, and re-evaluations of human beings who are responsible for the decisions of households and firms in economic processes.[19]

§1 The mechanism of unstable growth

Jevons attempted a mechanical explanation of the business cycle in his "sunspot theory," which—notwithstanding its mathematical argumentation—is only of historical importance. Hicks, Samuelson, and others explain the business cycle, with the aid of the multiplier and the accelerator, as a "mechanism of unstable growth." Their assumptions result in a growth mechanism that is not only self-explanatory but also operates independently of all historical conditions of human existence. As in Jevons's sunspot theory, human activity plays no part in its operation.

Samuelson published his essay on the "Interactions between the Multiplier Analysis and the Principle of Acceleration" in 1939. He described this mechanism in his textbook as follows:

> Suppose, in a situation of unemployment, we get income growing again. The rising income induces, via the accelerator, new investment. The new investment induces, via the multiplier, further rises in income. Hence, the rate of growth of output may be 'self-warranting.'

But how can a system grow forever at 6 or 7 percent if its labor force grows only at ½ or 1 percent and workers' productivity grows only at 1 or 2 percent? It can't.

The self-warranting expansion, even if we are lucky enough to get and keep it, must ultimately bump into the full-employment ceiling. Like a tennis ball (and unlike a wad of gum), it is likely to bounce back from the full-employment ceiling into a recession. Why? Because the minute the system stops its fast growth, the accelerator dictates the end of the high investment supporting the boom. Like an airplane that falls once it loses its motion, the economic system plummets downward.

Similar accelerator-multiplier analysis may explain the ultimate end of a recession and the onset of an upturn. When output plummets downward rapidly, the acceleration principle calls for negative investment (or disinvestment) greater than the rate at which machines can wear out. This wear-out rate puts a floor on how fast disinvestment can take place, and hence a floor on how far it (the SS-II intersection) can push the economy below its break-even point.

Bumping along such a basement floor means firms will eventually work down their capital stock to the level called for by the low floor level of income. Then the acceleration principle calls for a termination of disinvestment! Our image must shift from gum, ball, and airplane to that of a cork. Once we stop pushing it down, it's buoyed back up again. A new cycle can begin . . . [20]

Hicks, in his *Contribution to the Theory of the Trade Cycle*, does not use the images of mechanically rebounding balls, plummeting airplanes, or corks that are mechanically buoyed back to the surface, but even he speaks of a "ceiling" and a "bottom" within which growth moves when it deviates from the "equilibrium path." He also assumes "that an upward displacement from the equilibrium path will tend to cause a movement away from equilibrium"[21] and claims, like Samuelson, that "the only way in which the capital stock can be reduced is by a cessation of reinvestment."[22] On the basis of these and similar assumptions, the real growth path deflects upward until it hits the "full-employment ceiling" and rebounds from it because "the induced investment" is now no longer high enough "to support a growth of output along the path."[23] However, once the fall in real growth has begun, it must continue for the time being, but it cannot fall ad infinitum, because, writes Hicks, "the slump must have a bottom."[24] "Just as the bottom to the slump is inevitable, so (provided that autonomous investment maintains its upward trend) recovery is inevitable."[25] The growth path oscillates between ceiling and bottom.

In human society, however, automatic mechanisms do not exist. Like David Hume's comparison of trading nations with water in communicating tubes, Samuelson's comparisons of economic phenomena with tennis balls, airplanes, and corks, or Hicks's asumption of a "ceiling" or a "bottom," are misleading.

The "mechanism of unstable growth" assumed by Samuelson, Hicks, and others is not borne out by reality:

1. The (investment) accelerator is not inevitable. Its appearance is dependent on certain historical conditions, which are not necessarily present or only partly present in the advanced industrial nations of today.
2. The multiplier model, like the pure accelerator model, ignores any influence from different experiences, various expectations, and changing valuations which accompany "unstable growth."
3. The assumption of a "fullemployment ceiling" from which the business cycle automatically rebounds like a tennis ball, is arbitrary; slumps often begin even when the "full-employment ceiling" has not been reached.
4. The claim made by Samuelson and accepted by Hicks that the natural wear-out rate represents the lower limit of economic disinvestment in a slump is not in accordance with the conditions of a changing and developing economy.
5. The effects of economic development on employment are not taken into account at all in the multiplier-accelerator mechanism.

§2 Historical conditions of the accelerator

Samuelson, Hicks, Domar, and many other economists tacitly assume that in contrast to other human phenomena, economic events continue to exist unchanged; they are assumed to be timeless and are therefore not subject to historical change. Therefore, they also discuss the accelerator principle without stating the assumptions which make its analytical value relative.

Among the premises which are frequently not mentioned are: (1) full capacity utilization in all the industries involved, (2) competition between firms, (3) no customer preferences, (4) constant technology (a stationary economy), and (5) a closed economy.

The authors also assume that entrepreneurs do not learn anything from their experience and therefore neglect everything which might reduce or eliminate the accelerator. Finally, they assume that valuations are given.

The accelerator, however, is not inevitable, but depends on certain conditions:

1. If there is spare capacity in an industry, new orders do not induce any net investment. If, for example, the consumer goods industry is only operating at seventy percent of total capacity, then even a fifteen or thirty percent increase in demand for consumer goods does not produce any additional demand for investment goods.[26]

2. *The accelerator only operates when there is competition between firms.* It is competition which forces firms to undertake the over-hasty investment described by the accelerator model. However, firms learn from their experiences. In the primary industries, which experienced extremely rapid acceleration in the nineteenth century, firms started as early as the 1870s to restrict competition by means of cartels or market-dominating horizontally integrated concerns. (As the founding of the European community has meant that national cartels are no longer adequate to restrict competition, attempts have been made to combat the effects of the accelerator by means of European cartels.)

3. If customer preferences come into play, there is no longer a need for cartel agreements to spread sudden orders over the future. Industries which sell a varied range of high-quality products can make use of delivery dates even if they do not dominate the market, provided that their customers are prepared to wait months or even years for a special product. If the quoting of delivery dates becomes the norm, the extent of a firm's investment will be largely independent of its sales at a particular point of time.

4. As the rate of acceleration depends on the life expectancy of capital goods,[27] acceleration fluctuates with the rate of technological development. If the rate of technological development is relatively slow, then machines can be used for forty or fifty years, as they were in the last century. The acceleration coefficient is then correspondingly large. If, on the other hand, the rate of techno-

logical development is relatively fast, as it has been in recent decades,[28] then machines become prematurely obsolete; they must be replaced by new, more efficient machines before they are worn out. The rate of acceleration falls correspondingly. In the pure model, the acceleration coefficient is fifty if the life expectancy is fifty years and is only ten if the life expectancy is ten years. The shorter the life expectancy, the higher the annual new investment and the lower the acceleration effect of each (additional) net investment.

5. Economies which are subject to unstable growth are not stationary. They are developing economies. Before a rise in consumption, therefore, there is often not only reinvestment but also net investment; there is *investment in rationalization* as well as *investment in development*, which are required for the production of new products or at least new models, for example in the automobile industry. In a developing economy, the stability of growth therefore depends less on the consumption of given goods than on the continuity of economic progress and therefore on the rate and the stability of investment in rationalization of production and development of new or better products. This investment is not subject to any kind of mechanism.

6. The advanced economies of Western nations are in any case not closed economies at present. Additional demand for capital goods therefore falls not only to domestic suppliers, but may shift to other countries, which may at the same time be suffering from underutilized capacity.

The accelerator is therefore not a phenomenon which continues unchanged for all time. Whether and to what extent "acceleration" becomes noticeable depends on whether and to what extent there is reserve capacity, whether and to what extent competition is restricted by market-dominating cartels and concerns, whether and for how long customers are prepared to wait for delivery of their orders, whether technological development permits the use of long-lived or only short-lived machinery, whether and to what extent investment in rationalization and development is being undertaken, and last but not least, whether we are dealing with closed economies or whether and to what extent international trade has been liberalized. Due to the dependence of the accelerator on historical conditions, Tinbergen may perhaps have been premature in concluding at the end of his essay "Statistical Evidence on the Acceleration Principle"[29]: "Summarising, it may be said that the accelerator principle cannot help very much in the explanation of the details in real investment fluctuations, with the possible exception of railway rolling stock."[30]

§3 Relevance of experiences and expectations to multiplier

The multiplier does not behave independently of the experiences and the expectations of households and firms. Nevertheless, Keynes and his successors, such as Samuelson and Hicks, view marginal propensity to consume as a constant value. Keynes believed that expectations average out; Samuelson and Hicks make no mention at all of either the expectations or the experiences of firms and households.

In reality, however, (average) marginal propensity to consume does not remain constant. It is high in a boom and low in a slump, because optimistic expectations prevail in a boom and pessimistic expectations in a slump. Therefore marginal propensity to consume also changes when the government influences expectations with the aid of autonomous investment. If government economic policy succeeds in reversing previously negative expectations, households no longer assume that their incomes will fall due to short-time working or unemployment. They are now confident that their real income will rise and that their jobs will be safe. The behavior of the population is reversed at the same time as their expectations.[31] People no longer "save" to the same extent as before as a safeguard against the risks of the future, but instead now catch up on their previously postponed purchases of consumer goods, especially consumer durables.

The expectations of firms are reversed at the same time as those of (private) households. While firms were previously reluctant to invest, they will now undertake the previously neglected investment and also initiate expansion programs in order to cope with the expected increase in sales. The upturn in the economy will also stimulate investment in rationalization and development. In this case, the autonomous investment induces private investment, which Kahn and Keynes have excluded from the multiplier model in keeping with their assumptions, but which Samuelson includes in his analysis, at least partially, without pointing out this deviation from Keynes's general theory to his readers.

Whether and to what extent expectations are reversed depends on the past experiences of households and firms and therefore on their learning processes. After a severe, long-lasting depression, as in the thirties, households and firms will only revise their expectations slowly and belatedly. After a long boom, the expectations of households and firms will become optimistic much more quickly, as was the case after the recession of 1966/67 in Germany during the Erhard government.

The influence of changing historical conditions also makes itself felt in another respect. Autonomous investment does not take place outside space and time. It is an historical event. Its effect is therefore not independent either of the type of government (dictatorship or parliamentary democracy) or of any individual legal rights of the unemployed. The same amount of autonomous investment therefore has different effects. In a dictatorship, government expenditures regularly take place without delay. In a federal democracy, in which additional expenditure must also be made by individual states, there are delays which not only diminish the intended effect but may even lead to the opposite result. Most of all, the "deployment of labor" differs between a dictatorship and a democracy. In a dictatorship, the unemployed are put to work on building roads or "digging holes" (Keynes) regardless of the job for which they are qualified. In a parliamentary democracy, in which even the recipients of benefits have a right to "suitable work," the same kind of policy is not of much use if the unemployed are clerks, foremen, chefs, or part-time workers. Finally, in a dictatorship, wages are usually frozen during any period of underemployment, while in a democracy, powerful unions achieve wage raises despite already existing unemployment. These considerations also show that the problems of unstable growth are historical phenomena which depend largely on governments and government action and cannot be discussed in terms of scientific mechanisms.

§4 Nonexistence of the "full-employment ceiling"

The statement that expansion rebounds from the "full-employment ceiling" like a tennis ball is not borne out by experience either. There is no "full-employment ceiling" in the shape of a rigid limit which cannot be influenced by economic policy, nor can it be maintained that expansion never turns down until the limit of full employment is reached:

1. It is possible to influence the "labor potential." If the domestic work force is not large enough, despite working overtime, the labor potential can be expanded by recruiting foreign workers, as shown by the experience of some European countries in the last two decades. In West Germany, the proportion for foreign workers in the total work force at times exceeded twelve percent.

2. Many booms collapse long before they reach the full-employment ceiling. At the beginning of the Great Depression of the thirties, neither Germany nor the United States had full employment. Nor can it be claimed that before the slumps which occurred in the United States or Great Britain after World War II, expansion had hit the full-employment ceiling. In less developed economies, even during a boom unemployment often exceeds ten percent and in some cases even thirty percent.[32]

The idea that expansion rebounds from the full-employment ceiling like a tennis ball is not realistic.

§5 The physical wear-out rate and the influence of revaluations

"When output plummets downward rapidly," writes *Samuelson*, "the acceleration principle calls for negative investment (or disinvestment) greater than the rate at which machines can wear out. This wear-out rate puts a floor on . . . "[33] The physical wear-out rate, however, is only relevant to a stationary model in which there are no revaluations in the course of adjustments and in which no technological progress takes place.

In the real world in which values are not by nature "given," this kind of "floor" does not exist, for two reasons:

1. In a developing economy, the obsolescence of machines no longer depends, or no longer mainly depends, on their physical wear-out, but on their technological competitiveness. Under these circumstances, relatively new machines become unusable as soon as they become technologically obsolete. The value of technologically obsolete machinery tends to be nil.

2. In prosperity and depression, economic valuations also

change. During the Great Depression, even new machines had to be written down to their scrap price, because the slump in sales meant that they were not needed and there was no demand for them. The concept of cost, which is not only found in Ricardo or Marx but also underlies the theories of Samuelson and Hicks, fails to recognize the empirically substantiated fact that in a slump, a machine can become completely or practically worthless, despite the cost bound up in it.

The basic error of which Hicks, Samuelson, and Domar are guilty consists of attempting to explain a human or social phenomenon such as unstable growth by means of a physical mechanism which is unaffected by experiences, expectations, reevaluations, innovations, and government action. Neither the accelerator nor the multiplier operate with the inevitability of natural laws.

The accelerator principle ceases to operate when competition has been replaced by monopoly, or when such strong preferences have arisen that firms are able to spread additional orders over the future with the aid of delivery dates. Nor does the liberalization of international trade leave the operation of the accelerator unscathed. The effects of the multiplier are influenced by learning processes, by the type of government, by the economic system, by legal rights, by expectations, etc.

Neither of the models takes the economic development into account. Samuelson's theory of the multiplier-accelerator mechanism also fails to recognize the significance of investment in rationalization of production and development of new and better products for the stability or instability of "growth." Finally, the concepts of a rigid "full-employment ceiling" and a "bottom" formed by the physical "wear-out," between which the growth path supposedly oscillates back and forth, are in stark contrast to reality.

There is no such thing as a monocausal or, more accurately, a monofunctional explanation of the business cycle, just as there is no such thing as a uniform illness or a cure-all medicine. Every business cycle or every unstable growth always has a number of causes, causes which in particular change in economic history. The performance of the business fluctuations is influenced by learning processes as well as by mistakes of economic policy—or economists' errors.

SECTION 4: Inflation-Employment Mechanism

> Yet, in truth, there is no remedy except to throw
> over the axiom of parallels and to work out a
> non-Euclidian geometry. Something similar is
> required today in economics.
>
> John Maynard Keynes

Economic theories change with different (historical) experiences; this is evidence that a science is still developing. While Keynes was still postulating that price increases were not possible in a period of underemployment, provided no bottlenecks occur, some time later the Keynesian school put forward the theory that unemployment falls as inflation increases.

§1 The Phillips mechanism

Phillips[34] has analyzed the supposed relationship between inflation and employment. Samuelson and Solow have described the relationship between price increases and unemployment, taking into account changes in money wages, by means of the so-called Phillips curve (Figure 7). The horizontal axis of this diagram

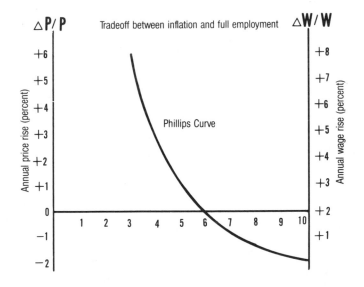

Fig. 7. The Phillips curve depicts the crucial tradeoff "between degree of unemployment and wage-price creep" (Samuelson).

shows the rate of unemployment, while the left-hand vertical axis represents the annual percentage rise in prices (rate of inflation) and the right-hand vertical axis the annual percentage rise in wages. The reason for the displacement of the scales is an assumed increase in productivity of two percent.

According to this curve, the following mechanism operates: If an increase in productivity of two percent is accompanied by a deflation rate of two percent, the rate of unemployment rises to ten percent. If prices remain constant and the value of money remains stable, unemployment is six percent. If the rate of inflation rises to six percent, underemployment falls to approximately three percent. If the increase in productivity rises from two to three percent, the Phillips curve shifts downward; the higher productivity enables higher wages to be paid.

Although Samuelson calls the Phillips curve "realistic,"[35] the "mechanism" interrelating inflation, employment, and productivity on which it is based is nonexistent. Although there are relationships between employment on the one hand and price and wage increases on the other, these by no means always operate in the same way. Employment does not necessarily rise as inflation increases, nor does a certain rate of inflation or deflation inevitably correspond to a certain rate of unemployment. Deflation is neither a necessary or a sufficient cause of underemployment:

1. As Hume was already aware, deflation can, if foreign trade is operating, lead to a reduction in imports and an increase in exports, and thus improve the country's employment position. The same applies to a country whose rate of inflation is lower than those of other countries, as shown earlier.
2. Underemployment can occur as a result or as an accompanying phenomenon of price increases, as in the case of stagflation (see §2).
3. Learning processes influence the effects of inflation and depend in their turn on the rate and the duration of inflation (see §3).

§2 Underemployment during inflation ("stagflation")

Underemployment during inflation is a phenomenon which has been known for centuries and which has various causes. These cases include:

1. a favorable trade balance which may cause a reduction in exports and an increase in imports (David Hume);
2. the Keynesian policy of deficit spending which is no longer pursued in a closed economy, but in an open economy;
3. economic power, which enables prices and wages to rise regardless of the employment situation;
4. international disturbances which lead to a decrease in foreign trade despite worldwide inflation;
5. previous export surpluses due to an undervalued currency that enables the labor potential of the economy to be increased by importing foreign workers; this increase then turns out, after elimination of this dumping, to be no longer justified (and cannot be successfully combated through deficit spending).[36]

1. Stagflation as a consequence of misunderstanding Keynes's general theory

There is no doubt that Keynes has based his general theory on a model of a closed economy. The employment policy that he recommended therefore applies without limitation only to a closed economy; this fact has been largely overlooked.

In a closed economy, additional expenditure financed by deficit spending increases employment. In an economy which is part of an international economy, on the other hand, the opposite occurs (as shown in Chapter 3), particularly when exchange rates are fixed, as in the period following Bretton Woods. In this case, the cause of stagflation is the influence of domestic inflation on foreign trade. If exports fall and imports rise, underemployment increases not in spite of but precisely because of deficit spending.

2. Stagflation as a consequence of power

Price increases together with constant or increasing unemployment also occur when firms have the power to raise their prices regardless of sales or whether unions have the power to win wage increases regardless of the state of the labor market.

(1) If a firm or a cartel dominates the market, it becomes possible to raise prices when sales are falling. Firms which, in contrast to the model firms of economic theory, are not aware of cost and sales curves (especially since in reality, wages, taxes, exchange

rates, etc., do not remain constant, as neoclassical economics assumes) try in this way to compensate for the decrease in profits which would otherwise occur.

From the point of view of the firm, this "target pricing" will be (more or less) effective if the price was previously too low or has become too low due to cost increases, revaluations, or a change in the market structure. From the point of view of the economy, however, such price increases have an unfavorable effect. The price increase will cause sales to decrease, and as sales fall, so does employment. This is particularly so when price increases cause purchases to be transferred from domestic to foreign markets.

(2) Union wage increases that are not justified by productivity may have a detrimental effect on the employment situation, for two reasons: (a) such wage increases cause plants to become unproductive (this is also the case in a closed economy), (b) it now becomes more economic to produce the goods abroad.

In both cases, which in fact often coincide, stagflation results.

The behavior of both market leaders and union leaders can of course be influenced, like any kind of human behavior, by learning processes. If, for example, firms learn that price increases reduce their profits or endanger their freedom to regulate their own (administered) prices, they will in the future be more wary of raising their prices in times of falling sales. If unions learn that wage increases which are not supported by productivity bring about unemployment, they will show more moderation in their future wage claims. This kind of caution on the part of the unions was evident in the Federal Republic of Germany during the first twenty-five years of its existence.[37]

If unions have no power, as is usually the case in a dictatorship, they are also incapable of influencing wage levels. In totalitarian economies, whether of the Soviet or the fascist variety and regardless of whether unions are banned or have been turned into an arm of government, the danger of excessively high wages does not exist.[38] The problem of stagflation is therefore only encountered in dictatorships in exceptional cases; exploitation and stagflation are incompatible with each other, so that from this point of view, stagflation is the lesser evil.

3. Disturbances in international trade together with world inflation

When an international economy which is already suffering from worldwide inflation, as in the 1970s, encounters problems, such as those caused by the quadrupling of oil prices, world level of employment will be unfavorably affected. This is particularly the case if the oil producing countries do not spend their additional revenue on imports, while the countries paying this revenue are forced to restrict their imports of manufactured goods due to the oil price rise. Here too, human decisions are responsible for a result which contradicts the mechanism shown in the Phillips curve.

4. Stagflation as the end result of currency dumping

In a period which tends, under the influence of the post-Keynesians, toward inflationary increases in the money supply, an export surplus due to an undervalued currency may also cause stagflation. If a country's exchange rate is undervalued, the labor market permits an inflow of foreign workers, some if not all of whom turn out to be superfluous when the exports decrease. If exports are no longer subsidized and imports no longer artificially increased in price, inflation and unemployment coincide.

A proportion of the underemployment which affected the Federal Republic of Germany in the seventies originated from this problem. As early as the end of the fifties, the fixed exchange rates of the Bretton Woods monetary system had caused the Deutschmark to become increasingly undervalued. West Germany at this time had less inflation than most of the other countries and the labor productivity of the German economy was also rising more sharply than that of most other economies. The result was an accelerated rise in German exports while imports lagged behind; this created additional jobs which could not longer be filled by the domestic work force. A considerable proportion of the approximately two and one half million foreign workers who entered West Germany from the beginning of the sixties onward found their jobs as a result of the international undervaluation of the Deutschmark.[39]

When that undervaluation was eliminated due to the restoration of flexible exchange rates,[40] the situation changed. Exports stagnated or at least grew at a slower rate than imports. The unemployment thus produced is not revealed if and insofar as a corresponding number of foreign workers return to their country of origin. If they do not—because foreign workers are treated as people, who in a social world cannot be just shunted back and forth—then underemployment occurs, even if the money supply is simultaneously increased. In a purely mechanical world, as the classical and neoclassical economists imagine it to be, such a phenomenon is of course impossible.

5. Other causes of stagflation

These are not the only causes of stagflation. Stagflation will also occur if, at a time of prevailing inflation: (1) a gap in demand arises because foreign workers leave or because the population falls due to a decrease in the birthrate, or (2) the labor supply increases because training periods are shortened, the number of soldiers drafted is reduced, or a greater number of housewives come onto the labor market.

If foreign workers return home or the population falls as a result of a decrease in the birthrate, the level of demand in the economy falls. Bars and stores whose customers were the foreign workers who have left have to close. If the birthrate decreases, factories which produced baby clothes or toys will make workers redundant.

If an army is slimmed down, the effect is twofold; the armed forces' demand for uniforms and equipment falls while the labor supply simultaneously rises.

In addition, a government can artificially promote voluntary unemployment by means of excessively high unemployment benefits. If, during a boom, firms pay wages (actual wages) in excess of the minimum wage tariffs agreed upon by unions and employers and if unemployment pay is calculated as a percentage of these actual wages, while firms now only hire new workers at the tariff wage, the rate of benefit may be the same as or even higher than the tariff wage. If, for instance, the actual wage for a qualified worker was 180 percent of the tariff wage and if an unemployed worker receives benefit amounting to 68 percent of his last actual wage (as has been the case in the Federal Republic of Germany), unemployment pay is almost a quarter higher than the tariff wage. The same effect results if unemployment pay is tax-exempt and the time in which a worker is unemployed is restricted to only a few months of the year. Such provisions have an unfavorable effect on employment, because they reward laziness and punish work, while also increasing the tendency to work illicitly, which in return falsifies the unemployment statistics. This policy is bad not only for the government, which is losing tax revenues due to illicit work, but also, and indeed primarily, for the working population, which has to bear the cost of this subsidization of "pseudo-unemployment."

In all the cases discussed in the preceding paragraphs, the relationship assumed in the Phillips curve does not apply.[41] The belief that any kind of underemployment can be cured by increasing the money supply is untenable; in fact, this belief was held neither by Keynes nor by the mercantilists.

§3 Influence of human learning on the effect of changes in the value of money

The effect of periods of inflation and deflation is not independent of human behavior, and this in its turn is not independent of the duration and velocity of changes in the value of money. By way of example, three results of human learning processes will be discussed here: (1) anticipation of price changes, (2) the interchange of liquidity preference and "investment preference," and (3) the change from hoarding money to hoarding goods.

1. Anticipation of price changes

People who are faced with appreciable price rises for the first time behave differently from those who are used to appreciable rates of inflation. In the first case, there is absolutely no serious attempt at defence. Even when there are strong, independent unions, wages will lag behind prices, which has a favorable effect on employment. In the second case, workers and their unions have learned that rising prices devalue their wages. They will therefore anticipate the price rises which they expect in the future in their wage increases. Wage increases then run ahead of price increases, which has an unfavorable effect on employment, as already indicated by Haberler.

2. The interchange of liquidity preference and investment preference

Slumps encourage liquidity preference; booms encourage investment preference.

If entrepreneurs and managers learn that prices are falling, debtors are becoming lazy, and creditors are getting tough, they postpone investment in both stock and capital goods for as long as possible. This is the main cause of the prevailing "liquidity preference" which Keynes observed during the Great Depression of the thirties, but which he unjustifiably generalized.[42]

If, on the other hand, entrepreneurs and managers learn that prices and incomes are rising, they will begin to bring forward purchases and investment into the present which they would otherwise not have done until some time in the future. They stretch their liquidity because they expect the value of money to fall and that the economic recovery will again make it worthwhile to invest in growth and development. This is a phenomenon which occurs in every boom. Firms which behave differently even endanger their competitive position, like the American company Montgomery Ward, whose president pursued a policy of liquidity preference during a period of increasing prosperity; the experience of the thirties led him to expect a new Great Depression, while his competitors at that time were investing in development and rationalization.

3. The change from hoarding money to hoarding goods

According to Keynes, the hoarding of money is a chronic tendency which is peculiar to mankind. Households and firms, however, do not only spend more at certain times than they earn, by dissaving or buying on credit, but may also learn that it may be better to hoard goods rather than money.

If entrepreneurs, for instance, discover that the money which they receive for their goods becomes worthless from one day to the next, they are no longer prepared to exchange their goods for money. The money economy then increasingly becomes a barter economy, which has an unfavorable influence on consumption and above all on investment. During a period of "galloping inflation" investment tends to be nil—not because firms are unwilling to invest, but because the shortage on the market of capital goods prevents them from investing.

The effects of changes in the value of money on supply and demand vary with the rate and the duration of inflation and with the learning processes of entrepreneurs and managers.

§4 The results

Households and entrepreneurs are neither automatons nor robots. They do not only influence the economy in which they live; they are permanently influenced by it. Any attempt to interpret economic phenomena as mechanisms results in a dehumanizing of economic theory. This applies to Hume's foreign trade mechanism no less than to the neoclassical market mechanism. It also applies to the post-Keynesians' attempts to construct a growth or a business cycle mechanism by combining the accelerator and the multiplier or to build a mechanical relationship between inflation and employment. All these attempts inevitably come into conflict with experience, because they fail to take account of the fact that the behavior of the economy is determined by human beings who learn from experience and who shape their economic activity in accordance with their expectations, which are in turn influenced by learning processes.

As a result of human freedom of action, economic theory is far more complicated than any natural science. Any attempt to avoid this problem by transforming the science of the human economy into a pseudo-natural science makes as little sense as the efforts of the Historical Schools to pursue economic theory on the basis of historicism. Both these approaches obscure the object of analysis which it is the theoretical economist's job to investigate.

Economists will have to learn that economic science is a *science of the economic society of human beings, in which there is not simply one solution for each problem but a multiplicity of possible choices as a result of human ability to learn and human freedom to act.*[43] The uniqueness of man as a being who intervenes in the economy by his actions and who learns from economic history means firstly that it is impossible for economic theory to contain any analogies with scientific mechanisms and secondly that it is possible to pursue an economic policy. In a world of mechanisms, as in the models of classical and neoclassical economists, there is no way of manipulating the economy; to this extent it was only logical for David Ricardo to reject economic policy in general.[44] Economists such as Keynes, Hicks, Samuelson, Solow, Arrow, or Klein are less consistent in recognizing the necessity (and therefore the possibility) of economic policy while continuing to teach the existence of economic mechanisms in which human actions and human behavior play no part.

CHAPTER 5

"Infinite" Values in Economic Theory

'Marginalthinking' or, in other words, 'marginal concepts' play a central role in economic theory.
Erich Schneider

Economists tend to work in models outside space and time with infinite values, infinite curves or curves which are at least unlimited within the model, although there is nothing infinite or unlimited in the real world.

As metaphysics operates with transcendental values, so meta-economics works with infinite elasticity, infinite sales, unlimited utility and cost curves or, unlimited demand and supply curves, infinite periods of time, and an infinite speed of adjustment.

SECTION 1: Infinite Elasticity, Infinite Sales, and Unlimited Supply

§1 Infinitely elastic and perfectly inelastic demand

In the model world of economists, demand can be "perfectly elastic" and "perfectly inelastic." If demand is perfectly elastic at a given price, this means, according to Erich Schneider, "that the household is prepared to demand any quantity at this price."[1] The elasticity of demand E_d is, as Samuelson puts it, "infinite," resulting in the equation $E_d = \infty$.[2] In this case, the "demand line" D is infinite and runs parallel to the horizontal axis (Figure 8).

Although many authors make use of this concept, it is not defensible: (1) It is unrealistic. (2) It is based on an illogical argument. (3) It contradicts other statements by the same authors.

1. In reality, no household is prepared to buy "any quantity" at a particular price or the same quantity "at any price." In reality there is neither infinite elasticity nor perfectly inelastic demand; infinites and absolutes lie outside the world of mankind.

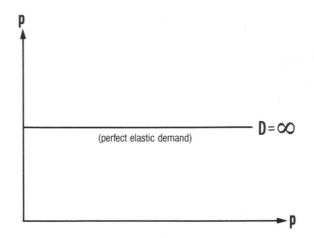

Fig. 8.

2. The assumption that households (or firms) cannot influence the price should not lead to the conclusion that they "demand any quantity at this price." This is an error of logic; the former has nothing to do with the latter. The fact that a consumer cannot influence prices does not mean that he will not demand more at a lower price and less at a higher market price. *Even when a consumer is unable to influence prices, the quantity he demands depends on the price.*

3. Authors contradict themselves when they assume on the one hand that the demand curve slopes downward and on the other hand work with "demand lines" which run parallel or vertical to the horizontal axis.[3] Neither Edgeworth's indifference curve analysis, as used by Erich Schneider, nor the so-called "law of diminishing marginal utility," on which Samuelson bases his "theory of demand and utility," is compatible with "infinitely elastic" or "perfectly inelastic" demand. The real demand curve is not related to one price but shows the varying demand corresponding to different prices.

In fact, a "demand line" L always relates only to a particular price which is given by the associated (real) demand curve D, as shown in Figure 9. If the given price is P_1, the quantity is determined by point E_1; consumers demand quantity M_1 at price P_1. If the given price is P_2, the quantity demanded is determined by

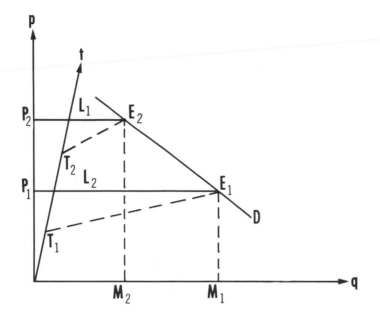

Fig. 9. Households' demand at different prices (at different times T_1 and T_2). The demand D is limited at any given price: Neither households nor firms have am infinite demand.

point E_2; consumers demand quantity M_2 at price P_2. This is important in three respects:

1. *In reality, the demand line relates to a point on the (real) demand curve.* The so-called demand line is only produced by joining this point to the vertical axis (however, there is no real need to do so).

2. *The demand line is always limited by the (real) demand curve.* There is no such thing as infinite demand.

3. Due to the false assumption of an infinite demand line, neoclassical theory concludes that the supply curve and the demand line (or the demand curve) always intersect. *In fact neoclassical theory has only dealt with an extreme case.*

§2 Unlimited sales

In the model of perfect competition, it is assumed that a firm is able to sell an "infinite quantity." Its "price-sales function" is "unlimited." It can, as Samuelson expresses it, "sell all it wants to along its horizontal *dd* curve, never depressing market price.[4] This statement in its turn confuses two different things: (1) the inability of a firm to influence the price, and (2) the quantity it sells. In addition, the "price-sales function" *dd* is not derived from the firm's sales but from households' demand.

If a firm cannot influence prices, there is only one point on its sales curve which is real. However, it does not follow from this that the firm can sell any quantity it wants to, even though one textbook author borrows this fallacy from another. No real firm buys or sells infinite quantities. No firm can sell all it wants to. Every firm's sales are restricted by its customers; this is particularly so under competitive conditions. *The more intensive the competition, the more suppliers have to act in accordance with their customers' wishes.* If this were not the case, competition would in reality be perfect when the influence of customers has dropped to zero. It is this and only this which the theory of "unlimited sales," which is found in almost all textbooks, would have us believe. Anyone who wrongly applies mathematics can also show, as we have known since the time of the Greek philosopher Zeno, that fast-running Achilles will only catch up with the leisurely turtle in infinity.

The theory of infinite sales in perfect competition therefore contains three gross and (strictly speaking) unpardonable errors:

1. It fails to recognize that in reality, infinity does not exist. *The sales of each and every real firm are limited, as is the demand of each and every household (or firm).* A firm sells only a certain quantity at a given price. If the market price were lower, it would sell more; if the market price were higher, it would sell less. The comments on Figure 9 apply here by analogy; the neoclassical economists have confused the lines drawn parallel to the horizontal axis through the price-sales point with the sales curve and have wrongly assumed that this price-sales function is infinite.

2. It fails to realize that a price-sales function is always derived from the firm's associated real sales curve, which is always finite and downward-sloping, even when the firm cannot influence the market price. *Every "price-sales line" G relates to a single price, while the real sales curve V shows the varying sales volumes corresponding to different market prices* (Figure 10).

3. It supposes competition to be perfect when customers, who should really be the object of competition, no longer have any

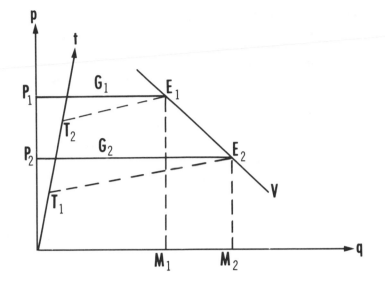

Fig. 10. Sales of a firm at different prices (during periods T_1 and T_2). At price P_1 the firm sells quantity M_1 and at price P_2 it sells quantity M_2. The associated "price-sales lines" G_1 and G_2 terminate at E_1 and E_2. As there is no infinite demand, so there are no infinite sales.

influence on a firm's sales. This stands the purpose of competition on its head; anyone *who believes that competition is perfect when customers cannot exert any influence on prices, quality, or product differentiation has entirely misunderstood the tasks of competition in the service of the consumer.*[5]

The dependence of competing firms on their customers can only be shown when the two-dimensional models of traditional theory are abandoned. The description of economic reality requires more complicated models, as Keynes has already pointed out in another context.

§3 Unlimited cost curves

In the neoclassical equilibrium model of *perfect competition* not only a firm's price-sales function is assumed to be infinite, but cost curves are also unlimited, although this is not usually stated expressly. In this case, there is always a point of intersection of its sales curve V and its marginal cost curve MC, which according to these assumptions is identical to its supply curve. Figure 11 shows the usual representation of this equilibrium outside space and time. Sales curve V (which is supposed to be identical with the households' demand curve D) and marginal cost curve MC intersect at G. To maximize its profit, the firm sells quantity M at price P. Mathematically, this solution cannot be faulted. A firm maximizes its profit when it can choose a level of output which produces the equation MR = MC.[6] As the parallel course of the price-sales function means that MR = P, a firm therefore maximizes its profit when it chooses the sales volume which produces the equation MC = P. In this situation, any kind of policy is impossible, because the price is assumed to be a datum and there are neither different qualities nor customer preferences.

However, the assumption of an unlimited supply curve is no more in keeping with economic reality than an infinite price-sales function. A firm's sales, as shown in the preceding paragraphs, are limited by its customers. The supply of a firm which exists in space and time (and all the firms in the world without exception exist in space and time) is limited by its capacity or by its ability to

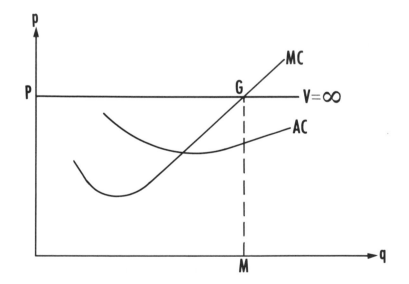

Fig. 11.

deliver. Figure 12, on which the third axis measures capacity i, shows that at a given capacity I, a firm can only produce quantity M_e. Its marginal and average cost curves terminate at E. The marginal cost curve and the sales curve do not intersect, if the marginal cost curve ends before the sales curve is reached.

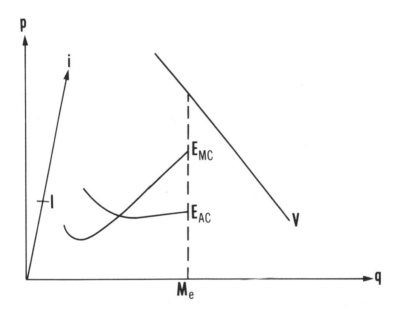

Fig. 12. Marginal cost curve E_{MC} and sales curve V do not intersect if the curve E_{MC} ends before the sales curve V is reached. This can be the case if capacity as well as inventory are limited.

As its inventory is also limited, the only course remaining open to it is to invest in expansion, but this takes time and also depends on the investment decisions of top management, which are in turn determined by their past experiences and future expectations.

SECTION 2: Influence of Sales and Output on "Market Structures"

§1 The economic questions

By assuming unlimited or infinite values (and curves), the theory of market structures has blocked access to the economically relevant questions which are fundamental to the contrast between monopoly and competition. These questions are:

1. Is a firm able to determine its own sales or do its sales depend on its customers?
2. Does a firm not need to worry about its customers because they have practically no other choice, or is a firm forced to pursue marketing policies in order not to lose its customers (or to win new customers)?

Before these questions can be answered, however, it must also be pointed out that the real world which is to be analyzed differs from the neoclassical world of market structures in two respects:

1. In the real world, there are—in economics as in politics—no absolute, only relative, equilibria which are firmly *fixed in space and time and are characterized by their transitoriness.*
2. In these relative equilibria, the quantities produced, supplied, and sold are not identical, nor can they be mathematically determined; they are, like prices, the result of entrepreneurial decisions which—and this is the main point—are largely dependent on whether the market is subject to competition or monopoly.

§2 Influence on competition

In the model of perfect competition, entrepreneurial policies are impossible. If price is a datum and there are neither different qualities nor customer preferences, it is impossible for the firm to carry out any entrepreneurial functions.

Real competition, however, is of a different kind. Every firm makes decisions on prices and qualities, as it does on the choice of its employees, its production processes, its capacity. In contrast to a monopoly, however, a competing firm has to act in accordance with its competitors. It cannot determine its prices, its qualities, and its after-sales service independently, as a monopoly can, if it does not want to lose customers to its competitors, thus making less profit or suffering losses. Its entrepreneurial decisions, and thus both the price and the quality of its goods, are to this extent determined by its competitors.

If a firm's sales and cost curves are no longer unlimited or infinite, the sales curve and the supply or cost curve no longer necessarily intersect. There are two main reasons for this: (1) the finiteness of sales, and (2) the finiteness of supply, or, if inventories and delivery times are ignored for the time being, the limitation of capacity (and therefore of output).

This can even be shown to be the case in equilibrium.

1. The influence of limited sales on "competitive equilibrium"

If sales are no longer infinite but limited by a firm's customers, the relative equilibrium shown in Figure 13 may result. In this diagram, on which the third axis k represents a firm's customer preferences, the price-sales line terminates at E_v; the firm's customers only amount to quantity K. Due to competition from other firms, the firm can only sell quantity M_r, and not quantity M_{th}, at this price (and this quality). In this case it is the customers, and not the marginal costs, which determine the firms's sales (and its real sales curve V). It is the customers who force the firm to produce "under conditions of individual diminishing costs."[7] Sraffa's attempt to explain this situation with the aid of monopoly thus turns out to be unnecessary.

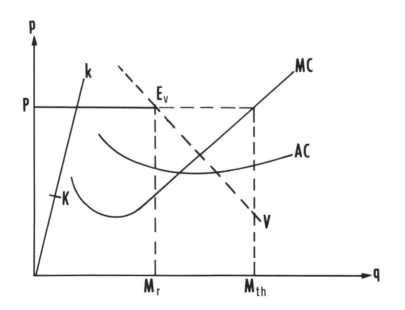

Fig. 13.

2. The influence of limited supply on competitive equilibrium

If supply is no longer unlimited, the *relative* equilibrium reproduced in Figure 14 becomes a possibility. Due to its limited capacity I, shown on the third axis i, the firm is unable, due to the
unexpected flood of customers, to fully satisfy the demand. The
finiteness of the marginal cost curve MC means that it does not
reach the price-sales line. The supplyer is now able to choose
between quantity M_a and quantity M_1 (or any quantity between
the two). In the first case, he sells the quantity corresponding to
his maximum output. In the second case, he is already selling
products which he will manufacture at a later date. Here, too, it
is ultimately the customers which prevent the curves intersect-
ing. Their demand exceeds the present ability of the firm to
deliver the goods.

While the solution reproduced in Figure 13 hardly presents any
particular difficulties, the situation depicted in Figure 14 will at
least seem strange to those used to thinking in terms of absolute
equilibria. How, they ask, can a firm which despite the existence

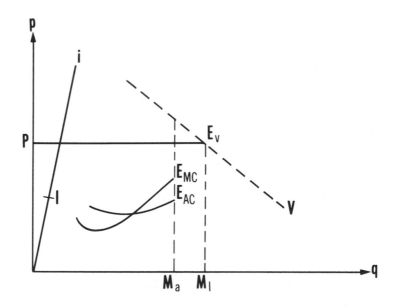

Fig. 14.

of competition chooses a price which is above the end of its marginal and average cost curves be in equilibrium? The answer to this by no means unjustified question is twofold: (1) We are dealing not with an absolute equilibrium, but with a relative and therefore a transitory equilibrium. (2) The firm believes that it makes sense to choose price P because that price permits it to take orders which enable it to maintain full employment for the foreseeable future at a time of falling demand, at the same time preventing the loss of customers to its competitors.

The assumption that a firm always sells the quantity which it produces in fact conflicts with reality. A firm may: (1) sell products in the present which it has manufactured in the past, and (2) make purchases in the present for goods which it will only produce at a later date.

In the first case, goods are taken out of inventory, and in the second case, the firm will quote delivery times.

Only when it is unrealistically assumed that there is no space or time, which eliminates any kind of differences, are production and sales identical and unlimited. However, things are different in the real world, which is made relative by space and time. In this world, production and sales frequently take place at different times. In this world, there are firms whose sales are limited by their customers, as well as customers who due to the particular quality of the product or to special personal relations are prepared to wait for their goods. In this world, manufacturers know from experience that an increase in orders may be temporary, so that even lengthening delivery times does not yet justify a "further flow of resources into or out of the field"[8]: and thus an infringement of Chamberlin's condition of equilibrium. Instead, they will spread additional orders over the years to come, in order to ensure full employment for both their plants and their employees. Their supply curve is therefore not identical to their marginal cost curve (or any other cost curve), as already shown in Chapter 1 for other reasons.

3. Real competition as a process versus "perfect competition"

In reality, however, competition is not an equilibrium, but a process which has to fulfil economic functions in society. These functions do not exist if sales and supply are assumed to be infinite or unlimited.

The social functions of (real) competition are:

(1) *to lower the market price to the price of the marginal producer;* real competition therefore brings about what the theory of perfect competition assumes to be "given";

(2) *to adjust supply to (quantitative) demand, which changes in time and space;* real competition induces firms to increase their supply by windfall profits when there is a sellers' market and forces them to reduce their supply (and their production) by losses when there is a buyers' market, at the same time producing the equilibrium which the theory of perfect competition assumes to be "given";

(3) *to introduce new or at least better products;* because competing firms use innovations as a means for making higher profits (or for surviving) and also as a means for escaping from competition; real competition therefore creates new markets (e.g., for automobiles, TV sets) and causes old markets to shrink or disappear (e.g., for horse-drawn carriages, movie theaters), consequently producing the markets which the theory of perfect competition assumes to be already "given";

(4) *to introduce new methods of production which reduce costs and enable real income to rise,* thereby bringing about the "marginal producer" and the "marginal consumer" which the theory of perfect competition assumes to be "given";

(5) *to adjust the quality of the products to the individual wishes of the demanders;* real competition (and not monopoly, as Chamberlin and his followers believe) is therefore responsible for the product differentiation which enables consumers to have freedom of choice, which they would not possess if a uniform good were sold at a uniform price, as assumed by the theory of perfect competition;

(6) *to inform the producers of changes in the quantities and qualities of the commodities which the consumers wish to buy;* with the help of the demanders' "voting power," real competition provides the information which the theory of perfect competition assumes to be given if it postulates "perfect knowledge of the market" (*vollkommene Markttransparenz*);

(7) *to direct resources from shrinking markets to growing or developing markets* by re-evaluating factors of production lower in shrinking and higher in developing industries; competition thus brings about the allocation of resources which the theory of perfect competition assumes to be "given";

(8) *to educate people to behave economically and to become efficient* because real competition punishes uneconomic behavior and rewards efficiency, whereby people and not public authorities (or members of government) make the final decision.

In short, real competition is not an equilibrium in which sales are infinite and cost curves are unlimited, as the followers of the marginal utility school believe. *Competition is a social process in which*—to stress only the main points—*supply is adjusted to demand and new and better products as well as new and cheaper methods of production are developed, thus on the one hand improving people's standard of living and on the other hand preventing bottlenecks by replacing exhausted resources by new or other factors of production*[9] (e.g., the replacement of wood by coal, of coal by oil, of oil by atomic energy).

In a competitive society (*Konkurrenzwirtschaft*), no firm can exist which produces (or offers) the same products in the same way year after year. An automobile company which keeps on producing its 1950 models unchanged and with the same methods of production will have gone out of business by the seventies. A department store which in 1980 offers the same goods in the same way as in 1960 would be unable to find enough customers to survive. In a competitive society, changes take place in the goods, the methods of production, and the markets, and there is nothing which is infinite, unlimited, or "given."

§3 Influence on monopoly

Economists also assume that monopoly operates with unlimited cost and sales curves. Therefore, the relevant textbooks do not contain any representations of monopoly in which the marginal revenue curve and the marginal cost curve do not intersect.

In the real world, however, in which there are no markets outside space and time, this is not necessarily the case. If two curves are no longer unlimited, then it is still possible, but no longer inevitable, that they will intersect. The curves may now terminate before they reach each other.

In reality, therefore, the normal representation of *monopolistic equilibrium* is only one of several possibilities. In reality, (short-term) supply is limited by the capacity and the expectations of the firm and sales are limited by the firm's customers, which makes it possible that marginal revenue and marginal cost curves no longer meet. In such cases, the monopoly point does not lie on the actual sales curve, but outside it.

The mathematical monopoly point may be economically irrelevant for two reasons:

1. *As a result of intensive competition from substitutes:* if cigarettes become too expensive, people may change to smoking cigars, chewing tobacco, or smoking a pipe. When there is effective competition from third markets, a market monopoly cannot charge more (for a given quality) than a certain price (or go below a certain quality) without losing customers to the suppliers of substitute goods. If the higher price does not compensate for the loss of sales, it is not worth his while to charge more than this economic upper price limit. On the contrary. By shifting his sales curve to the left he would worsen his position and diminish his profit. His actual sales curve therefore ends before it reaches Cournot's monopoly point.

2. *As a result of limited capacity:* if an inventive (creative) firm succeeds in establishing a new market and therefore a temporary monopoly (creative monopoly), its production capacity may be too low, if the new product makes an impact on consumers, to fully satisfy the demand. In this case, however, its sales curve does not terminate before it reaches the mathematical monopoly point, as in the first case, but both this curve and in particular the marginal revenue curve now lie above the marginal cost curve which is prematurely terminated by the limited capacity.

If, therefore, the unreal assumption that sales and cost curves are unlimited (and equilibria timeless) is abandoned, there are two cases which in economic terms are much more interesting then Cournot's or Amoroso's mathematical solutions:

1. In the case of a well-established product, the competition from substitutes can be so intensive that the monopolist cannot go above a certain upper price limit without losing so many customers that it would not pay him to breach this upper price limit. If this upper limit is below the mathematical monopoly price the marginal revenue curve MR terminates in point E before reaching the marginal cost curve MC; due to the intensity of competition from third markets, he is now unable to attain the mathematical monopoly point (Figure 15). This produces the following result: *the more intensive the competition from substitutes, the lower the price to*

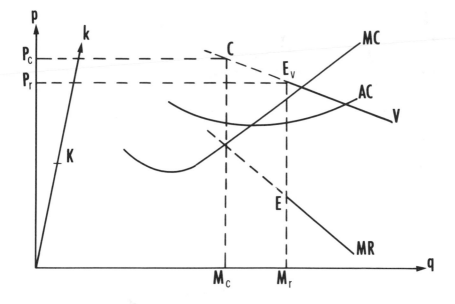

Fig. 15. The third axis k represents the competition from substitutes, the sales curve V terminates at E_v and the marginal revenue curve MR consequently terminates at E. Due to the intensity of competition from third markets the monopolist cannot attain the mathematical point C. If he charges more than price P_r, he loses customers to his competitors on third markets and his sales curve shifts to the left due to the loss of customers. If the monopolist does not want to lose an appreciable number of his customers, the only course left open to him is to sell quantity M_r at price P_r. In this case, turnover is higher and price lower than in pure monopoly.

be paid by the consumers, and the greater the quantity (and the better the quality) they obtain at this price.

2. In the case of a firm which has established a new market by launching a new product, the monopoly's supply can be insufficient to satisfy the demand at the theoretical monopoly point. The marginal revenue curve MR now lies above the end of the marginal cost curve E_{mc}. Here, too, the monopoly point is unattainable. The temporary monopoly (creative monopoly) thus gains the possibility of choosing between several alternatives (Figure 16).

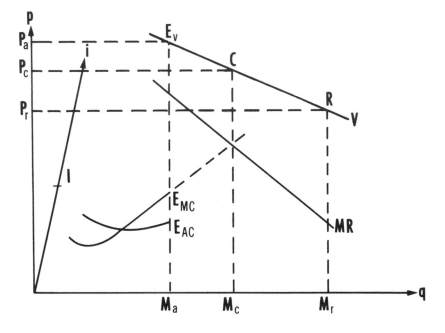

Fig. 16. The third axis represents the capacity i of an inventive firm, the marginal revenue curve MR lies above the end of the marginal cost curve E_{MC}. The capacity level I is much too low for the level of sales, and the firm is unable, for the time being, to invest in expansion, perhaps for financial reasons. In this situation, the temporary monopoly is able to choose a price which is higher than the theoretical monopoly price. If it chooses price P_a, it sells quantity M_a, which it produces at maximum output. If it chooses price P_c, it sells quantity M_c. This gives rise to delivery times, which are symbolized on the diagram by the distance $\overline{M_a M_c}$. It can, however, also choose price P_r and sell quantity M_r; then the delivery times become even longer.

(1) It chooses price P_a and sells quantity M_a, which corresponds to its output at full capacity utilization. In this case, the quantity sold is equal to the quantity produced.

(2) It chooses a lower price, e.g., price P_r or P_c, and is thus selling products in the present which will only be produced at a later date. In this case, its sales are considerably higher than its output; this gives rise to the delivery times which are familiar in the real world.

In both cases, price and quantity are no longer mathematically determined, but fixed by entrepreneurial policy, which is shaped by past experiences and by expectations of future developments.

If, therefore, the false assumption that cost and sales curves are unlimited is abandoned, it can be demonstrated that: (1) Various kinds of combinations are possible even in the case of monopoly. (2) The various results no longer necessarily or inevitably occur.

The closer economic analysis is to reality, the less Böhm-Bawerk's supposed "laws of nature" apply, and the more important entrepreneurial decisions become; the model worlds of Cournot, Amoroso, etc., are entirely devoid of these entrepreneurial decisions.

SECTION 3: Infinity in Macroeconomics

The tendency of economists to work with infinite values is not limited to the theory of market structures, but also appears in macroeconomic theory. Keynes states, in connection with the description of the theory of the multiplier, that if a community attempts "to consume the whole of any increment of income, there will be no point of stability and prices will rise without limit."[10] In reality, however, there are neither price rises "without limit" nor the "infinite geometric progression" which crops up in many textbooks in the same context. If the propensity to consume is unity and the single autonomous investment amounts to one billion dollars, total equilibrium income rises by exactly this amount and not a cent more. If the propensity to consume is below unity, the additional consumer income gradually disappears from "circulation," which results, at the end of the process which takes place in space and time, in the re-establishment of an equilibrium income which is the same as it was before.

"Infinity" is a mathematical marginal concept which is unsuitable for analyzing real economic problems. There is no such thing as infinity in the social sciences. For mankind and for human society, infinity only exists either as a "marginal concept" (Immanuel Kant) or in that transcendental world which lies entirely outside human experience. In the world of economic realities, which is firmly fixed in space and time, there is nothing unlimited or infinite. Economists who deal with infinite values or infinite progressions are no longer pursuing economic theory, but metaeconomics.

CHAPTER 6

The Elimination of Power

I have been given a name which does not befit
me. I have been called Nature, but I am entirely
Art.

Voltaire

Neoclassical theory has almost eliminated economic power
from its object of analysis by the choice of its premises.[1] If cost
and sales curves are already "given" before economic activity begins (and all that is left is profit maximization), it follows that:

1. Economic power can exist only in the case of market power.
All other types of economic power are eliminated by the artificial
restriction of the object of analysis.

2. Firms can only influence sales prices, and trade unions can
only influence wages by restricting supply. A situation in which
one partner is more powerful than the other and can therefore
impose his will on him is impossible. Neither the classical nor the
neoclassical economists examine revaluations, especially the use
of revaluations, as parameters of action, although economic
power, like any other kind of power, may be based on the superi-
ority of a partner: even in economics it is possible that one partner
is in command and the other has to obey.

3. Even market structures such as monopoly are subject to a
mechanism which deprives them of any freedom of action and
makes any arbitrariness on their part impossible. However, there
is no power without the possibility of arbitrariness. Economic
power is not to be found in (absolute) equilibria, but in economic
processes which develop in space and time.

In a world which is subject to Jevons's law of indifference in
which neither products nor production processes change, firms and
households possess perfect knowledge and all values apart from
price and quantity are eliminated, all power is restricted to merely
varying prices and quantities. Since, moreover, changes in price and
quantity must also take place in accordance with given mathematical equations (because otherwise firms and households are not

behaving rationally), even a monopoly is not free to make its own decisions. It is as powerful—or as powerless—as an automaton.

However, it is illogical to transfer the results of these models to the real world because the assumptions do not apply to reality. Economic activity is not identical either with profit maximization or with utility maximization. In real economic life, neither products and production processes nor cost and sales curves are "given," but the result of economic decisions, and valuations are not constant but can be used as parameters of action. *The real job of an entrepreneur or top manager begins before cost and sales curves can be drawn and is practically finished by the time cost and sales curves can be presented.*[2] Finally, in the real world there is no perfect knowledge, nor do entrepreneurs or managers act according to mathematical equations, but are able to make entrepreneurial decisions based on their past experiences and their expectations for the future.

The neoclassical economists believe that economic laws are stronger than economic power. However, the "opposing forces which are purely economic in nature and which are finally victorious" (Böhm-Bawerk)[3] are derived from the models the economists themselves have invented. To apply these results to the real world is nothing but a self-deception. In reality, power is not restricted by "natural laws." The "opposing forces which are purely economic in nature" are in fact only logical conclusions from artificial premises. They are neither "economic" nor are they "natural," but simply metaeconomic.[4]

SECTION 1:   Market Power

When the arbitrary premises underlying the neoclassical models are abandoned, it becomes evident that a monopoly (like any other firm) does not only have price and/or quantity as its parameters of action. In real economic life, every firm possesses many parameters of action (besides price and quantity), which the neoclassical economists have precluded by their assumption that cost and sales curves are given before any economic activity begins. It also becomes evident that firms which hold a permanent monopoly and firms which compete with each other do not differ in their parameters of action, but in the way they use them. *A monopoly uses the same parameters of action in a different way from a competing firm because it is not forced by competition to care about its customers.*

This statement is only shocking to those who are used to thinking in the traditional patterns of neoclassical economists. It becomes reasonable if neoclassical doctrines are thrown aside and the parameters of action available to entrepreneurial policy in real life are analyzed.

§1 The entrepreneurial parameters of action

A firm which produces goods has, in the course of time, to make the following decisions, among others, with regard to:

1. the types and the number of products to be included in its production program;
2. the production processes to be used;
3. the purchase of raw materials and semifinished products to be used in production;
4. the hiring, training, and dismissal of employees;
5. the manufacturing quality, which can be either improved or reduced;
6. the characteristics which are to distinguish the products to be manufactured (e.g., top speed, gasoline consumption, design, acceleration, durability, or comfort in the case of an auto);
7. the nature and the size of inventories;
8. the manufacturing capacity and therefore decisions on whether to enlarge or contract the size of the plant(s);
9. rationalization investment by the use of proven technologies which increase labor productivity and reduce the wage costs per unit of production;
10. customers' and suppliers' credit, advance payments, taking out of bank loans, etc.;
11. sales organization, e.g., the employment and the number of representatives, sales offices;
12. the increase in or the reduction of customer services and the influencing of the customers by means of argument, advertising, sales promotion, etc.

In a *developing* economy, where new methods of production and new products are created, the entrepreneurial decisions also include:

13. expenditure on research and development, etc;
14. acceptance of the risk involved in the introduction of entirely new, as yet unproven or at least not fully proven production technologies, which will without doubt initially increase costs due to production holdups, etc., but by means of which the management hopes to gain an advantage over its competitors in the future;
15. acceptance of the risks resulting from the production and sale of entirely new products, since the management does not know at first whether these products will be successful; if they are, however, they will give the company a temporary monopoly on the new market which that company has itself created.

Moreover, every real-life firm is able not only to decide (within certain limits) on the level of its selling prices, but also to vary its output independently of its sales. It can sell more than it produces, giving rise to (extended) delivery times, and it can produce or offer more than it can sell, thereby increasing its inventory. Whether it does the former or the latter depends not only on the prices, but also on the qualities of its products, the nature of its sales service, the effectiveness of its advertising, (and also on the state of the market), etc.

The use which firms make of their parameters of action depends not the least on the pressure of competition to which they are subject. The greater the pressure of competition, the more their decisions must be in the interest of their customers, so that they do not lose customers to their competitors, or even so that they can lure customers away from their competitors. This, therefore, gives the following general rule: *the greater the pressure of competition, the less firms can adjust the application of their parameters of action to their own interests and the more they have to care about the wishes of their customers.* It is not Adam Smith's "Invisible Hand," but competition from other firms which ensures that the individual interest of firms furthers the wealth of people, i.e., in this case the wealth of the consumers.

§2 *Monopolistic misuse of entrepreneurial parameters*

A firm which has a (permanent) monopoly of a market needs to pay no or very little attention to its customers. It can make decisions which are to its advantage and to the disadvantage of its customers. As a result of the power which the (permanent) monopolist has gained over the market due to the elimination of competition, he can, for example:

1. standardize his products and thus restrict his product range without reference to the individual desires of his customers in order to save costs, without passing on these savings to his customers;
2. reduce the manufacturing quality in order to increase his profits to the detriment of his customers;
3. use inferior and therefore cheaper raw materials and semi-finished products;
4. reduce the durability and therefore the life of his products, thereby forcing his customers to increase their demand;
5. abstain from reinvestment or net investment or even disinvest in order to make or to perpetuate scarcity profits to the detriment of his customers;
6. abstain from rationalization investment, because he has no competitors to force him to reduce his costs and because the increased profits, if any, do not seem to be worth the effort involved;
7. reduce his inventory and therefore force his customers to increase their inventories;
8. largely or fully ignore qualitative changes in demand, e.g., those brought about by fashion, because he has no competitors to force him to act in accordance with the qualitative wishes of his customers;
9. charge his customers excessive interest, fees, etc., thereby gaining additional income;
10. reduce his sales efforts because and insofar as his customers have to come to him and not vice versa;
11. reduce or entirely abandon customer service without reducing his prices accordingly;
12. cease trying to attract customers, as under competition, and instead let his customers feel their dependence so that they become ready to value his products more highly.

Due to his lack of interest in *development* of new or better products and production methods, a monopolist can also:

13. reduce or even completely abandon expenditure on research and development;
14. fail to employ entirely new production technologies, because he is afraid of the risk involved, and because he has no competitors to spur him into taking on this risk; and
15. dispense with the introduction of entirely new products or product qualities, because he can do without the additional costs, risks, and problems involved. In contrast to firms which compete with one another, a (permanent) monopoly is therefore usually uninterested in technological progress.

A monopoly is also able to maximize its profits by (simultaneously) raising its price and cutting the quantity offered for sale.[5] However, this is only one strategy among the many entrepreneurial possibilities which a monopolist has at his disposal.

The power of a (permanent) monopoly is therefore by no means restricted to the variation of quantity and/or price; nor is the power of a monopoly due to the fact that it has parameters of action not available to competing firms. Its power, on the contrary, comes from the ability to pay little or no attention to customers due to the nonexistent or insufficient pressure of competition. If a (permanent) monopoly arises, the customers in this market are no longer protected by competition from one-sided entrepreneurial decisions.

Of course, even a permanent monopoly is not forced to use its parameters ruthlessly. All types of power are characterized by the fact that their holders are able to perform a certain action, but can equally well refrain from doing so if they wish. The (permanent) monopoly of the real world is not bound by a mathematical equation; its parameters are not parameters of *re* action as in Cournot's theory, but parameters of *action*, which cannot exist without freedom to act. In reality, therefore, there are not only generally harmful monopolies, but also monopolies which benefit the public, which the prevailing monopoly theory generally passes over in silence, apart from the exceptions such as Baumol's sales maximization model, [6] which is in its way no less one-sided than Cournot's monopoly.

As a result of their unreal models, Cournot and the proponents of equilibrium theory have not only entirely misrepresented the nature of the permanent monopoly, [7] but have also largely if not fully underestimated the economic harm which the misuse of entrepreneurial parameters can inflict.

In the model world which Cournot and his followers have constructed, there is no economic power apart from market power (and option fixing) and even this type of economic power has been degraded beyond recognition. However, if the unreal premises of this school (constant valuations, perfect knowledge, constant products and productions methods, etc.) are abandoned, it becomes apparent that economic power has various causes and can occur in various forms.[8]

SECTION 2:   Partner's Power

> The seller, whose horse is only worth two
> pounds, constrains you by violence and threats
> to buy it for ten pounds.
> > Jeremy Bentham

If the unreal assumption is made that human valuations can neither change nor be changed, it follows that nobody can make revaluations by its own or be forced to make revaluations by others. And if all economic activity consists of individual acts of exchange which occur in isolation and therefore outside space and time, a business relationship between two partners which develops over time is impossible.

In the real world, which is what economists really ought to be analyzing, these premises are invalid. In this world, economic valuations can change and be changed. In this world, human relationships which have developed over time play a part. In this world, therefore, one can be dominant and another dependent, and one is able to command and the other has to obey, whatever the state of the market.

§1   The basic problems

Dominance-dependence relationships, in which the dominant partner imposes his will and therefore his valuations on the dependent partner, are relevant both for individuals and between economies. Households are dominant when there are slaves, serfs, or other dependent servants. Manufacturers or state enterprises dominate their work force if the latter are not protected by free trade unions. Nations are dominant when they rule colonies or satellite countries, and firms are dominant if their trading partners are dependent upon them.

The dominant firm uses the valuations of the dependent firm as parameters of action. It forces the dependent firm to make revaluations which are in its (the dominant firm's) interest, without taking account of the resulting disadvantages for the dependent firm.

Slaves, which even in the days of Walras, Jevons, or Menger were traded on Brazilian markets just like other products, without even one of these economists having recognized this phenomenon [9] were forced by violence to make revaluations. The legally free but economically dependent workers in the days of antiunion legislation had to let their wages and their working hours be dictated by their employers, in spite of the fact that many employers competed for the workers on the labor market. In the same way, dependent firms have to obey the instructions of the firms which dominate them whatever the state of the market. [10] The dependence of a firm can be legally justified. (e.g., the "domination agreements" permitted under § 308 of the German Companies Act), or can be based on economic links, as with the dominance-dependence relationships to be discussed here, which are usually founded on business relationships which have grown up over time and usually last for a fairly long period.

A dominant partner allows a dependent firm *to choose only between the lesser of two evils,* namely, either to follow his dictates or to lose him as partner (which may even endanger the existence of the dependent) (*partner's power*). The dominant role can be played by either the supplier (supplier's power) or the demander (demander's power). [11]

§2 Option fixing—a special case of partner's power

Ragner Frisch's [12] concept of the "option-fixer" deals with a special case of partner's power. According to Frisch, an option-fixer has the power to offer his partner the choice of taking a certain quantity of goods at a certain price or getting nothing at all. Frisch's option-fixer therefore restricts his partner's choice. He thus forces his partner to move from his marginal utility curve to his average utility curve or from his marginal cost curve to his average total cost curve, and in this way obtains his partner's differential return.

Frisch starts out from the assumption that a supplier acts according to his marginal costs and a demander according to his marginal utility. However, as we saw in Chapter 1, this does not match up to the real world and even in the neoclassical models applies only to so-called perfect competition.

The important point with regard to this chapter, however, is something different. Frisch fails to realize that (1) a firm which causes its partner to change the curves which supposedly determine his decision forces that partner to make *revaluations* (which lay outside neoclassical theory). He overlooks (2) the fact that there is no reason why such an influence should be limited to a given system of curves. Revaluations[13] can also lead to a shift of the curves themselves. The costs of a firm are not the result of the market forces alone, but are also influenced by a firm's individual situation. A firm's cost curves shift downward if it is forced to revalue (or to influence) its costs. Costs which can be changed individually are not only "calculated costs" (including "calculated risks," "calculated interest for the firm's own capital," the "entrepreneurial salary") but are also all other costs which are dependent on the firm's individual position. This is true (1) for the royalties or bonuses of the employees and executives. It may even be true (2) for the workers' wages if the local union or the firm's laborers agree to lower wages (or to work more for the same wage, as the pilots of PANAM in Berlin offered to do in 1981) because otherwise their employment appears to be endangered. A firm can furthermore obtain (3) lower purchase prices with the help of the argument that otherwise it would be forced out of business and its suppliers would therefore lose an important customer. The cost curves of free and dependent firms are not identical, because a dominant firm can force its business partner not only to give up its producer surplus, but also (and this is relevant alone in this connection) to revalue (or at least to influence) its costs.

The cost curves are therefore governed by the same kind of relativity which according to Myrdal[14] governs the utility curves: they have no material content as long as the value systems on which they are based remain unknown.

Lastly, Frisch has failed to see that option fixing is only a special case of the general phenomenon which François Perroux[15] has called "dominance." A dominant firm rules over its partner

(partner's power). It can force the firm which is dependent on it to make revaluations *without* ordering it to purchase or supply a particular quantity. A dominant firm generally does not commit itself to its own future obligations. If it is a demander, for example, it forces its supplier to lower its prices (and to improve the quality) without itself promising to buy any particular quantity. The quantities it buys depend completely on its future decisions.

Frisch's failure to recognize this may be due to the fact that he still thinks in terms of constant sales curves and that he still has in mind individual, isolated acts of exchange, although we are now generally dealing with business relationships which have grown up over time and which will continue into the future.

§3 Supplier's and demander's power

A firm which dominates one or more partners can be both a supplier and a demander (or a creditor and a debtor). [16]

Supplier's power was enjoyed, for example, by the U.S. automobile manufacturers before the Automobile Dealer Franchise Act was passed. The large automobile concerns knew that every dealer was dependent upon them but that they were not dependent upon every dealer. While their dealers soon went out of business if they stopped supplying autos and spare parts, the automobile concerns could change dealers at will. They used their dominance to force their dealers to take more cars than they wanted to, or to take old models which could not be sold except at a loss or to prevent them from engaging in lucrative sidelines such as the financing of cars, so that they could themselves make extra profits in this way. [17]

Demander's power is held, for example, by supermarkets, department stores, or industrial concerns which induce their suppliers to grant them preferential prices or to supply them with higher quality products than are supplied to other customers by threatening to stop doing business with them otherwise. If a firm has demander's power, it can also force its supplier to lend employees for stock-taking at no charge, to bear the costs of advertising or renting shelf space, even to deduct a proportion of its previous year's profit as an anniversary gift.

Neither the automobile firms (e.g., Ford or Chrysler) nor the supermarkets, mail order firms, or chain stores who use (or used) these practices have (or had) monopolies or monopsonies on the market. In each case, the unequal distribution of power comes entirely from the fact that any dominated firm is dependent upon its partner, while for the dominant firm all the partners which are dependent upon him are "replaceable."

In its report[18] of 1977 the German Monopolies Commission included "demander's power" under market power (*Marktmacht*), without carrying out any empirical studies. Although the Monopolies Commission's assumption is in line with the neoclassical model world, it is incorrect:

1. A partner can exercise demander's power (or supplier's power) even if it has only a one-thousandth or a one ten-thousandth share of the market. The relevant point is not his market share, but the proportion he sells to or buys from his *partner*. (In many cases the share of sales does not play any role at all.)

2. The market share of a dependent partner can therefore be many times greater than that of the dominant partner. The dominant supermarket may have no more than a one-thousandth share of the jam market, while the firm from which he buys his jam has a share of eight or ten percent. The dominant firm does not dominate the market but its partner.

3. One and the same firm can be both dominant and dependent at the same time. Thus, breweries in many cases dominate bars or inns (in which they have invested capital) and are dependent upon supermarkets, even if the same product (e.g., bottled beer) is being traded.

4. A firm can be both more or less dominant and more or less dependent on the same "relevant market." The prices differ according to the distribution of power. In this case a firm gets (or pays) different prices for the same product, in an extreme case a different price from every customer.

5. A dominant firm achieves its aim not by varying the quantity (or price) but by means of commands.

6. The effects of price and quantity are therefore not the same:

(a) A demand monopoly (monopsony) obtains a lower price, according to neoclassical theory, by demanding *less* than a competitor. A dominant demander, on the other hand, purchases a larger quantity at a lower price from a supplier which he forces to make revaluations (and also reconsiderations) with regard to his costs.

(b) A monopoly obtains a higher price by reducing the quantities offered for sale. In contrast, a dominant supplier forces his customers to take a larger quantity at the same (or even a higher) price. For example, at the time when General Motors was able to fully exercise its dominance, its dealers were forced "just before the close of the season . . . to take quantities of cars that they couldn't possibly sell except at a loss."[19]

Anyone who includes partner's power under monopoly (or monopsony) is therefore confusing two phenomena which are entirely different in every respect.

Lastly, the phenomenon of partner's power exists independently of buyers' and sellers' markets:

1. The American automobile manufacturers dominated their dealers without reference to the state of the automobile market. In the same way, dominant retailers dominate the suppliers which are dependent on them without reference to business fluctuations. Even in times of prosperity a supplier cannot lose important customers without getting into difficulties, while department stores or supermarkets sell so many different goods that the loss of one supplier is practically meaningless to them.

2. The existence of buyers' and sellers' markets does not explain why some traders pay more and other traders pay less for the same good at the same time.

The phenomenon of a dominant partner has nothing to do with size either. Even big concerns and their affiliates (such as Nestle, Unilever, ITT, or Oetker) can be dominated by relatively small supermarkets. General Motors, the largest automobile concern in the world, was dominated (at least until 1961) by the much smaller chemical firm of Du Pont.[20]

In neoclassical economics, which in this case agrees with Marx's axioms, the view has become accepted that the most dangerous or perhaps even the only enemy of the competitive economy is monopoly. This is not true. Faced with a monopoly, thanks to competition from substitutes, firms can usually transfer to other (relevant) markets, and thus to other partners.[21] A dependent firm does not have this option. It is legally or economically dependent on its partner.

SECTION 3:   Other Types of Power

§7   *The economic relevance of size*

If it is assumed that all firms are of equal size (or infinitely small), the size of a firm cannot be a cause of economic power. Thus, there cannot be any small firms which are powerless or large firms which have supremacy solely because of their size and the strength of their financial resources.

However, the size of a firm is economically relevant, for various reasons. A firm selling several products and operating in many markets can take profits it has made on one market and invest in other markets to improve its position in those markets. A company with large financial resources can withstand economic crises better than a firm with smaller resources; it also has the power to use its capital strength to force weaker firms to close down or to merge. A large firm can also use its national economic significance as a parameter of action. During the Great Depression, the Brüning government in Germany let hundreds of small banks go to the wall, but rescued the big banks with the aid of tax revenues.

§2   *Insider power*

If "perfect knowledge of the market" is assumed, all firms then possess the same knowledge and Bacon's famous phrase "scientia potestas est" would surprisingly not apply to the economy.

However, knowledge is also unequally distributed in the economy and becomes power if a firm (or a household) exploits its superior knowledge to the detriment of others.[22] A Rothschild who learns about Napoleon's defeat at Waterloo before everyone else, thanks to his courier service, exploits the power which he thus obtains to indulge in speculation in the same way as a bank which uses its insider information in it own interest or a company executive who buys shares before others learn of a successful business deal or sells shares before outsiders find out that the company has suffered losses.

By using his superior (or earlier) information, an insider brings about a redistribution of income and wealth to his advantage and to the disadvantage of those who are less informed.

An insider has no more a monopoly on a market than does

(usually) a dominant business partner. His power is based on his knowledge, not on his market position.

§3 *Power of control*

The power of control which managers exercise over firms in the East and West cannot exist if economic power is exclusively the result of market power. This kind of power cannot exist either if private property is looked at as the only source of power, as do many socialist authors who believe that the elimination of private ownership will free human society from exploitation forever.

However, Berle and Means[23] rightly pointed out as long ago as 1932 that power in modern joint-stock companies can become independent of property. If the shares of a firm are distributed among many shareholders, the shareholders lose control over their firm, this control now being exercised by the management more or less on its own authority. In the case of proxy voting power of banks for shares deposited with them, which exists, for example in West Germany, the chairman of the board of management may even become all-powerful. The board of management of the Deutsche Bank AG held more than fifty percent of the share capital represented in the general meeting. It could therefore not only elect its supervisory board and if necessary its sucessor(s), but could also formally approve its own actions, like a dictator. On the other hand, in English-speaking countries, where there is no bank's proxy voting power, holding even ten or twelve percent of the shares can be sufficient to dominate a shareholders' meeting and to pack the board with one's own people. In both systems, those who exercise the control can therefore issue instructions which are less in the interests of the (other) shareholders than in their own interest.

Even this form of power, which is individual to the modern economy, has nothing to do with market power. Firms and not markets are being controlled in this case.

§4 *Power of transnationality*

If it is assumed that the legal system has no economic consequences, the existence of corporations is not relevant either. The transnationality which occurs when a corporation possesses legally independent companies in various countries would then also have no economic significance.[24] However, transnationality does in fact influence competition. Its influence is the greater the more important the measures of national economic and financial policy are, which a multinational corporation can circumvent with the aid of its affiliates in other countries.

Transnational or multinational corporations are economically one firm but legally many firms. Due to the separation of the legal and economic unity of a firm, which has been artificially created by the legal system, a multinational corporation, in contrast to companies which are restricted to one country, has the power to obtain for itself certain competitive advantages. A multinational corporation can (1) shift profits and losses into the countries of its choice by means of transfer pricing between its companies and thus escape national tax laws, (2) treat currency dealings within its empire as internal transactions (legally or illegally) and in this way avoid restrictive national monetary and foreign exchange policy measures, and (3) plan flows of products among its constituent firms independently of the competitive situation and counteract thereby the liberalization of international trade (remembering to some respect the central planning of a state economy).

Transactions between companies of the same corporation which are based in different countries count as foreign trade from the point of view of the countries involved, but they are internal transactions from the point of view of the multinational corporation. As a result of this artificially created double role, multinational corporations gain advantages which one-sidedly distort competition between multinational and national companies to the detriment of the firms which are limited to one country. The power of transnationality also has nothing to do with market power, but it can be a means to gain power over markets.

§5   Power of pressure groups

If it is assumed that the state either does not exist at all or at least exists only as an "overall economic datum"[25] economic policy decisions therefore cannot be manipulated by private firms. The same conclusion is reached if it is assumed, along with many classical economists, that the state is powerless against the natural laws which prevail in the economy. In both cases, pressure groups would be irrelevant.

In fact, the state intervenes in economic activity by its legislation and by its administration. If firms have political power, they are therefore in a position to influence national laws (e.g., antitrust legislation) or government action (e.g., the placing of orders or participation in subsidies).[26] This type of power has nothing to do with market power either, in spite of the fact that in reality it plays an important role and affects the distribution of income and wealth.

Economic theory's lack of interest in economic power is fatal in several respects: (1) It prevents an analysis of the causes of concentration and restricts policy on concentration to curing only the symptoms. (2) It prevents an analysis of the forms to which competition deteriorates and consequently contributes to the fact that power instead of efficiency becomes more and more a decisive factor in competition. This fact is also important for competition (or antitrust) policy: cartel agreements against deteriorated competition in which power becomes decisive instead of economic efficiency, and cartel agreements against efficiency competition do not have the same economic effect. (3) It prevents the full realization of the constitutional state; formal equality before the law is worth little if different positions of power have different legal consequences and the mighty can use the law to his advantage.

In a world in which economic power has not yet been tamed, human rights are restricted or entirely suppressed.

SECTION 4: Temporary Power in Competition

If competition is defined as "perfect" when many firms, all of which are equally weak, offer a uniform good at a uniform price, every kind of power is thus eliminated from competition. Real competition, however, differs from this textbook model in the same way as "a bombardment" compares "with breaking down a door."[27] It is a process or, to be more precise, a collection of processes which, when they operate, adjust supply to the changing wishes of the demanders (adjustment competition) and introduce new and better products as well as new and cheaper production processes (development competition). Both processes give rise to temporary economic power. [28]

§1 Temporary power in adjustment competition

In adjustment competition, power switches back and forth between suppliers and demanders. To this extent, it is determined by space and time.

An excess of supply over demand produces a buyers' market. In this case the buyers are in the stronger position and can force the sellers to accept lower prices. The sellers, or some at least, suffer losses until they have adjusted their supply to demand by reducing their production.

If, on the other hand, demands exceeds supply, a sellers' market exists. In this case, the sellers are more powerful than the buyers. Consequently, they reap scarcity profits which stimulate them to increase production and/or to undertake net investment.

In both cases prices are determined not by costs but by scarcity. In both cases of adjustment competition, the redistribution of power is dependent on the prevailing degree of scarcity and serves to eliminate over- and underproduction on individual markets, thus preventing imbalances in the economy.

§2 Temporary power in development competition

In development competition, creative entrepreneurs gain economic power which is eroded by their imitators and thus by their (future) competitors.

A firm which creates a new market through innovations obtains a temporary monopoly of efficiency ("efficiency monopoly"). A firm which markedly improves an existing product or reduces its costs by means of a cheaper production process does not obtain a temporary monopoly; it nevertheless gains a competitive advantage (and increases its "differential return").

In these development processes, economic power arises as a result of a special performance, i.e., the introduction of new and better goods or the raising of labor productivity. As a result, the satisfaction of society's requirements is improved. (Temporary) economic power and the pressure of competition are the causes of economic development; without the expectation of gaining a temporary monopoly or a competitive advantage, new ideas would in general not be utilized in the economy.

If the prices are determined from the outset by the socially necessary costs, as assumed by Smith or Ricardo, or by the socially necessary working hours, as stated by Marx, there are no incentives to stimulate firms to engage in competition in adjustment and development. *Prices do not fulfil economic functions if they coincide with costs; they only carry out these functions if they deviate from costs.*

Losses induce firms to restrict their production, scarcity profits stimulate them to expand their production, and the expectation of additional or monopoly-type profits spurs them to introduce new products and product qualities as well as cheaper production processes. If prices are (always) determined by costs, neither competition in adjustment nor in development are possible, and the national economic functions resulting from temporary power in competition are not carried out. Just as there is no economy without power, there is no adjustment or development in competition without economic power arising and declining again. The struggle for temporary power preserves competition; the existence of permanent power kills it.

CHAPTER 7

Interactions Between the State and the Economy

> The misdeeds of governments are public and
> conspicuous.
>
> Bernard Shaw

Classical economists, such as Adam Smith or David Ricardo, have regarded the state as a necessary evil for reasons of order and security. According to them, the state has nothing to do with economic problems and its influence on the economy is certainly not a subject for economic analysis. Marx saw a stateless economy as an ideal for the future because he identified the state with the ruling class. The marginal utility school has in its turn ignored not only the state but also space and time, by assuming the existence of a perfect market, and has thus ignored any kind of historical development. Only in the Keynesian school does the state play a larger role, but even here it is limited to the function of a deus ex machina which combats unemployment by means of autonomous investment. None of these schools deals with the interactions which take place between the state and the economy.

However, the state and its activities are not "data" for the process of economic development nor are they "data" for firms and their pressure groups whose particular task is to influence the state in their own interest.[1]

SECTION 1: Influence of the Economy on the State

The state changes with the economy. This is shown by the many government laws passed after the rise of the factories during the nineteenth century to protect not only women and children but also male workers. The introduction of a state unemployment insurance scheme in the German Reich in 1927 was also a response to urgent social and economic problems. Notable examples of the influence of the economy on the state are the government laws which were enacted during the thirties in countries such as the United States, France, Germany, and Great Britain under the influence of the Great Depression and brought about far-reaching changes in the social and legal systems of these countries. The environmental pollution resulting from increasing industrialization and motorization have also presented governments with new legislative tasks. The idea that the state pursues an existence which is independent of the economy, which is still discernible in many of the current textbooks of economic theory, is therefore untenable. The more democratically a nation is governed or the more the government takes account of the interests of its citizens, the more a state adapts itself to the changing demands of economic life.

SECTION 2: Influence of the State on the Economy

There is no social economy without a state. Even the Industrial Revolution, which was regarded by classical economists such as Adam Smith as a kind of natural phenomenon, is the result of state intervention. This era of development of new and cheaper capital and consumer goods which has lasted from the eighteenth century until the present day and is unparalleled in the entire history of mankind, was only made possible by two government measures: (1) the abolition of compulsory guild membership, without which economic development would have been outlawed by the rules of the guilds, and in particular (2) the patent laws passed before the start of the Industrial Revolution, without which there would not have been sufficient incentives for the development of new or better products and new or cheaper production processes.

In an economy with compulsory guild membership and without patent rights, the breakneck speed of economic development and the growth in both the satisfying of society's needs and the population which this brought about, which are decisive for the last two hundred years, could not have been achieved.

State intervention has both positive and negative effects on the economy. A particularly striking example of the harmful effect which government activity can produce is the Great Depression. This unique event of economic history cannot be explained without (1) the reparations which the victorious countries imposed on the defeated countries and whose disastrous consequences Keynes had already pointed out in the twenties, (2) the high tariff barrier policies of countries such as the United States and the use of import quotas by countries such as France, (3) the neutralization of inflowing money and to this extent "state hoarding" in France and the United States to avoid stagflation,[2] and finally (4) the destruction of the world's monetary system by national exchange control in most European countries.

If the industrialized countries were now to change back to high tariff barriers, import quotas, or exchange control, a new Great Depression of a similar size would be the inevitable consequence. On the other hand, the recovery of the international economy, thanks to the Havana conference and the Kennedy Round, has had a positive effect on the international economic activity and has probably contributed more to the raising of the international level of employment than Keynesian full employment policy in the postwar period.

Even economic systems are not natural phenomena, as they were assumed to be by Smith, Ricardo, Say, and many other economists up to the present day, nor are they the result of inevitable developments, as Fourier, Proudhon, or Marx believed. They are the result of state activity. Neither a competitive economy nor a state monopoly economy[3] grows up without the state. The "social market economy" of West Germany has been created just as much through state intervention as has been the economy of the Soviet Union. It is also the state which is responsible for economic policy in the West and which enacts four-year or five-year plans in the Eastern block countries. Even the international economy which followed the mercantile age grew up because nations under England's influence abolished trade barriers. The international economy which has developed since World War II is also the result of agreements between nations, as is the present international currency system.

SECTION 3: Confusion of the Results of State Intervention with Natural Phenomena

Economists who look for "natural laws" usually overlook the transitory causes which make economic relationships into temporary historical phenomena. Thus, classical economists not only failed to recognize that the so-called Industrial Revolution was sparked off by state actions (prohibition of guilds, patent laws), but also overlooked the fact that the phenomena which they described as the results of "natural laws" are in fact due to state intervention.[4]

According to Ricardo, for example, the "natural price of labour" is that price "which is necessary to enable the labourers, one with another, to subsist and to perpetuate their race, without either increase or diminution."[5] In fact, wages in Ricardo's day were not "natural" but were the result of state antiunion legislation. "The masters," as Adam Smith described the situation at that time, "being fewer in number, can combine much more easily; and the law, besides, authorises or at least does not prohibit their combinations, while it prohibits those of the workmen. We have no acts of Parliament against combining to lower the price of work; but many against combining to raise it."[6]

With the abolition of antiunion legislation, which was one-sidedly directed against the workers, and with the permitting of free and independent trade unions, the Ricardian "natural law," which was largely adopted by Marx, has disappeared. If wages tend to increase from year to year as a result of union demands, as in the United States or West Germany, the theory that wages are determined by the means of subsistence necessary to maintain the laborer[7] ceases to be tenable.

From the historical facts of his day, Karl Marx concluded that "within the capitalist system all methods for raising the social productiveness of labour are brought about at the cost of the individual labourer." He argued from this "that in proportion as capital accumulates, the lot of the labourer . . . must grow worse."[8] As long as the antiunion legislation is in force, this theory of impoverishment is in accordance with empirical data. After this legislation has been abolished, this phenomenon is no longer observable. The real wages of domestic servants, formerly one of the most harshly exploited groups of workers, have risen approximately thirtyfold over the last fifty years.[9] Real wages in so-called "socialist countries" have been less mobile upward.

The fact that economic phenomena can be the result of state intervention has also been overlooked by Keynes and his followers. In his *General Theory*, Keynes not only failed to recognize that state action could cause underemployment. According to him, the savings of private households and the liquidity preference of private firms were alone responsible for the unemployment of the thirties. He also disputed that deficit spending causes inflation at the time of underemployment, provided that no bottlenecks arise. However, this is in fact only true if states regulate prices by means of price laws and price commissioners, as was then the case in Germany and Great Britain.[10] However, it is not necessary for states to intervene in price formation in this way. If the state allows prices to follow the free interplay of supply and demand, price increases even occur in industries with a high level of underemployment, as is happening at the present time.

In keeping with the historical conditions of the thirties, Keynes has also based his general theory on the premise that the economies in which underemployment exists are "closed economies." At that time, nations had indeed sealed off their economies from each other as far as possible by means of exchange control, high tariff barriers, etc. However, this kind of "fencing off" is not necessary. Now that the governments of the Western nations have restored the international economy, these premises no longer apply to the nations in the free world.

Finally, a country's type of government is by no means irrelevant to the success or failure of its economic policy. In a democratic society such as the Federal Republic of Germany, for example, an unemployed person cannot be forced to do laboring work on expressways, canals, or parade grounds if he was previously working in an automobile factory as a fitter or a welder. In a dictatorship, the individual rights are less developed. There it is possible to create work without such difficulties by building roads and canals. There is also no right to strike and interest rates are usually low. Even phenomena such as the multiplier and the accelerator are not independent of the economic order laid down by the state.

Economists have to be aware of these interactions between politics and economics if they are not to fall victim to the error of confusing the effects of national laws with natural laws. Just as the economy is not a mechanism, the economic and social order is not a "datum," but is subject to human organization.[11] Anyone who overlooks the role of human beings in the state and the economy fails to recognize that all judgements[12] or conclusions only become relevant when the conditions relating to them are realized. If this were not so, economic policy would be impossible.

CHAPTER 8

Logical Inconsistencies and Incorrect Observations

> One goes to a psychiatric ward to learn to
> appreciate normal human behavior.
> Paul A. Samuelson

A scientific discipline such as political economy, of which the object of analysis is far more complicated than that of any natural science, requires both a complete mastery of the apparatus of logic and a special aptitude for empirical observations. Even economists, however, are not free of errors of deduction and thus of logic, or of errors of induction and thus of perception.

SECTION 1: Logical Inconsistencies

> We must throw out concepts and theorems that
> are logically self contradictory . . .
> Joan Robinson

Logical inconsistencies become apparent when theorists, in the course of their analysis, change the concepts from which they started out, without taking note of the resulting divergences.

It is logically inconsistent, for example, for Ricardo to transfer the theory of the "natural tendency of profits . . . to fall"[1] from his model of a stationary economy to a developing economy. In a stationary economy, in which capital goods neither become technologically obsolete nor lose their value on shrinking markets, "the gradual growth of constant capital in relation to variable capital must," according to Marx, "necessarily lead to a gradual fall of the general rate of profit."[2] In a developing economy, however, fresh capital is repeatedly required, not only because in many cases increasingly longer production detours are taken[3] but also and particularly because capital goods in excellent condition repeatedly become worthless due to the development of new production processes and new markets. The faster the rate of technological development, the sooner capital goods which are still usable or even almost new have to be taken out of service. The trend of a falling profit rate is not only "happily checked at repeated intervals by the improvements in machinery," as Ricardo thought, but becomes considerably overcompensated for. Conclusions derived from a model of a stationary economy cannot be transferred to a developing economy.

It is also logically inconsistent for Marx to initially define surplus value as the "excess over the original value"[4] and thus as the difference between revenue and cost and later to identify it with profit,[5] "which for the capitalist has all the charms of a creation out of nothing"[6] and, on the other hand, to explain that even a communist society must withhold a proportion of the surplus value from the worker.[7] Thus, Marx states: "This surplus-labour appears as surplus-value, and this surplus-value exists as a surplus-product. Surplus-labour in general as labour performed over and above the given requirements, must always remain . . . A definite quantity of surplus-labour is required as insurance against accidents, and by the necessary and progressive expansion of the process of reproduction in keeping with the development of the needs and the growth of population . . . "[8]

The contradictions into which Karl Marx is falling here are the result of his applying a concept of surplus value which he has derived from a model of a stationary economy to a developing economy, where new products and production processes are created. In a stationary economy, in which the same products are perpetually manufactured in the same way and in which supply and demand always coincide without reference to space and time, "surplus labour" is superfluous not only for risks ("insurance") but also for net investment. In a stationary economy with no state (and therefore no taxes) the difference between revenue and cost appears as profit with no cause. However, there is no economy without the state and no economic development without risks, net investment, and technological obsolescence of capital goods. In a developing economy, there is not only "reproduction." Production itself is in constant change.

In a developing economy there are first of all the "adjustment losses," caused by fluctuations in demand and other economic phenomena (the "accidents" of Marx) and secondly the "development losses" (which Marx does not mention) linked with the emergence of new markets and the disappearance of old markets. If, for example, movie theaters are being increasingly superseded by television, the equipment invested in movie theaters loses its value. In the same way, no new markets emerge without additional expenditure on new products. In a developing economy, are two factors: (1) technological obsolence in excess of physical wear-out, because out-of-date equipment must constantly be replaced by technologically more efficient capital goods, and (2.) the need to use part of the "surplus value" for net investment which becomes necessary in a developing economy for three reasons:

(a) as *expansion investment,* because real per capita income grows, resulting in an increase in demand,
(b) as *rationalization investment,* which is triggered by the introduction of new and cheaper production processes, and
(c) as specific *development investment,* which is inevitably associated with the emergence of new products and the rise of new markets.

It is therefore illogical to transfer results derived from a model of a stationary economy to a developing economy in which national income and wealth increase with technological progress.

It is also logically inconsistent if economists state on the one hand that falling real income causes an increase in demand for inferior goods, shifting the demand curve for these commodities to the right, and on the other hand adopt the widespread claim that the demand curve in the so-called "Giffen paradox" has an abnormal slope,[9] although real income has fallen in this case as well. Thomas E. Holland even distinguishes three different types of products: "normal, inferior and 'Giffen' products."[10] However, there is no such thing as a "Giffen product," nor is the slope of the demand curve in the so-called Giffen paradox abnormal. None of the innumerable textbook authors who spread this fairy tale have tested the Giffen paradox with the aid of income elasticity. Otherwise, they would have seen that demand for inferior goods always increases with decreasing real income, regardless of whether the drop in real income is due to a decrease in money incomes (e.g., in wages) or to a rise in prices.

The authors who hold to the theorem of "Giffen products" over-look two things: (1) that in the so-called Giffen paradox from which they start out, real income is falling although money wages remain the same, as Alfred Marshall has already stated.[11] Here drop in real income is caused by the rise in price of the good which is essential for staying alive; (2) that the poor of London cannot increase their demand for this good without at the same time reducing their demand for superior goods. Even this is a general phenomenon which can be observed whenever real income falls appreciably. The demand curve for inferior goods moves to the right, while the demand curves for superior goods at the same time shift to the left, because real income has fallen. Nor is this in any way affected by the fact that the cause of the drop in real income is the rise in price of the inferior good; the rise in the price of bread forces the poor to increase their consumption of bread and to lower their consumption of meat and fat.

It is also logically inconsistent for authors such as Jan S. Ho-gendorn to state on the one hand that demand for a good shifts to the right if this good is valued more highly than before or if "a greater liking" occurs,[12] while on the other hand saying only a few pages earlier (drawing on Thorsten Veblen) that the demand curve for prestige goods has an abnormal slope.[13] In fact, the "leisure class" does value many goods by price. However, as in any case of "a greater liking," the demand curve shifts to the right. The fact that the higher valuation is based on the higher price and not on other characteristics makes no difference.

Logical inconsistencies are also committed by those economists who by means of the so-called "budget lines" introduce income into Edgeworth's and Pareto's models, which operate with happiness or with natural values such as units, kilograms, or liters. They thus bring in (at least indirectly) exactly those prices which Edgeworth and Pareto are trying to explain by means of their analysis. Neither incomes nor the budget lines fit into these models, which operate with natural pleasure and physical products. Income only exists when there are prices, i.e., when goods have to be paid for. The budget line which represents the income available is incompatible with Edgeworth's concept of happiness and Pareto's acts of choice. Even in Gossen's law of pleasure equaliza-tion, the problem is not the shortage of money but the shortage of time, which makes the complete satisfaction of all needs impossible—a problem which may even arise in paradise, where neither prices nor income exist.

It is also logically inconsistent for Sraffa, Chamberlin, and Robinson to infer the monopoly of a firm from the heterogeneity of a good.[14] This conclusion would only be permissible if the good and the firm were identical with each other. However, this is not the case, according to their own definitions. Both Sraffa and Chamberlin assume that not only material, personal, and spatial but also temporal differences in a good justify a monopoly. If this were correct, even a shop which sells a hundred or a thousand hot dogs each at a different time would have a hundred or a thousand different monopolies. The derivation of "company monopolies" from the lack of "product homogeneity" is therefore an error of logic, even though it is included in innumerable textbooks.

Sraffa, Chamberlin, and Robinson were indeed aware that they were changing the premises when they embarked upon the attempt to replace the theory of perfect competition with another theory. However, they were by no means fully aware of the meaning of the change. None of these authors recognized that the equilibrium of perfect competition is entirely unreal simply due to its lack of reference to space and time; instead, each of these economists followed the line of searching for a model of competition which conformed to reality better than the old model of perfect competition. Although these authors abandoned Jevons's law of indifference to a certain extent, they not only stuck to looking at equilibria but chose Cournot's monopoly as the model which conformed better to reality, without taking into account the fact that this model was also constructed outside space and time (and therefore outside human history). With the statement that each firm possesses "the monopoly of its output," they had only changed the market structure, not its basic premises, and therefore had not dealt with its unreality.

Another logical inconsistency, found in many textbooks, is the theorem of the "kinky demand curve,"[15] which originated with Paul M. Sweezy. Sweezy initially confuses the firm's sales with its demand. He examines in what ways the sales of a firm change if the firm varies its sales price. However, the sales curve is not "kinky" either. If a supplier raises his price without his competitors also raising their prices, he loses customers. Some of his former customers buy the products of competitors, who are now cheaper than he is. His sales curve consequently shifts to the left, and the sales curves of his competitors, who now have more customers than before, move to the right. If, on the other hand, he cannot lower his price without his competitors doing the same, there is no movement of customers. Consequently no shift of the sales curves takes place, because every competitor keeps his customers[16] (and demand has not changed either). In other words, the individual sales curves of firms remain unchanged (with given total demand) if there is no change in the competitive and sales relationships.

Sweezy's theorem thus contains two errors of logic: (1) the confusion of the demand and sales of a firm, and (2) the assumption that the sales curve is "kinky," although it shifts when a firm gains or loses customers.

The confusion of demand and sales prevents the analysis of sales problems in economic theory. The textbooks which do not differentiate between the demand and the sales of a firm do not analyze sales curves and the causes of their shifts.

SECTION 2: Oversimplifications and Their Consequences

> When the results of a theory seem to flow specifically from a special crucial assumption, then if the assumption is dubious, the results are suspect.
>
> Robert M. Solow

Economists tend to make oversimplifications, without realizing that in so doing they change the object of analysis, thus leaving the way open for wrong interpretations.

One oversimplification, as mentioned above, is the identification of the demand for commodities with the demand of households.[17]

This oversimplification, which is found in almost all modern textbooks, enables the authors: (1) to talk of the "demand curve of firms" when they mean the sales curve of firms; (2) to restrict firms' demand to factors of production (labor etc.), this demand being determined by "marginal productivity," and (3) to determine demand for commodities by means of marginal pleasure (marginal utility) in accordance with Gossen's laws, Edgeworth's indifference curves, or Pareto's acts of choice.

All these conflict with reality. Demand for commodities is not identical with households' demand. Households' demand for commodities is not solely or even mainly determined by marginal utility (happiness). Firms' demand for commodities is finally determined neither by marginal productivity nor by marginal utility:

1. Firms have a much higher demand for commodities than do households. Before an auto or a dishwasher reaches a household, a large number of firms will have demanded hundreds or thousands of products which go to make up the auto or the dishwasher. Firms consequently have far more demand curves for commodities than do households.

2. Marginal utility or marginal pleasure does not determine either households' or firms' demand for commodities. Households do not choose the goods that they acquire on the basis of the pleasure; their choice of the goods they demand is guided by prices and the money in their pocket. Firms have no pleasure at all. Therefore, their demand cannot be derived from "indifference curves." Their demand does not depend on the "marginal productivity" either; children's toys or some other consumer goods on sale in a department store have no productivity at all. In fact, the demand of firms depends on their past sales, on their expectations with regard to the future, and on the financial resources they have available.

The falsification of the object of analysis becomes particularly clear in the case of demand monopoly (monopsony). According to most textbooks a monopsony is a household which exploits its market power by purchasing less than would a competitor under the same circumstances. This statement contains four errors: (1) Monopolies which demand commodities are found not among households, but among firms (and public authorities). Private households do not dominate markets. (2) Firms' demand for commodities cannot be derived from marginal utility or from indifference curves. (3) A monopsony maximizes its profit not by buying less of a cheap good but by buying more. The cheaper a firm can buy, the cheaper it can sell and the higher are its sales. (4.) The strategy of a monopsony, like that in the case of demander's power, can only be explained by abandoning the crucial premise that in real life economic values are given and constant. A demander who dominates a market can force his suppliers to make revaluations and is therefore able to buy more at a lower price.

Other oversimplifications of a similar type are: the identification of demand with consumption, of production with supply, or of the supplier with the producer.

It is also an oversimplification for Marx, drawing on David Ricardo, to count "skilled labour . . . only as simple labour intensified, or rather, as multiplied simple labour, a given quantity of skilled (labour) being considered equal to a greater quantity of simple labour."[18] This oversimplification permits these authors to equate the "natural wage" with the wage of an unskilled worker. However, this is wrong for several reasons:

1. It generalizes the historical situation of the unskilled laborer at the time of Ricardo and Marx.
2. It hides the fact that even when anti-tradeunion legislation was in force only a proportion of workers received the supposed "natural wage." (Question: Why is a wage "natural" if it only applies to the unskilled?)
3. It also fails to recognize that as development progresses, the proportion of unskilled laborers in the work force falls, because their work is increasingly taken over by machines.[19]
4. It conceals the basic qualitative difference between various kinds of human activity. A "smaller quantity of skilled labour" cannot be equated with "a larger quantity of simple labour." This is especially true for creative activities. Daimler and Benz are no more the multiple of a mechanic than Michelangelo is the multiple of a decorator or Goethe the multiple of a common or garden variety writer. Mental work is not quantifiable, and creative activity is not a multiple of receptive activity. With their oversimplifications, Ricardo and Marx have eliminated precisely the factor which has determined the economic face of the nineteenth and twentieth centuries: the creative activity and therefore the ability of human beings to create new things which has led to economic development and thus to a permanent revolution in both the supply and the production of goods.

A further oversimplification, which ignores basic economic problems, is evident when Ricardo, as well as more than a few present-day economists, only speak "of commodities, of their exchangeable value, and of the laws which regulate their relative prices" when these commodities "can be increased in quantity by the exertion of human industry, and on the production of which competition operates without restraint."[20] However, this definition contrasts starkly with reality: (1) Famines would be impossible if grain, rice, or beef cattle could always be increased by the exertion of human industry. New markets, on which the products are protected by industrial secrets or patents, would then also be ruled out. (2) Even if goods "can be increased in quantity," competition does not operate "without restraint." In reality, competition is restricted by market-dominating cartels or trusts, syndicates, multinational corporations, etc. Is a good sold by a cartel or a monopoly not a commodity?

Ricardo's definition of "economic goods" thus gives us a model world which is in fact stripped of all the important economic problems and in which it is impossible to analyze the scarcity which varies in space and time.

Another oversimplification is to be found in the theory of market structures that falsifies the object of analysis by the assumption that cost and sales curves are given. This assumption results in the exclusion of any kind of entrepreneurial influence on cost and sales curves,[21] thereby in fact preventing the firm's management from undertaking any kind of entrepreneurial policy. Changes in products, in production processes, and in the sales organization are by definition impossible, as is investment in rationalization or development. A model of this kind leaves no room for the question of whether an increase in a firm's sales is due to improvements in product quality, to advertising, or to a reduction in durability. Nor is it possible in this model to discuss the question of whether or when a firm is in a position to reduce its costs by means of cheaper production processes or by worsening the quality of its products (for instance by using inferior materials). As long as cost and sales curves are assumed to be given, it is not possible either to examine the influence of voluntary or obligatory revaluations on the positions of cost and sales curves. A model which is oversimplified to such an extent that price and quantity are the only variables, largely if not totally eliminates the problems of economic power, especially if by applying Jevons's law of indifference, all material and personal differences are ignored.

The economic power in such radically oversimplified models

then appears as a purely quantitative phenomenon, which is thus deprived of all qualitative and personal differences. Human ability and human behavior seem to be entirely meaningless. Everything depends solely on the number (or the quantity) of firms in the market: one = monopoly, two = duopoly, a few = oligopoly, many = competition. The exclusion of all variables which cannot be measured purely quantitatively thus leads to an (almost) complete lack of the significance of economic problems.[22] It is therefore hardly surprising that one group of economists, such as Eucken or von Stackelberg, assume that the intensity of competition increases with the number of firms in the market, and other economists, such as Ott, teach the opposite,[23] while Cournot identifies competition with duopoly. However, the number of firms is not significant for the intensity of competition. In reality, human abilities play the decisive role: the competitor's ability to adjust his firm to changing historical conditions and his ability to create new or better products and better or cheaper methods of production.

Finally, another oversimplification views the existence of private and public ownership as the main difference between decentralized and centralized planning. This applies to all authors who, like Eucken, allocate all "market structures," including oligopolies, duopolies, and monopolies to the market economy.[24] However, whether an economy or a market is decentralized or centralized does not depend on the kind of ownership: (1) There are competing firms which are largely or wholly owned by the state (as was Volkswagen for a long time, and still is as far as control is concerned) or are "common property" (e.g., the Bank of Gemeinwirtschaft, owned by the German Federation of Trade Unions). (2) In every monopoly, whether it is publicly or privately owned, production, investment and, as far as possible, sales are centrally planned.

Although the question of ownership is not unimportant, the basic economic difference is the contrast between competition and monopoly. Planning is decentralized under competition and centralized in every monopoly. Competition forces firms to pay attention to the interests of their customers. A monopoly, whether publicly or privately owned, is not under this obligation. For these reasons as well, the "theory of market structures," which is still found in many present-day textbooks, is misleading.

The oversimplifications of the classical and neoclassical schools have not made easier the analysis of economic problems. The reverse is true. Oversimplifications such as the reduction of economic processes to a succession of equilibria or the exclusion of all economic variables apart from price and quantity impede an understanding of the economic problems of the real world, which develop in space and time and are characterized by qualitative differences. Oversimplifications falsify the facts. They not only hinder but prevent economic anaylsis.

SECTION 3: Transformation of Hypothetical Statements into "Absolute Truths"

> Definitions are dogmas; only the deductions from them are knowledge.
>
> Karl Menger

Modern economists no longer demand absolute standards as did Smith, Ricardo, or Marx. They create absolutes by ignoring the premises from which their relationships were derived. They define their concepts without making it clear that every definition turns a hypothetical statement into a dogma.[25]

A typical example of this is the treatment of the accelerator in almost all textbooks. According to Erich Schneider, the accelerator is a relationship which is expressed by the equation[26]

$$I_{ind} = \beta \cdot \frac{dC}{dt}.$$

According to Samuelson, the accelerator principle shows "a tremendous pulse in investment spending as a result of a moderate increase in consumption sales" and "links the level of investment to GNP's rate of growth."[27] However, neither the equation nor its interpretation expresses the relativity which is inherent in these phenomena in real life: (1) The accelerator which has been observed in reality depends on historical conditions which are not generally realized. (2) The theoretical significance of the accelerator principle applies solely under the premises from which it has been derived. It is hypothetical.

The pure accelerator model assumes not only a stationary economy, as mentioned by Samuelson,[28] but also the following premises:

1. no reserve capacity in the domestic consumer and capital goods industries,

2. no imports or exports (i.e., a closed economy),
3. no change in the life of machinery,
4. no cartel agreements between firms, etc.,
5. no customer preferences.

Each of these premises makes the significance of the doctrine relative or even makes it meaningless:

1. If there is reserve capacity in domestic industries, the net investment which initiates the accelerator does not take place.
2. If trading relations with other countries exist, any additional demand may be distributed throughout the world.
3. If the life of machinery changes, the acceleration effect does not remain constant. If, for example, the average life of machinery drops from twenty to ten years, the acceleration coefficient is halved, and the repercussions of the oscillatory process are reduced correspondingly.
4. If firms conclude cartel agreements to escape the pressure of competition,[29] they can extend delivery times. The more firms spread additional orders over the future, the less evident is the accelerator.
5. If customers have strong preferences for particular quality products (e.g., for autos from Daimler-Benz), a firm can make its customers wait even without cartel agreements. It does not have to "simultaneously" expand its capacity, as in the accelerator model, but can pursue a long-term investment policy.

As the accelerator model is limited to a stationary economy, it also conceals the fact that in real life, in which new and cheaper products are always being created, the stability of growth depends primarily on investment in rationalization and development.

The accelerator equation (which many unfortunate students have to learn by heart) contains none of the above premises. It entirely ignores the hypothetical nature of the statement and thereby pretends to be a mechanism which does not in fact exist.

Samuelson, like all other authors who "formalize" in the same or similar ways, infringes the rules of logic in two respects: (1) He transforms a hypothetical statement into an unrestricted and thus apparently universally valid statement. (2) He transfers conclusions from the pure accelerator model to reality.

The theory of the accelerator as expressed in terms of absolutes is thus neither logically nor empirically tenable: (1) logically, because a hypothetical conclusion is presented as a universal truth, (2) empirically, because it fails to take into account that historical conditions change.

A further example of a concept expressed in terms of absolutes is the multiplier equation developed by Kahn and Keynes. The multiplier is defined by Samuelson as the "number by which the change in investment must be multiplied in order to present us with the resulting change in income," adding, in similar fashion to Keynes, "a whole endless chain of secondary consumption respending is set up by my primary $1,000 of investment spending."[30]

First of all, this definition contains an error of logic, or at least an inaccuracy, which is confusing to the reader. If the individual investment in question is once and for all, as in the Samuelson's example ("my primary $1,000 of investment spending"),[31] there is no change at all in equilibrium income.[32] Although the "primary $1,000 of investment spending" does initiate a chain of secondary consumer respending, the amounts spent become increasingly smaller (as Samuelson also shows in his example),[33] finally disappearing completely from circulation in the new equilibrium. Although the sum of all the increases which take place in the process and therefore over the course of time is, at a marginal propensity to consume of two-thirds, three times the primary spending; at no time, not even during the process, does the national income rise to three times the incremental investment. Thus, Samuelson, like Keynes before him,[34] has here confused the sum of all the periodic increases with an increase in national income in the new equilibrium. A change in the equilibrium income has not taken place, as becomes apparent at the end of the process.

Secondly, the definition given above can be challenged for other reasons. Like the traditional accelerator equation, it fails to mention the premises from which the theory of the multiplier is derived. Examples of these premises are: (1) a closed economy and thus an economy without exports and imports, (2) a stationary economy and thus an economy in which no investment in rationalization and development takes place, and (3) a constant "marginal propensity to consume" and thus the elimination of learning processes and expectations.

If the economy is not closed, the price increases resulting from autonomous investment may, in reducing the country's international competitiveness, have a harmful effect on the national level of employment. The theory of the multiplier makes no mention of this.

The international competitiveness of a country is, in general, increased not by autonomous public investment but by investment in rationalization and development. The normal multiplier equation has no relevance here either; it is therefore not possible to derive from it the (wrong) conclusion that in a market economy "autonomous investment" should have priority over the promotion of economic development.[35]

When there is an appreciable surge in investment, whether it originates from the state as in Keynes or from inventions as well as in Samuelson, the marginal propensity to consume is not constant but variable. The reversal of expectations, which Kahn, Keynes,and Samuelson do not even mention, is of decisive importance here. The marginal propensity to consume increases if it is expected that the "autonomous investment" will produce rising instead of hitherto falling prices and falling instead of hitherto rising unemployment.

The traditional multiplier equation[36]

$$dY = \frac{1}{1 - \dfrac{dC}{dY}} \cdot dI$$

is therefore not as unproblematic as its supporters would have us believe: (1) As a result of formalization, which fails to take account of the premises, it changes a hypothetical judgment into an absolute statement. This transformation is logically incorrect; the pure doctrine of the multiplier applies neither to an open economy nor to a developing economy. (2) As a result of the incomplete formalization which ignores all process-related values such as innovations, experiences, expectations, revaluations and therefore assumes a constant marginal propensity to consume, it is claimed that equilibria apply to situations which are really steps in a process. This transformation is also logically unjustified and empirically wrong; an economy does not move from equilibrium to equilibrium.

The objections raised against the traditional accelerator and multiplier equations apply equally to the "multiplier-accelerator model" which is supposed to explain unstable growth. This model is neither logically correct, because it presents hypothetical judgments from the model of a closed, stationary economy as absolute truths, nor does it reflect the real world, because it ignores important elements in processes which operate in space and time, e.g., innovations, experiences, expectations, and revaluations and assumes the existence of equilibria where there are none. In reality, unstable growth is a chain of "unique events" (*Niehans*) which are caused by different and changing factors and which cannot be explained by one model alone. Mathematically, Samuelson's multiplier-accelerator model cannot be faulted; economically, however, it contains no material evidence.

The inclination to change hypothetical judgments into absolute truths by omitting their premises is apparent in almost all cases in which neoclassical economists present their doctrines in mathematical terms. This is understandable to a certain extent. Absolute truth can be stated in the form of simple definitions or equations. Relative statements, i.e., statements which are only true under certain conditions, are far more complicated. The primitive mathematical tools which the neoclassical economists usually use are not adequate for presenting them.

A science does not become exact just because it uses mathematical symbols, especially since there is nothing to prevent formally correct equations being factually wrong. Theorems which are presented in the form of mathematical equations are only exact when they contain all the premises from which they are derived. The omission of the premises under which a conclusion is valid falsifies the result.

SECTION 4: Sham Proofs

§1 *Tautologies*

Tautologies do not replace proofs, but they are often used in economic theory in their place. Tautologies of this kind are most often encountered when economists, in their search for the economic absolute ("thing in itself") ignore the real problems of human economic behavior. However, since the "thing in itself" is barred to human vision, as the philosopher Kant taught, the only course left to those who are searching for the absolutes in a social science such as economics is to offer sham proofs.

A tautology is found, for example, in Adam Smith, when in his search for absolutes he explains prices in terms of costs making up the goods, although costs are obviously nothing more than prices. The costs of raw materials and semifinished products are given by their prices. Interest payments are prices which have to be paid for loans, and wages are prices which have to be paid for labor. Even Ricardo described wages as the price of labor. All these prices are as relative and as transitory as the prices of the finished products. The prices of raw materials and semifinished products remain no more constant than do the prices for loans or labor. In a world in which wages rise with labor productivity and workers' real income fluctuates with the fortunes of the economy, Ricardo's attempt to postulate the subsistence level as the natural measure for wages has turned out to be a major and a disastrous error. In a market economy, in which new and cheaper products are always being created, new markets arise and old markets disappear, and sellers' markets change to buyers' markets, in such a world prices are not solely determined by costs but by scarcity. The belief that the true and absolute value of all goods is to be found in the costs is metaphysics or, more accurately, metaeconomics.

Other examples of tautologies are Say's theorem and Keynes's equilibrium with underemployment.

§2 Formalization as proof

As long ago as 1913 Knut Wicksell pointed out that mathematical equations are not proofs in his *Vorlesungen über Nationalökonomie* (Lectures on Political Economy).[37] Although the language of mathematics has the advantage of being precise, it can be misused just as easily as any other language. In the same way as the grammatical correctness of a sentence has nothing whatsoever to do with its factual accuracy, the formal correctness of a mathematical formula has no bearing on the factual accuracy of the statement it contains. Mathematical forms of expression, like the words of a language, are factually neutral, and can be used to express inaccurate and factually incorrect statements.

The famous equation for the profit maximization of a Cournot's monopoly $MC = MR$ is perfectly correct in formal terms, but it does not prove that a real monopoly, whose cost and sales curves are not "given," acts solely, if at all, in accordance with marginal costs and marginal revenue. It only shows that a sole supplier who knows his cost and sales curves and is not able to influence them maximizes his profit in this way. Thus far, Cournot's monopoly corresponds to the naive idea that some neo-Marxists have of an entrepreneur (or manager): his only function is to maximize his profit. Cournot's monopoly does not carry out real entrepreneurial functions.

The present as well as the future effects that a monopoly has on the satisfaction of society's needs are not apparent in an equation in which all entrepreneurial methods of influence and thus all kinds of entrepreneurial policy have been ignored. The formal or mathematical correctness of this equation proves nothing whatever about its economic usefulness.

The equation $P = MC$, which in all the relevant textbooks determines the (absolute) equilibrium of perfect competition, cannot be faulted either in terms of formal logic. It does not prove, however, that a competing firm acts in accordance with its marginal costs in reality. Due to the unreal and scholastic premises from which it is derived, it contains no economic evidence that can be applied to the real behavior of competing firms: (1) The competitor of this model bears no resemblance to an entrepreneur (or manager). He is a "quantity adjuster" who has no entrepreneurial tasks (apart from profit maximization). (2) Despite the misleading name, the model has nothing to do with competition. A uniform good sold at a uniform price, may be due to a cartel; it never results from competition.

Competition is found not in equilibrium but in adjustment processes (and thus on buyers' and sellers' markets, etc.) and in development processes, in which new product qualities and production processes are used as a means of competition. In processes, prices are no longer determined by costs but by the relationship between supply and demand and thus by scarcity which varies in space and time. Competitive prices are not cost prices but scarcity prices; *only when and insofar as prices deviate from costs do they fulfil their competitive functions.* The fact that the equation $P = MC$ has been correctly derived mathematically does not prove anything about its economic relevance.

The statement that the demand curve is identical with the marginal utility curve cannot be faulted from the mathematical point of view any more than the equation $P = MC$. In economic terms, however, it is just as unusable: (1) It identifies demanders with households, which is factually incorrect; and (2) it contains not a factual but only a purely formal statement. "Marginal utility" (or marginal pleasure) for a person is a subjective and variable quantity. This quantity varies not only with the age and the experiences of a person, but also with his economic situation. The statement that free and exploited people or the rich and the poor act according to their "marginal utility curve" is, even if it is formally correct, without any real economic significance, because neither the free and the exploited nor the rich and the poor have the same marginal utility curve.

Neither indifference curve analysis nor Pareto's act of choice have changed human concepts of value into objective and measurable quantities. Here as well, the magicians who pull the rabbit out of the hat have put the rabbit in the hat in the first place by assuming, either openly or covertly, that human beings are "pleasure machines" who act solely in accordance with their wants, and that these wants and the pleasure resulting from them are invariable quantities due to the given demand structure, and are thus quantifiable values.[38] In reality, however, values are neither constant nor objective. Any psychologist and any medical student knows that human valuations are variable and subjective. Myrdal was therefore correct in saying in his book *Das politische Element in der nationalökonomischen Doktrin* (The Political Element in the Development of Economic Theory),[39] which appeared in 1932, that the theory of choice is a "meaningless mathematical scholasticism" and that the modern version of the marginal utility theory is "a subjective theory of value with no psychological content."[40]

SECTION 5: Confusion of Concepts

Although it is normal scientific practice to work with clear[41] concepts, there are numerous concepts in political economy which are ambiguous and can therefore be used in one sense, then in another.

The concept "capital" even today covers two different things. For Adam Smith, David Ricardo, and partly for Karl Marx, capital was the money paid for "materials and subsistence." "As soon as stock has accumulated in the hands of particular persons," according to Smith, "some of them will naturally employ it in setting to work industrious people, whom they will supply with materials and subsistence . . ."[42]

Capital, however, is also taken to include those capital goods which increase productivity and, since they consist of "manufactured means of production," are more accurately described as "production capital."

Financial capital and production capital are two entirely different things: (1) *Financial capital* is produced by thrift and as such is not productive. (2) *Production capital* (or capital goods) is the result of creative acts (no production capital without innovation!) and increases productivity. Without continuous development of capital goods (i.e., of machinery, semiautomated and fully automated equipment, etc.) the increase in general purchasing power which takes place over time and has been observed for decades is impossible.

The confusion of two such different things as financial capital and production capital has given rise to numerous errors. Karl Marx, for example, has been led by this confusion of concepts to derive the surplus value from the "variable capital" (which he identifies with labor) even when it is the result of production capital. However, the "relative surplus value" is produced not by labor but by the use of machines which increase productivity.[43]

At the beginning of the Great Depression, the Brauns Report commissioned by the German government confused the two concepts completely. It came to the conclusion that general domestic underemployment can only be combated by means of financial capital and thus by increased abstinence,[44] although anyone who is not confused by the ambiguous term "capital" ought to be able to understand that in a closed economy a production apparatus which is underutilized but is in all other respects fully available can only be brought into full swing by additional expenditure.

The British fell into the opposite error after World War II, which had largely destroyed their production apparatus, by stimulating consumption instead of investment. Capital goods, however, cannot be created by waste (following the teachings of Mandeville and Keynes), but only by abstinence from consumption (according to Senior). The British policy of stimulating consumption therefore prolonged poverty and turned Great Britain into a relatively underdeveloped country.

The confusion of "financial capital" with "production capital" (and vice versa) therefore has not only theoretical but also actual economic and political consequences.

Just as ambiguous as the concept of capital is the concept of saving, at least in the English-speaking world. "Saving" is taken to mean either (1) (real) *saving*, in which funds released by abstaining from consumption are invested, and (2) (mere) *hoarding*, in which the funds are not invested, with the result that a proportion of income is spent neither on consumption nor investment.

In an equilibrium, however, there is by definition no hoarding, so that here the Keynesian equation I = S always results.[45] In economic processes as they occur in reality, this is not the case. Hoarding plays as decisive a role in the process of depression as the creation of money does in the process of a boom. Households and firms have a preference for liquidity in times of depression and create money (or at least spend hoarded money) in times of prosperity. Hoarding as the mere abstinence from consumption, and saving, which can also be induced by means of price increases, must therefore be distinguished precisely; hoarding restricts the exploitation of given capacities, saving is economically not possible without investment in expansion, rationalization, and development.

The concept of investment is also used ambiguously. Keynes and his school, for example, use the concept in three different contexts in connection with: (1) the creation of capital goods, i.e., with the construction or retention of production facilities; (2) unsalable inventories which arise from a drop in sales, which are described as forced or unintentional investment;[46] (3) public expenditure, the "autonomous investment" which is often unproductive or the productivity of which is different in nature to that of labor-saving machinery.[47]

When supporters of the Keynesian school claim that it is useless to stimulate investment in a depression, this theory too, at least in this generalization, is only the result of an unclear concept. It doubtless makes little sense to replace worn-out machines if in a depression there is still unutilized spare capacity available. However, the repairing of factory roofs or the renovation of factory and office buildings (including glazing and painting) is a measure which is also rational in times of depression and is in all cases work-creating. Finally, the promotion of development investment for new and better products is especially worthwhile in a period of unemployment.

No less unclear is the concept of the "investment goods industry" used in the theory of the accelerator. According to the usual examples, such as are also found in Samuelson, for instance, this means the engineering industry. In the last century, in fact, the acceleration was to be seen primarily in the basic industries (coal, iron, steel, cement, etc.), in which the tendency to make cartel agreements was accordingly found very early on. In the engineering industry itself the accelerator effect has been less apparent, due to the technological progress which causes the products of this industry to become prematurely obsolete.[48]

There is also confusion in several respects about the use of the concepts "duopoly" and "oligopoly." First of all, the "market structures" which originated with Cournot are applied to a reality which operates in space and time, although these structures are equilibria in which time as principium individuationis (Arthur Schopenhauer) plays no part. Secondly, several authors confuse oligopoly and market leadership with one another. According to Robert Triffin, for example, in the case of "pure oligopoly" the "leadership position" is contrasted with the "position of follower."[49] John M. Blair at the start of his book speaks of the oligopoly of the steel producers in the United States, only to state later on that the U.S. Steel corporation is a "price leader."[50] However, if one firm is in a leadership position and the remaining suppliers are only followers, then this is not oligopoly but monopoly (or "partial monopoly," to use Walter Eucken's term).

The concept of the "price leader"[51] is also misleading. It originated with the economists of the nineteenth century, who did not know any other values than price and quantity and who therefore considered the market leader to be a mere price leader. In fact, a market leader does not only dictate prices (and quantities) but also, as the case may be, production processes, terms of payment, investments, qualities, etc. For example, when General Motor Corporation was still the market leader, it indicated to its competitors not only the size and the design of cars but also the investment quota.

A confusion of concepts, in fact a double confusion, occurs when concepts such as "imperfect" and "monopolistic" are used as synonyms, as, for example, by Joan Robinson and many other authors. On the one hand, these are two entirely different concepts:

1. *"Imperfection"* in the sense of Jevons's law of indifference occurs whenever there are any kind of temporal and spatial (or material and personal) differences. The "criterion of imperfection" is satisfied if there are differences in time, differences in space, differences in quality, or personal differences between sellers and buyers. The criterion of imperfection is, for example, fulfilled in the case of sellers' and buyers' markets or in any development processes, in which cheaper or better products come onto the market.
2. *Monopolistic influences* are present if competition is restricted by cartel agreements or if market leaders call the tune.

In fact, these concepts belong to two totally different areas. "Monopolistic" is an economic concept. "Imperfect," like "perfect," is a scholastic concept, which has no material content with respect to reality and to the economic phenomena which occur in it, but which only takes into account whether spatial and temporal differences are present or not. Jevons's criterion of imperfection is economically nonsensical because according to it, any kind of real competition, especially adjustment competition and development competition, would be "imperfect."

Ragnar Frisch's concept of "dynamics" is also based on a misunderstanding and cannot be understood without equilibrium theory. According to Frisch,[52] an analysis is "dynamic" if, as Erich Schneider puts it, "the values of the relevant variables in the relationships used for the explanation do not all refer to the same point in time or the same period."[53] *However, the introduction of time is not sufficient to explain economic processes if the traditional restrictions of the object of analysis to price and quantity are not abandoned.* The essential elements of booms and slumps, buyers' and sellers' markets, and growth and development can only be analyzed if prices are no longer assumed to be regulated by costs; and if changes in quality,[54] experiences, expectations, and evaluations, and especially the effects of innovations on supply and demand (and on employment) are included in the analysis.

Lastly, there are concepts in economics which can change like a chameleon. Among these are the concepts "capitalism" and "socialism." What Marx and his contemporaries understood by capitalism has little more in common with what is called capitalism today than the name. Marx's and Engels's ideas of a socialistic society differ radically from the economic systems which are today described as "socialistic." A concept which calls both a "community of free individuals"[55] and the hegemony of the Soviet Union "socialistic" is no more scientifically usable than a concept which lumps together the economic system of Marx's day and the economic order of the Federal Republic of Germany under one name.[56]

The concepts of socialism and capitalism are in fact based on wrong conclusions:

1. The classical idea of an absolute world, in which only reproducible goods are economically relevant, conflicts with reality. The concept of a world in which everyone acts solely in accordance with his needs belongs to metaphysics.
2. The assumption that in "capitalism," in contrast to "socialism," the "natural wage" remains at the subsistence level has nothing to do with natural laws, but was dependent upon a particular time. When there are free and strong trade unions, wages increase with productivity. Exploitation is not a natural phenomenon, nor is it inherent in a particular economic system.
3. In a stationary economy without space and time, prices are regulated by socially necessary costs (or socially necessary working hours) and values are absolutes. In the real world, prices are principally regulated by scarcity which, like markets, products, and values, changes in space and time.

To this extent, the concepts of "socialism" and "capitalism" are metaeconomic in origin.

SECTION 6: Arbitrary Choice of Premises

> All theory depends on assumptions which are not quite true. That is what makes it theory.
> Robert M. Solow

W. Stanley Jevons considered it "curious, moreover, that, when we take the theory of the lever treated according to the principle of virtual velocities, we get equations exactly similar in form to those of the theory of value. . . ."[57] This is not curious, however, but is the logical result of the premises assumed by Jevons and the marginal utility school. If firms and households are assumed to behave like levers, then "exactly similar" equations result. These premises, however, are arbitrary; a lever neither thinks nor acts nor creates new things and has no expectations, no experiences, and no valuations.

Arbitrariness in the choice of premises begins, but does not end, with the exclusion of all economic variables which cannot be reduced to price and quantity. It is arbitrary for Keynes to assume in the theory of the multiplier that autonomous investment affects neither the "marginal propensity to consume" nor the "marginal efficiency of capital" and consequently induces neither an increase in the propensity to consume nor a rise in private investment. Only those who assume that the economy moves from equilibrium to equilibrium can regard the marginal propensity to consume as constant and the effect of additional government expenditure on firm's investment as nonexistent.

It is also arbitrary to make the assumption that technological progress is a given value which is expressed by the coefficient β and is independent of business fluctuations and the existent economic order. Schumpeter has already pointed out that "new combinations" occur in great numbers at the start of a boom, while they are almost nonexistent or occur only here and there in a slump.[58] Even those who consider Schumpeter's theory to be an exaggeration and take the phenomenon which he described to be a result of economic development rather than a cause cannot deny the existence of interactions between the state of the economy and economic development.

Nor are the nature and the speed of economic development not independent of the choice of the economic system. In countries with a free market economy not only existing consumer goods such as private cars, motorboats, and watches are improved from year to year, but also a whole range of entirely new products such as radios, TV sets, electric shavers, washing machines, and dishwashers are created. In a state monopoly system like the Soviet Union a similar development in the consumer goods sector is not to be found. If there are new or better consumer goods they are usually imitated from market economies. This undeniable fact calls into question the theory that technological progress is independent of the economic order.

It is also arbitrary to assume that both competition and monopoly belong to the market economy. This assumption is only true if the analysis is restricted to price and quantity and every market structure is defined as an equilibrium outside space and time.[59] If this unjustified falsification of the object of analysis is abandoned, it becomes apparent not only that there is a basic difference in every respect between competition and monopoly but also that Eucken's "centrally administered economy"[60] is nothing more than a state monopoly system, which is just as inimical to progress as a private monopoly, at least in the consumer goods sector. Competing firms adjust to the changing wishes of consumers, lower their prices to the socially necessary costs under the pressure of competition and improve the satisfaction of society's needs by developing new consumer goods and cheaper production processes. Monopolies, regardless of whether they are privately or state owned, normally do none of these. They let the consumers do the adjusting and restrict technological progress to developments which are in their own interest.

Moreover, it is arbitrary to assume the existence of markets outside space and time or of infinite and unlimited supply and demand curves.[61] The assumption of an infinite speed of adjustment, on which many economists base their analyses, is just as nonsensical as the statement that under perfect competition firms cannot influence prices because these firms are "infinitely small" or are "atomistic" in size.[62]

It is also arbitrary, and therefore wrong, to fail to mention premises. Thus, in discussions of market structures such as "perfect competition" or "homogeneous monopoly" it is generally not mentioned that these are equilibria developed on the basis of Jevons's law of indifference. The consequence is that authors such as Schneider[63] or Woll regard "the sale of the same good of a supplier at different prices"[64] as possible, thus standing Jevons's law on its head, or that other authors postulate the equilibrium model of "perfect competition" as an "analytical example" (Samuelson) or an economic policy ideal (Lenel) without taking into account its lack of reference to space and time.[65] It is just as arbitrary for results which are ascertained on "perfect markets" to be unreservedly transferred to "imperfect markets," although the former are defined as being outside space and time and the latter are firmly fixed in space and time.[66]

Furthermore, it is arbitrary to assume that firms behave in the same way during economic processes as in equilibrium, although processes which take place in space and time are necessarily governed by different criteria from those applying to equilibria outside space and time. The assumption that oscillatory processes can be symbolized by a "cobweb" is about as far away from reality as it is possible to be.[67] Processes cannot be explained as a succession of equilibria; adjustment and development are not processes "by which the economy moves from one equilibrium point to the next."

Another example of arbitrariness is the tendency, which originated with François Quesnay and was revived by the Keynesian school, to represent economic activity purely as *circulation,* in which production, consumption, etc., alternate like the sun and the moon.[68] Anyone who compares the flows of goods and services which existed at the time of Quesnay or Hume with the flows of goods and services of today can see that it is not so much the perpetual return of the same features as development and thus progress which is characteristic of the market economy. As there are no "given" markets which continue to exist unchanged there are also no "given" and unchangeable products and valuations.

It is also arbitrary to assume that economic phenomena are functional mechanisms. They, in fact, consist of interpersonal relationships, in which deliberate decisions, actions, creations, and thus valuations which repeatedly have to be re-examined are of decisive importance. These in their turn are based on experiences and expectations which change in space and time. To this extent, any analogy to the natural sciences is mistaken. The inevitability of functional relationships is nonexistent in a social science such as economics.

A further example of arbitrariness is the assumption, also found in the writings of many renowned economists, that the science of economics is perfectly free to choose whatever premises it likes. This assumption is in keeping with scholasticism, which makes deductions from premises which are arbitrarily selected and bear no relation to experiences. *An empirical science excludes any kind of "science fiction."* In an empirical science it is impossible to make assumptions just because they correspond to the opinions or the wishes of the author. In an empirical science any premise which is not supported by the experiences which are to be analyzed is wrong.

Finally, it is also arbitrary for Lawrence R. Klein to assume in his *Textbook of Econometrics* that the cobweb theorem is proven econometrically and statistically,[69] although the theory that an oscillatory process moves from equilibrium to equilibrium (and also operates in the model of perfect competition) has never been proved and never can be proved because a process is not a succession of equilibria and perfect competition does not exist. Economics only becomes a science if it is restricted to results which are logically derived from premises that correspond to the conditions of the experience to be analyzed. In contrast to scholasticism, an empirical science requires two things: (1) logical correctness, and (2) premises which conform to reality.

Many results of theory are logically correct but untrue,[70] because they have been derived from arbitrary premises. An economic theory which is based on premises which contradict experience is metaeconomics.

CHAPTER 9

From Metaeconomics to Economic Science

I believe that it is necessary to make a thorough
overhaul of basic theory under the slogan History
versus Equilibrium.

Joan Robinson

Is the world ruled by strict laws or not? -This
question I regard as metaphysical.

Karl R. Popper

SECTION 1: Balance

Both classical and neoclassical economists have oversimplified their basic models to such an extent that the real economic
problems are only present in them in a distorted form or are no
longer present at all. To be able to postulate strict laws and equilibria, they have ignored not only the processes of adjustment
and development which take place in reality but also the scarcity
which varies in space and time. In their eagerness to oversimplify
the problems, they have excluded all problems which cannot be
expressed in terms of price or quantity, as if the satisfaction of
human needs was only a quantitative problem and not also, or
even mainly, a qualitative problem in many respects. The notion
presently current in Eastern bloc countries that running an economy is a problem of quantitative planning targets to this extent
corresponds to the basic model of neoclassical economists.

The extent to which the real problems are distorted by this
approach is demonstrated not only by a concept of competition
which excludes any kind of competitive activity but also by the
fate allotted to the entrepreneur in the doctrines of the classical
and neoclassical economists. For the classical economists, the entrepreneur is a capitalist whose purpose is mainly to provide financial capital. According to the neoclassical economists, the only
function of an entrepreneur is to maximize his profit in accordance with given formulas. This caricature of an entrepreneur,

which might have come out of some malicious satire, has no economic functions at all.

His product is given and he cannot change it.[1] Production capacity and manufacturing processes are also data in the theory of market structures.[2] Problems of adjustment are simply eliminated by the assumption of given sales curves or an infinite speed of adjustment. There are no fluctuations in sales. The development of new and better products is impossible in a model world in which the future does not exist. The entrepreneur or manager finds his market ready for him and need not fear that it will disappear one day (something which unfortunately happens all too often in the real world). As his cost curves are also given, the manufacturing of the product also presents no difficulties. He is relieved of worries about the introduction of new manufacturing processes. Investment *policy* is as unknown to him, as are sales and quality policy or personnel and financial problems.

The difference between a monopoly and a competing firm is thus restricted to price and quantity. The monopolist can at least determine his price himself, albeit by a formula which no manager has ever used, but must then demand the price calculated according to the stipulations of this theory. A competing firm is relieved of even this task. The "market" has made price into a datum for him, which by definition he cannot change at all. The only activity which remains for him is "quantity adjustment."

Like managers (or entrepreneurs), households are also deprived of (practically) all functions. The customers[3] cannot influence the quality or the range of the goods they are offered in any of these "market structures." They are unrealistic in the same way as managers who do not operate any kind of price, quality, product range, personnel, financial, sales, or investment policies.

In this metaeconomic world, both the monopolist and the competing firm are nothing more than parasites. What they do can also be performed by an automaton. They are therefore expendable without any loss to the economy. There is no reason why they should not be expelled or, as Marx said, expropriated.

The metaeconomic theory does also not permit any distinction between manufacturing and trade. If only acts of exchanges outside space and time take place and if the sum of all exchanges is identical to the economy of society, as in Walras, manufacturing then appears to be a phenomenon which is outside real economic activity. Economic activity thus degenerates to trade; but in a model world in which nothing changes and everything is assumed to be in unlimited supply or reproducible, this trade fulfills no economic function, as Marx recognized.[4] The suspicion results that the entrepreneur is not only superfluous but in fact harmful. In a world in which by definition economic goods are not rare or scarce but everything is reproducible, but in which not every worker has everything he wants, there is a disharmony, the responsibility for which can only lie with the "capitalist system." The elimination of "capitalism" thus opens the gateway to a paradise in which once the "expropriators" have been expropriated, everything is again available in abundance.

Due to an ingenious error, Marx has in fact taken the stationary picture of the world which is concealed behind classical theory to be the true ideal, with which he contrasts the contradictions of the real phenomena with disgust. Although he fully recognized—and this distinguishes him from classical economists—that competition, when it operates, reduces prices to the socially necessary costs, he, nevertheless, regarded the classical model world, in which prices are already a priori identical with the socially necessary production costs, as the final stage.[5]

In a stationary model world there are neither new markets nor an increase in real incomes. In it, the amount of supply and production remain constant; thus misery and poverty cannot be eliminated by an increase in productivity and by a widening and an improvement in supply of the goods, but only by a redistribution of wealth. To this extent, Ricardo and Marx were working along the same lines in that they regarded the solution to the problem to lie not in an increase and an expansion of production but solely or at least primarily in the distribution of the GNP. Like the supporters of the marginal utility school, they failed to recognize that distribution of the GNP is indeed an economic problem, but it is neither the only one nor the sole deciding factor. The redistribution of a given GNP is a once-and-for-all event, while an increase in the GNP by means of the employment of more efficient capital goods can be repeated again and again. A radical redistribution of wealth and a constant GNP are mutually dependent. A radical redistribution of wealth and a continual increase in the GNP are mutually exclusive, because such a redistribution causes the sources of investment in expansion, rationalization, and development to run dry.

Mankind does not live in a world in which all economic goods "can be increased by the exertion of human industry." Suitable incentives are therefore required to induce those responsible for production to eliminate bottlenecks, develop new products and production processes, and cease production of out-of-date products. An economic system which does not make such incentives available is faced with the problems which characterize the Soviet economy, because and insofar as it has been designed in accordance with the concept of a stationary model: a lack of progress in the consumer goods sector, insufficient flexibility of the factors of production, which cannot be shifted from dying to growing markets, and inadequate quality, because the system basically operates with the classical values of price and quantity.

The basic model of both the classical and the neoclassical economists has led to a disastrous falsification of economic questions. The economic problems facing every society, both in the West and the East, arise not from a stationary world but from a changing and developing world,[6] in which familiar energy sources and products become scarce and new types of goods and means of production are developed, and in which firms and households repeatedly have to change their ideas and their valuations. The real economic world, which is the only true object of analysis for political economy, is governed by transitoriness. As human beings who have created this economic world are only on the earth for a limited time, so markets are born and die, while the goods traded on these markets are in a constant state of change. In the real world, which economists have the task of analyzing, an enterprise does not simply grow up because "stock has accumulated in the hands of particular persons" (Smith), nor are the tasks of its management (regardless of whether the firm is operating in the East or the West) limited to quantity adjustment or to the calculation of prices. In a changing and developing economy, a firm only benefits society when its production, quality, investment, and innovative policies are all in the interests of its customers.

The tendency of economists to create absolutes, to oversimplify, and to generalize has had disastrous consequences, not only for the East but for the West as well. The tendency to create absolutes has favored the emergence of scientifically untenable ideologies without which the prevailing conflict between capitalism and socialism[7] would never have achieved its historic significance. Their tendency to make radical oversimplifications has caused economists to bypass the problems of the real economy, in which households do not solely act in accordance with physical values such as pleasure or marginal utility but with prices and incomes, and in which supply is neither solely nor mainly determined by costs, but by scarcity which varies in space and time. Only when prices deviate from costs do they fulfil their task in the real competitive economy of adjusting supply to demand. And only when there are profits (and losses) is there sufficient incentive for the development of new products and production processes. Finally, the tendency of economists to generalize conclusions or experiences has led repeatedly to mistakes. The Western world would have been spared a good deal of worry over the last few decades if Keynes's general theory had not been applied to an international economy for which it was not designed, and if the economic policy makers had regarded the problem of employment less from the point of view of a stationary economy and more from that of a developing economy.

Oversimplification, generalization, and the creation of absolutes are therefore not as harmless as traditional theory would repeatedly have us believe, even if those factors are not blamed for serious wrong developments.

There are two basic reasons why the present methodology applied to economic theory should be abandoned: (1) the scholastic arbitrariness in the choice of premises, which is wrong in an empirical science, and (2) the erroneous developments in both ideology and economic policy, which would not have been possible if economic theory had not been transformed into metaeconomics.

SECTION 2: Solution of the Dilemma

> It is the business of economics . . . to collect facts, to arrange and interpret them, and to draw inferences from them.
>
> Alfred Marshall

> All this . . . indicates work to be done, provided that we give up the search for grand general laws and are content to try to enquire how things happen.
>
> Joan Robinson

The dilemma of economic theory results from a peculiarity inherent in all social sciences. Its object of analysis is not nature but human society, in which man has the ability "to create new things" and is thus in a position to shape the society in which he lives according to his own ideas. On the other hand, however, its object of analysis is not economic history either. Like any other theory, economic theory consists of the recognition of possible relationships.

In the first place, political economy does not deal with regularly recurring phenomena from which natural laws can be derived, as do the natural sciences. The observations which an economic theorist makes and the experiences he gains vary over time, because economic science, like all social sciences, is a science of human society. Economics is in constant change due to the problems it is faced with and the solutions found by human beings for these problems. The phenomena which can be observed in the social sciences have nothing to do with absolute truths, but instead resemble "unique events" (Niehans), because *Man shapes the society in which he lives due to his ability to create new things*.[8] The changes in past economic and social orders and in past international economic and monetary systems bear witness to this, as do the achievements of "creative entrepreneurs," who introduce better and cheaper products or even create entirely new markets.

Secondly, however, political economy's object of analysis is not economic history either. The economic history of society is the economic historian's field of study. The object of economic theory does not consist of the relationships which have been realized in the past, but of all relationships which may become reality, regardless of whether these relationships have become history or not. In other words, its *object of analysis is not the historical economy but the conceivable economy*. It comprises all possible relationships and is not restricted by history.

Because political economy is a science of human society, it follows that the "method of isolating abstraction" which has been so successfully used in the natural sciences, is not sufficient on its own in economic theory, although both classical and neoclassical economists have assumed that it is.

Because economic theory's object of analysis is not the historical economy but the achievable and thus the conceivable economy, it follows that it is not sufficient to collect historical facts, as the historicizing schools have mainly done.

The changeability and thus the relativity of economic problems makes it necessary to incorporate possible variants into the analysis with the aid of the "method of premise variation." The economic theorist cannot be content with isolating one relationship at a time; his task is *to make all relevant relationships the object of his analysis by varying the premises and models.*

The method of premise variation which can also be called the "method of varying abstraction," analyzes the economically relevant relationships step by step or, more precisely, model by model. For example, it does not restrict itself to analyzing competition or monopoly under the oversimplified assumption that cost and sales curves are "given" (thus excluding any real economic activity even before any analysis is commenced). Instead, it also incorporates those parameters of action without which there would be neither cost and sales curves nor Schumpeter's "creative entrepreneur." Nor is the method of premise variation content with analyzing the phenomenon of underemployment solely (1) with the aid of a model of a closed, stationary and static economy, in which, moreover, there is a surplus of all factors of production, as in the thirties. Instead it incorporates all economically relevant variables into the analysis one after the other. It analyzes, in terms of models, (2) unemployment as a consequence of breakdowns in the international economy, (3) unemployment as a consequence of fluctuating technological progress; it analyzes (4) unemployment not only as a (supposed) equilibrium but as a process, in which expectations, valuations, and experiences change, and it deals (5 and 6) with models in which unemployment is accompanied not by a surplus of capital goods and raw materials (nature) but by a shortage of capital goods or of raw materials.

The method of premise variation, as its name implies, changes the variables in its models to gain a full picture of economic relationships.[9] However, the two-dimensional models as preferred by the marginal utility school are no longer adequate for this purpose. Three-dimensional models, as illustrated in Figures 2, 4, and 12 to 16, are required for varying the premises. In addition to the economic relevance of price and quantity, which are the only variables that neoclassical economics examines, the other economically relevant variables can then gradually be incorporated into the analysis: product quality, the expectations, (re)valuations, and experiences of human beings, economic development and thus the emergence and disappearance of markets, the influence of state activity, etc. The synthesis of the results then produces a theory which shows all the most important variants and thus permits a general overview which keeps economists from making premature oversimplifications and generalizations and from creating absolutes.

In social sciences such as economic science, the premises from which conclusions are drawn must: (1) correspond to the possible experiences, and (2) be varied until all the important relationships have been dealt with.

This kind of process, which makes equal use of induction and deduction, avoids both the errors of the historical school authors who collected experiences without analyzing them, and the mistakes of the classical and neoclassical school authors, insofar as they limited themselves to the isolation of individual relationships (and the creation of absolutes from them). Their results will therefore not be natural laws[10] either, as searched for by Hume, Smith, Ricardo, Marx, or even Samuelson. Instead, an economic theory of this kind will make possible an overall view of the relevant relationships and thus at the same time enable the economic policymakers to take measures which correspond to the historical conditions of the particular economic situation. An economic theory which contains all the relevant variations is a precondition for an economic policy which is capable of finding appropriate solutions for the unique events of our historical existence.

In view of the economic problems to be solved and in view of the significance of these problems for the future of human society, it is high time that economists devoted themselves to their real tasks, which do not remain constant in space and time: the analysis of the real world in all its complexity, in which neither products nor energy sources are infinitely reproducible or unlimited, in which there are famines when foodstuffs become rare goods, in which the human ability of mankind to create new things plays a decisive role, in which expectations, valuations, and experiences change with economic events and in which state action influences national and international economic relationships.

Notes

Introduction

1. Tjalling C. Koopmans, "Is the Theory of Competitive Equilibrium With It?," *American Economic Review*, Vol. 64 (May 1974), pp. 325, 326.
2. *Ibid*, p. 326. Phyllis Deane has applauded the willingness of new-generation economic historians "to experiment with more than one paradigm." Book Review, *Economic Journal*, Vol. 92 (September 1982), p. 720.

Chapter 1

1. This even applies to textbooks which describe economic theory as a science of scarcity. Cf. Heinz Kohler, *Economics: the Science of Scarcity* (Hinsdale, Ill., 1970), pp. 4–5, 18 ff.; Dennis J. Weidenaar and Emanual T. Weiler, *Economics* (Reading, Mass., 1976), pp. 3 ff.
2. Cf. Plato, *The State*, Book 5.
3. Cf. Adam Smith, *An Inquiry into the Nature and Causes of the Wealth of Nations*, 4th ed. (London, 1786), Book I, Chapter V.
4. Cf. David Ricardo, *On the Principles of Political Economy and Taxation*, 3rd ed. (London 1821), in *The Works and Correspondence of David Ricardo*, edited by Piero Sraffa (Cambridge, 1951), Vol. I., Chapter "On Value."
5. Cf. Karl Marx, *Capital. A Critique of Political Economy*, translated from the third German edition (London, 1970), Vol. I (Hamburg, 1867), p. 17.
6. Cf. Adam Smith, op. cit., Book I, Chapter V.
7. The economic problems which result from changes in values and value relationships will be discussed in detail in this and subsequent chapters.
8. On the theory of economic revaluations, cf. my book, *Markt und Macht* (Market and Power), 2nd ed. (Tuebingen, 1973), pp. 3–16.
9. Cf. Immanual Kant, *A Critique of Pure Reason* (Kritik der reinen Vernunft), quoted in the original version of this book, from the German text of 1781, edited by Karl Kehrbach (Leipzig, n.d.), p. 235.
10. *Ibid.*, p. 250; see also p. 77, where Kant says, "Thoughts without content are empty, perceptions without concepts are blind."
11. Cf., for instance, Paul A. Samuelson, *Economics*, 11th ed. (New York, 1980), p. 408 ("psychologic utility"), pp. 503–4 ("marginal-physical products"), p. 506 ("physical MPs").
12. W. Stanley Jevons, *The Theory of Political Economy* (London, 1871), pp. 44–46.
13. Léon Walras, *Elements of Pure Economics*, translated by William Jaffé (London, 1954), pp. 66, 117, 120, 128, 143, 204–6. Wicksell has already pointed out that Walras was confusing marginal utility and scarcity. Cf. Knut Wicksell, *Vorlesungen über Nationalökonomie auf Grundlage des Marginalprinzips* (Lectures on Political Economy) (Jena, 1913), Vol. I, p. 80.
14. Francis Y. Edgeworth, *Mathematical Psychics. An Essay on the Application of Mathematics to the Moral Sciences* (London, 1881), pp. 77-78; see also pp. 8-9, 15-16, 21-22. Edgeworth's concept is taught in most textbooks without mentioning that he measured "happiness," and not economic values, in his "lines of indifference." Cf. for instance, Willis L. Peterson, *Principles of Economics: Micro* (Homewood, Ill., 1971), pp. 26 ff.; Walter Nicholson, *Microeconomic The-*

ory (Hinsdale, Ill., 1972), pp. 46 ff. The introduction of economic values (income, price) into Edgeworth's concept of "indifference curves" is dealt with in Chapter 8 of this book under "Logical Inconsistencies."

15. Vilfredo Pareto, *Manuale di economia politica,* (2nd ed. 1921) in the English translation by Ann S. Schwier, *Manual of Political Economy* (London, 1972), p. 118.

16. Cf. for instance, Alfred Marshall, *Principles of Economics* 8th ed. (London, 1956), Book IV, Chapter III; Richard G. Lipsey and Peter O. Steiner, *Economics* 3rd ed. (New York, 1972), Chapter 11.

17. Although this is assumed by many economists, cf., for instance, Samuelson, *Economics,* op cit., pp. 21-27.

18. Ibid., pp. 52-54; Erich Schneider, *Einführung in die Wirtschaftstheorie* (Introduction to Economic Theory), Vol. II 12th ed. (Tuebingen, 1969), pp. 13 ff., 116 ff.; Edward Nevin, *An Introduction to Micro-Economics* (London, 1973) Parts Two and Three; Fred D. Levy, Jr., and Sidney C. Sufrin, *Basic Economics, Analysis of Contemporary Problems and Policies* (New York, 1973), pp. 20 ff, 29 ff.; cf. also the historic representation in Joan Robinson and John Eatwell, *An Introduction to Modern Economics* 2nd ed. (London, 1973), pp. 102 ff., 196 ff.; many modern authors show the various influences on supply and demand at the beginning of their writings, only to return later to the traditional, familiar statements; cf., for instance, Augustus J. Rogers, III, *Choice. An Introduction to Economics* (Englewood Cliffs, N. J., 1971), pp. 17 ff., and the writings listed in Note 22.

19. I speak of experiences (and not of experience) because I wish to stress thereby *the decisive difference between the social sciences (e.g., economics) and the natural sciences (e.g., physics).* In the natural sciences the same observation can usually be repeated. A stone always falls downward and a lever always works in the same way. *In the social sciences the observations change in space and time:* they are (more or less) unique. In economics, therefore, experiences vary with human activity, i.e., with economic policy, with technological progress (new and cheaper methods of production, new and better products, etc.), with the expectations and valuations of firms and households, with state laws, etc.

20. Cf. Joan Robinson, *The Economics of Imperfect Competition,* 9th ed. (London, 1950).

21. Cf. Edward H. Chamberlin, *The Theory of Monopolistic Competition, 3rd. ed. (Cambridge, 1960).*

22. It is an almost universally held view that products are demanded exclusively by households and supplied only by firms. Firms' demand is limited to the factors of production, i.e., "labor, capital and land." Cf. A. L. Bowley, *Mathematical Groundwork of Economics* (reprint, New York, 1965), pp. 40-45. The "demand for factors" is derived from households' demand and is determined by marginal productivity, cf. Samuelson, *Economics,* op cit., Chapters 22 and 27; Lawrence R. Klein, *A Textbook of Econometrics,* 2nd ed. (Englewood Cliffs, N.J., 1974), pp. 2-23; James M. Henderson and Richard E. Quandt, *Microeconomic Theory. A Mathematical Approach,* 3rd ed. (New York, 1980), pp. 5-36, 64-104; Milton Friedman, *Price Theory* (Chicago, Ill., 1962), pp. 12 ff., 74 ff; Kewal Krishan Dewett, *Modern Economic Theory, Micro and Macro Analysis* 12th ed. (New Delhi, 1966), pp. 52 ff., 189 ff.; Carl Brehm, *Introduction to Economics* (New York, 1970), pp. 41 ff., 83 ff.; Richard Attiyeh, George Leland Bach, and Keith Lumsden, *Basic Economics. Theory and Cases* 2nd ed. (Englewood Cliffs, N.J., 1977), pp. 54 ff., 73 ff.; Donald Dewey, *Microeconomics. The Analysis of Prices and Markets* (New York, 1975), pp. 25-26, 35 ff.; Lloyd G. Reynolds, *Economics. A General Introduction* (Homewood, Ill., 1963), pp. 93 ff., 104; Ernst Helmstädter, *Wirtschaftstheorie* (Munich, 1974), Vol. I, pp. 43 ff., 103 ff.; J. A.

Allport and C. M. N. Stewart, *Economics* (Cambridge, 1972), pp. 334 ff. ("the basis of demand") ; cf. also C. E. Ferguson, *Microeconomic Theory* (Homewood, Ill. 1966), pp. 9 ff.; *Introducing Economics* edited by B. J. McCormick (London, 1974), pp. 99 ff., 121 ff.; Kohler, *Economics*, op. cit., pp. 120 ff., 133 ff.; Willard W. Howard and Edwin L. Dale, Jr., *Contemporary Economics* (Lexington, Mass., 1971), pp. 31, 255; George J. Stigler, *The Theory of Price* (New York, 1961), pp. 42 ff., 68 ff., 96 ff.

23. The question of whether pleasure or utility can be measured or compared is therefore entirely irrelevant for economics; but cf. for instance, Kenneth J. Arrow, *Social Choice and Individual Values*, 2nd ed. (New York, 1963), pp. 9 ff.
24. Cf. Section 2, Chapter 9, of this book.
25. On this subject, cf. the comments of Gary S. Becker, *Economic Theory* (New York, 1971), p. 15.
26. Cf. Ricardo, op. cit., p. 12.
27. The economic problem of scarcity is also eliminated if it is assumed, as Carl Menger did, that the commodities are always available: "The volumes of goods are given in each actual case by the particular situation . . . ". Cf. Carl Menger, *Grundsätze der Volkswirtschaftslehre* (Collected Works of Carl Menger), (2nd ed.) (Vienna, 1923), Vol. I, p. 39; see also pp. 10-16, 32-56.

Chapter 2

1. Jevons, op cit., p. 91.
2. Cf. e.g., Heinrich von Stackelberg, *Grundlagen der Theoretischen Volkswirtschafts-lehre* (The Theory of the Market Economy), 2nd ed. (Bern, 1948), pp. 219 ff. (Part 4, Chapter 4); Piero Sraffa, "The Laws of Returns under Competitive Conditions," *Economic Journal*, 36 (1926), pp. 544-45; cf. also Marshall, op. cit., pp. 270-71.
3. Cf. Joan Robinson, *The Economics of Imperfect Competition*, op. cit., pp. 18-19, 88-91. The concept of the "perfect market," which only exists outside space and time, is also found in authors who deal with business administration, cf. Erich Gutenberg, *Grundlagen der Betriebswirtschaftslehre*, 14th ed. (Berlin, 1973), Vol. II, pp. 182 ff.; Günter Wöhe, *Einführung in die Allgemeine Betriebswirtschaftslehre*, 12th ed. (Munich, 1976), pp. 399-400.
4. Schumpeter believed that the markets for corn and cotton fulfill the conditions of a perfect market. However, there are not only differences in space and time, but also qualitative differences (e.g., corn with or without worms) and—last but not least—differences in the reliability of the suppliers. On perfect competition, cf. also Levy and Sufrin, *Basic Economics*, op. cit. pp. 46 ff.; C. A. Tisdell, *Microeconomics, The Theory of Economic Allocation* (Sidney, 1972), pp. 175 ff. Even on a stock exchange, which is often quoted as an example of a perfect market, the price varies before and after the fixing of the so-called "standard rate" (*Einheitskurs*), which can also be manipulated.
5. Cf. Kant, op. cit., p. 58.
6. Ibid., p. 51.
7. Von Stackelberg, op. cit., p. 221; Schneider, op. cit., Vol. II, p. 77.
8. Alfred E. Ott, *Grundzüge der Preistheorie* (Goettingen, 1968), p. 227.
9. Erich Schneider speaks of the behavior (*Verhaltensweise*) of the quantity-ad-juster, and thus assumes, like Eucken, that it is possible (in Eucken's words) that "given two different managers and *objectively* the same situation, one will behave as a 'competitor' and the other as a 'monopolist.' " This idea, however, is irreconcilable with the premises of the marginal utility school: absence of space and time, complete knowledge of the market, rational behavior, etc. Cf.

Schneider, op. cit., Vol. II, pp. 60 ff., 67 ff.; Walter Eucken, *Die Grundlagen der Nationalökonomie,*5th ed. (Godesberg, 1947), pp. 159-60.

10. Friedrich A. Hayek, "The Meaning of Competition," in *Individualism and Economic Order* (London, 1949), p. 92.

11. Cournot was unaware of the concept of the perfect market; however, his models are also static or comparatively static. Cf. Augustin Antoine Cournot, *Recherches sur les principes mathématiques de la théorie des richesses* (Paris, 1936). Chamberlin and Robinson incorporate customer preferences, product differentiation, etc., into the analysis and abolish to this extent Jevons's law of indifference; however, their line of argument cannot be understood without Cournot and without Jevons's law.

12. The equation MC=MR also applies to "perfect competition," except that here, MR=P.

13. Cournot op. cit., chapter 8 identifies competition with duopoly.

14. Ibid.

15. Cf. also Robert Triffin, *Monopolistic Competition and General Equilibrium Theory* (Cambridge, 1956) p. 103.

16. Cf. Von Stackelberg, op. cit., pp. 210 ff., and Bowley, *Mathematical Groundwork of Economics,* op. cit.

17. Cf. Sraffa, op.cit., pp. 535-50.

18. Wicksell explains the "surplus of retailers" by the existence of customer preferences (and monopolies). Cf. Wicksell, op.cit., Vol. I, pp. 142-43.

19. In addition to the works of Joan Robinson and Edward H. Chamberlin mentioned in Notes 20 and 21 of Chapter 1, the writings of Triffin, op. cit.; Hans Brems, *Product Equilibrium under Monopolistic Competition* (Cambridge, Mass., 1951); Donald Dewey, *The Theory of Imperfect Competition. A Radical Reconstruction* (New York, 1969), and Lawrence Abbott, *Quality and Competition. An Essay in Economic Theory* (New York, 1955).

20. Cf. Sraffa, op. cit., p.542.

21. Ibid, p.545.

22. Robinson and Chamberlin only partly understood the need for a new concept. This is shown by the fact that they continually used only two values in their diagrams, although they work with customer preferences, product differentiation, advertising, etc. Cf. Section 2, Chapter 9, of this book.

23. Perfect markets are by definition outside space and time (even if economists do not always remember this characteristic, which results from Jevons's law of indifference)! In contrast, the imperfect markets on which Sraffa's and Chamberlin's monopolies meet, exist in space and time, so that not only product differentation is possible, but the customers can be influenced by means of advertising.

24. John M. Clark's "workable competition" does not provide a way out of this blind alley. "Workable competition" is not a theoretical, but a pragmatic concept, which without deviating from the theoretical concept of equilibrium lists the characteristics which competition should have in practice. Cf. John M. Clark, *Competition as a Dynamic Process* (Washington, D.C., 1961).

25. Cf. Erich Preiser, "Wettbewerbspreis und Kostenpreis," in *Der Wettbewerb als Mittel volkswirtschaftlicher Leistungssteigerung und Leistungsauslese,* edited by Günter Schmölders (Berlin, 1942).

26. Ibid., p. 116.

27. "However, the individual seller and buyer exerts a certain influence on this price situation through his supply and demand; but on its own, this influence is imperceptible and is thus from his own point of view uninteresting." Wicksell, op. cit., p. 93.

28. Eucken, op. cit., p. 154; cf. also Schneider, op. cit., Vol. II, p. 75.
29. Samuelson, *Economics, op. cit., p. 39.*
30. Ibid., p. 590.
31. Cf. Erich Schneider, op. cit., Vol. II, pp. 142 ff.
32. Cf. Woll, op. cit., pp. 149-50; Ott, op. cit., pp. 189 ff. For a correct definition, on the other hand, see Wilhelm Krelle, *Preistheorie*, 2nd ed. (Tuebingen, 1976), Part I, pp. 38-39.
33. Cf. Erich Schneider, op.cit., Vol. II, p. 77; Woll, op. cit., p. 141.
34. Von Stackelberg also uses the same diagram to illustrate the price of the monopsony and the prices applying to "exploitation." Cf. Von Stackelberg, op. cit., p. 203, (Part 4, Chapter 2) Figure 39.
35. Taken almost word-for-word from Kalman Goldberg, *Our Changing Economy* (Boston, 1976), p.2.
36. Chamberlin, op.cit., pp. 56-57.
37. Erich Schneider, op. cit., Vol. II, p.124.
38. Samuelson, *Economics,* op cit., pp. 431, 432; similarly, von Stackelberg, op. cit., p. 60. Even in neoclassical equilibrium theory, the so-called "shutdown point" only exists in the unreal case of perfect competition. Both neoclassical monopoly theory and the theories of monopolistic and imperfect competition are aware of equilibria under conditions of individual diminishing costs and thus to the left of the so-called "shutdown point."
39. Cf. Alfred W. Stonier and Douglas C. Hague, *A Textbook of Economic Theory*, 4th ed. (London, 1972), pp. 151 ff.; Bernt P. Stigum and Marcia L. Stigum, *Microeconomics*, 2nd ed. (Reading, Mass., 1974), p. 130; Melville J. Ulmer, *Economics. Theory and Practice*, 2nd ed. (Boston, 1965), pp. 429-30; Lipsey and Steiner, op. cit., pp. 240-41; Karl Brandt, *Preistheorie* (Ludwigshafen, 1960), p. 46; Gutenberg, op. cit., Vol. I, p. 360; Vol. II, pp. 225-26.
40. "Verzögerte Angebotsanpassung und partielles Gleichgewicht" in *Zeitschrift für National ökonomie*, Vol. 5 (1934), pp. 670 ff.; in addition cf. to his predecessors, among them Ricci, Schultz, Tinbergen, Rodenstein-Rodan, particularly Oskar Lange's paper, "Formen der Angebotsanpassung und wirtschaftliches Gleichgewicht," in *Zeitschrift für Nationalökonomie*, Vol. VI (1935), pp. 358 ff.
41. Samuelson, *Economics,* op. cit., p. 381.
42. Leontief, "Verzögerte. . . . ," op. cit., pp. 671-72.
43. Ibid.
44. Cf. Samuelson, *Economics,* op. cit., p. 380, where he deals with shifts in the supply curve, and p. 381, where he discusses the cobweb theorem. Cf. also Donald A Nichols and Clark W. Reynolds, *Principles of Economics* (New York, 1971), pp. 47-48, 62 ff.; Basil J. Moore, *An Introduction to Modern Economic Theory* (New York, 1973), pp. 35, 41-42. Nor does the introduction of so-called "long-run supply curves" justify the explanation of oscillatory processes by equilibria. Cf. for example, Nicholson, *Microeconomic Theory*, op. cit., pp. 274 ff.
45. Cf. Samuelson, *Economics,* op.cit., p. 364.
46. Cf. my book *Kapitalismus, Sozialismus, Konzentration und Konkurrenz* (Capitalism, Socialism, Concentration and Competition), 2nd ed. (Tuebingen, 1976), pp. 82-98.
47. Cf. *Gunnar Myrdal, Das politische Element in der nationalökonomischen Doktrinbildung* (reprint, Hannover, 1963), p. 94, in which he describes the theory of choice as "empty mathematical scholasticism." Cf. also Section 4, of Chapter 8, of this book.
48. Cf. Jean-Baptiste Say, *Lettres à M. Malthus sur différents sujets d'économie politique* (Paris, 1820) and *Traité d'économie politique*, 6th ed. (Paris, 1841), Vol. I, Chapter XV.

49. That Say is assuming an equilibrium can also be seen from his statement that the amount of a good produced can only exceed the amount sold when too little of another good has been produced. The "market structures" of the marginal utility school even assume that output and sales are identical.

50. As Keynes wrote; cf. John Maynard Keynes, *The General Theory of Employment, Interest and Money* (London, 1936), p. 32. Although Marx takes as his starting point, when "we are only concerned with the pure phenomenon," the premise that every good produced is also sold, he states when analyzing crises: "No one can sell unless some one else purchases. But no one is forthwith bound to purchase, because he just has sold." Cf. Marx, *Capital*, op. cit., Vol. I, pp. 108, 113.

51. Keynes, *General Theory*, op.cit., pp. 32-33.

52. Ibid., p. 63. The idea "that saving and investment . . . can differ from one another" proves to be "an optical illusion" from the statical point of view. Ibid., p. 81; see also p. 74.

53. According to Keynes, positive and negative income expectations average out and are too uncertain "to exert much influence," ibid. p. 95.

54. Ibid., p. 135. The concept of the marginal efficiency of capital had previously been used by Wicksell, op.cit., Vol. I, pp. 211-22.

55. Keynes, *General Theory*, op.cit., pp. 48, 95.

56. Ibid., p. 95. Harrod makes the same assumption, when he writes "some producers find that the demand is falling off and others that it is increasing." Cf. Roy F. Harrod, *Towards a Dynamic Economics* (London, 1966), p. 81.

57. Even when the influence of expectations is recognized, their significance is played down. Cf. for instance, Milton Friedman, *Monetary Correction*, (London, 1974), p. 16. The importance of expectations is stressed by Erik Lundberg, *Studies in the Theory of Economic Expansion* (Oxford, 1955).

58. Keynes assumes a "liquidity preference" which is independent of the economic process and is determined solely by the objective interest rate level. Cf. Keynes, op.cit., pp. 168 ff.

59. Cf. Chapter 4, Section 4.

60. Gottfried Haberler, "Stagflation: An Analysis of its Causes and Cures," in *Economic Progress, Private Values, and Public Policy: Essays in Honor of William Fellner*, edited by Bela Balassa and Richard Nelson (Amsterdam, 1977), p. 312.

61. Cf. Evsey D. Domar, "Expansion and Employment" (1947); Robert M. Solow, "A Contribution to the Theory of Economic Growth" (1956); James Tobin, "A Dynamic Aggregative Model" (1955); Nicholas Kaldor and James A. Mirrlees, "A New Model of Economic Growth" (1962), all reprinted in *Macroeonomic Theory. Selected Readings*, edited by Harold R. Williams and John D. Huffnagle (New York, 1969). On the subject of the transformation of economic processes into equilibria, cf. also Kenneth J. Arrow, *Essays in the Theory of Risk-Bearing* (Amsterdam, 1971), pp. 177 ff.; Kenneth J. Arrow and F. H. Hahn, *General Competitive Analysis* (San Francisco, 1971); Fred R. Glahe, *Macroeconomics. Theory and Policy* (New York, 1977), pp. 358 ff.

Chapter 3

1. Schumpeter applied the expression "Ricardian vice" only to this case. However, since Ricardo also generalized phenomena observable in his time, this concept relates here to both types of generalization. Cf. Joseph A. Schumpeter, *History of Economic Analysis* (London, 1954), pp. 469 ff.; Helmut Arndt, "The Ricardian Vice", in *Festgabe für Friedrich Bülow zum 70. Geburtstag*, edited by Otto Stammer and Karl C. Thalheim (Berlin, 1960), pp. 37-49.

2. Ricardo, op. cit., p. 135. The question of how the remaining profit is distributed between the two countries is dealt with by many authors.
3. Many economists have transferred the theory of comparative costs from Ricardo's two-country model to a model containing many nations, without recognizing that this removes the precondition for the loss-making transaction: Why should a country complement a profitable transaction with a loss-making transaction when there is no longer any need to do so? Cf. John Stuart Mill, *Principles of Political Economy*, 7th ed. (London, 1871), Book III, Chapter 18; Jacob Viner, "The Doctrine of Comparative Costs." *Weltwirtschaftliches Archiv.*, Vol. XXXVI (1932 II); Levy and Sufrin, op. cit., pp. 380 ff; but cf. Francis E. Hyde and G. L. S. Shackle, *A New Prospect of Economics* (Liverpool, 1963), pp. 375 ff.
4. Cf. Frank W. Taussig, *International Trade* (New York 1936), p. 45; Gottfried Haberler, *Der internationale Handel* (Berlin, 1970) pp. 101-2, cf. also "The Relevance of the Theory of Comparative Advantage under Modern Conditions," in the same book. The theory of comparative costs operates with the physical unit of "hours of labour." Therefore, it cannot explain, as Haberler believes, "how the equalization" of capital movements occurs (ibid., p. 107). The different development of wages and productivity are not taken into account by Ricardo's theory, which wrongly identifies hours of labor with costs.
5. Cf. e.g., Klaus Rose, *Theorie der Aussenwirtschaft, 6th ed.* (Munich, 1976), p. 206.
6. Samuelson, *Economics*, op.cit., p. 628.
7. Ricardo overlooks the fact that those who receive less than the subsistence level become paupers and anti-social. In this respect he has already been corrected by Marx. Cf. Ricardo, op.cit., p. 93.
8. Marx, *Capital*, Vol. I, op.cit., p. 171.
9. Ibid., p. 172. Marx, like Ricardo, assumes a stationary economy, in which the number of laborers remains constant. Smith, Ricardo, and Marx included in the "means of subsistence" everything which a person needed to maintain himself.
10. As Ferdinand Lassalle called the Ricardian law of wages.
11. Cf. Donella H. Meadows, Dennis L. Meadows, Jørgen Randers, and William W. Behrens III, *The Limits to Growth* (New York, 1972) p.29.
12. Meadows, et al., op.cit., p.92.
13. Ibid., p. 29.
14. Ibid.
15. Ibid., p. 37.
16. Cf. Thomas Robert Malthus, *An Essay on the Principle of Population; or, A View of Its Past and Present Effects on Human Happiness*, 5th ed. (London, 1917), Vol. I, pp. 5 ff.; cf. also Meadows et al., op.cit., p. 36, Fig. 4.
17. Malthus, op. cit., Vol. I, p. 15.
18. Ibid., p. 5.
19. Ibid., Vol. II, pp. 306-80.
20. Malthus assumes *absolutely* constant rates of increase, and therefore does not base his writings, as is often claimed, on Turgot's "law of diminishing returns."
21. In the Federal Republic of Germany, for example, the technological revolution in agriculture has led to gross fixed assets per employee being higher in agriculture than in industry. In 1976 a job (*Arbeitsplatz*) costs an average of DM 150,000 in agriculture, but only DM 51,000 in the consumer goods industry, and only DM 53,000 even in the capital goods industry.
22. The fundamental importance of development competition for the shift in the "limits to growth" is not mentioned by either Malthus or Meadows.

23. Keynes, *General Theory*, op.cit., p. 3. The extent to which Keynes's general theory is to be understood as a reaction against the doctrines of his English predecessors is shown by James L. Cochrane, Samuel Gubins, and B.F. Kiker, *Macroeconomic Analysis and Policy* (Glenview, Ill., 1974), pp. 85 ff.; Michael R. Darby, *Macroeconomics. The Theory of Income, Employment and the Price Level,* (New York, 1976), pp. 263 ff.

24. Although Keynes has dealt extensively with international economic problems in another context, cf. John Maynard Keynes, *The Economic Consequences of the Peace* (London, 1919).

25. The resulting differences cannot be observed if only labor is regarded as a factor of production or if the three traditional factors of production are combined into two (labor and capital), as some authors do.

26. That a socialistic system, according to Senior's theory, must start with "abstinence" if it wants to expand its industry must seem paradoxical from Marx's point of view. However, Nassau W. Senior's *Letters on the Factory Act, as it affects the Cotton Manufacture* (London, 1837) could also have been written during the Soviet Union's first four decades of existence. Cf. "Senior's last hour" in Marx, *Capital*, op.cit., Vol.1, pp. 224-29.

27. Cf. Harrod, op.cit., p.92.

28. "Provided it is not too large," as Keynes adds, with reference to Spain's economic decline in the sixteenth century, cf. Keynes, *General Theory*, op.cit., p. 338.

29. Ibid., p. 245.

30. Ibid., p. 337. Many authors mention only two types of inflation: demand-pull inflation and cost-push inflation cf., e.g. Paul Burrows and Theodore Hitiris, *Macroeconomic Theory. A Mathematical Introduction* (London, 1974), p. 117.

31. Keynes takes a quantity theory of money as his starting point but then modifies it. The basis of his comments (which he himself puts in quotation marks and subsequently revises) runs: "So long as there is unemployment, *employment* will change in the same proportion as the quantity of money; and when there is full employment, *prices* will change in the same proportion as the quantity of money." Cf. Keynes, *General Theory*, op. cit., pp. 296-309.

32. In the German Reich, for example, from 1931, there were government-controlled prices (e.g., for branded goods) and price commissioners, and from May 1933 "trustees of labor" (*Treuhänder der Arbeit*), whose job was to supervise the observance of the wage freeze, which in fact already existed.

33. Cf. in this context i.e. Thomas F. Dernburg and Duncan M. McDougall, *Macroeconomics*, 5th ed. (New York, 1976), p. 213.

34. Cf. R.F. Kahn, "The Relation of Home Investment to Unemployment," *Economic Journal* 41 (1931), pp. 173 ff.

35. Keynes, *General Theory*, op.cit., pp.115-16.

Chapter 4

1. Cf., e.g., Samuelson, *Economics*, op.cit., pp.608-09; Ulmer, op.cit., pp. 652 ff., which, however, also deal with state activity; critical, e.g., Charles P. Kindleberger, *International Economics*, 4th ed (Homewood, Ill., 1968), p. 293.

2. Reprinted in David Hume, *Writings on Economics* (Edinburgh, 1955), pp.62-63.

3. Hume includes the price of all work or the advantage of the cheapness of labor and to this extent also the "income mechanism."

4. The expression "trade balance" is used here in the sense of Hume.

5. Hume, op.cit., pp.63-64.

6. Which did not exist in Hume's day.

7. Cf. Helmut Arndt, *Wirtschaftliche Macht* (Economic Power), 3rd ed. (Munich, 1980), pp. 150-155.
8. Cf. Keynes, *General Theory*, op.cit., p. 337.
9. Helmut Schneider understands "the *price-sales function* of a firm" to be " the functional relationship between the sales price and the quantity sold." Cf. Helmut Schneider, *Mikroökonomie*, 2nd ed. (Munich, 1975), p. 189.
10. Von Stackelberg, op.cit., pp. 185-186.
11. Henderson and Quandt, op.cit., p. 209.
12. Cf., for instance, ibid., pp. 190-192.
13. On this subject, cf. next chapter.
14. Cf. Section 1, Chapter 6, below.
15. John R. Hicks, *A Contribution to the Theory of the Trade Cycle*, 4th ed. (Oxford, 1961); cf. also Alan Coddington, "Hick's Contribution to Keynesian Economics," and Hicks's "Reply," in *The Journal of Economic Literature* (1979), Vol. XVII, pp. 970-88, 989-95.
16. Paul A. Samuelson, "Interactions between the Multiplier Analysis and the Principle of Acceleration," *The Review of Economic Statistics*, Vol. 21 (1939), pp. 75 ff.
17. On the present state of textbooks, cf., e.g., J. Carl Poindexter, *Macroeconomics* (Hinsdale Ill., 1976), pp. 418 ff.; Morris Perlman, *Macroeconomics* (London, 1976), pp. 139-40; Roger LeRoy Miller, *Economics Today*, 2nd ed. (San Francisco, 1976), pp. 216 ff.
18. Samuelson, *Economics*, op.cit., p. 216; cf. also D. C. Aston and J. H. Rickard, *Macroeconomics. A Critical Introduction* (London, 1970), p. 49; H. A. Marshall and J. R. Mould, *Economic Analysis. A Workbook* (London, 1971), pp. 113 ff.; Perlman, op.cit., pp. 9 ff.; Robinson and Eatwell, op. cit., pp. 110 ff.; Wykstra, op.cit., pp. 150 ff,; David C. Klingaman, *Principles of Macroeconomics*, (Belmont, Ca., 1976), pp. 94 ff.
19. The concept of mechanical movements in the field of macroeconomics is widespread. Even Friedman speaks of "mechanism" and "automatic reactions." Cf. Milton Friedman, "A Monetary and Fiscal Framework for Economic Stability," in *The American Economic Review*, Vol. 38 (1948), pp. 245 ff.
20. Samuelson, *Economics*, op.cit., p.248.
21. Hicks, *A Contribution to the Theory of the Trade Cycle*, op.cit., p.95.
22. Ibid., p.45.
23. Ibid., p.99.
24. Ibid., p. 103.
25. Ibid., p. 104.
26. Reserve capacity in the capital goods industry does not have the same effect, but still reduces the rate of acceleration.
27. It is usually not mentioned that the rate of acceleration is dependent on the machines' duration of life. Nevertheless, Samuelson gives an example from which the reader can derive this fact. Cf. Samuelson, *Economics*, op.cit., p.247. See also Poindexter, op.cit., pp. 161 ff.; Moore, op. cit. pp. 149 ff.; Frank C. Wykoff, *Macroeconomics. Theory, Evidence, and Policy* (Englewood Cliffs, N.J., 1976), pp. 188 ff. For a criticism of the oversimplifications of Samuelson and others, see Hugo Hegeland, *The Multiplier Theory*, (Lund 1954); on the premises of the acceleration principle, cf. my book, *Kapitalismus, Sozialismus . . .*, op.cit., p.93.
28. This especially applies to countries such as Japan or West Germany, who had to catch up technologically after World War II.
29. In *Economica*, NS 5 (1938), pp. 164 ff.
30. Ibid., p. 176. Some years later, J. Tinbergen, in his article "An Acceleration

Principle for Commodity Stockholding and a Short Cycle Resulting from It," established the existence of an "inventory accelerator." Cf. Tinbergen's paper in *Studies in Mathematical Economics and Econometrics* (in Memoria of Henry Schultz), edited by Oscar Lange, Francis McIntyre, and Theodore O. Yntema (Chicago, 1942).

31. The "rate of savings" in West Germany in 1973 was still 14.2%, rising to 15.7% in 1975 as unemployment increased. As expectations became positive and unemployment decreased, the "rate of savings" fell again to 14.4% in 1976.

32. The "full employment ceiling" also conflicts with the observations which Karl Marx made in the nineteenth century and which led him to assume the existence of a reserve army of industrial labor.

33. Samuelson, *Economics*, op cit., p. 248.

34. Cf. A. W. Phillips, "The Relation Between Unemployment and the Rate of Change of Money Wage Rates in the United Kingdom, 1861-1957" in *Economica*, NS 25 (1958), pp. 283 ff.; see also, e.g., Campbell R. McConnell, *Economics: Principles, Problems and Policies*, 6th ed. (New York, 1975), pp. 367 ff.; Cochrane, Gubins, and Kiker, op cit., pp. 248 ff.; Darby, op. cit., pp. 341 ff.; critical, for instance, K. W. Rothschild, "The Phillips-Curve and All That", in *Scottish Journal of Political Economy*, Vol. 18 (1971), pp. 245 ff.; Milton Friedman, *Unemployment versus Inflation? An Evaluation of the Phillips Curve* (London, 1975); Harold Wolozin, *Introduction to Economics. An Interdisciplinary Approach* (Boston, 1973), pp. 119 ff.; see also Poindexter, op. cit., pp. 370 ff.; Werner Sichel and Peter Eckstein, *Basic Economic Concepts*, 2nd ed. (Chicago, 1977), pp. 269 ff.; Perlman, op cit., p. 146; Moore, op cit., pp. 446 ff.; Wykoff, op cit., pp. 285 ff.; Wykstra, op cit., pp. 255 ff.; Miller, op cit., pp. 157 ff.; Kelvin Lancaster, *Modern Economics* (New York, 1973), p. 441; cf. also *Stability and Inflation* (Essays to Honour the Memory of A. W. H. Phillips), edited by A. R. Bergstrom et al. (New York, 1978); with regard to the "long-run Phillips-Curve," see also Edwin Mansfield, *Economics: Principles, Problems, Decisions*, 3rd ed. (New York, 1980).

35. Cf. Samuelson, *Economics*, op cit., p. 776.

36. Cf. under 4.

37. Cf. Helmut Arndt, "The German Experience: Inflation without Unemployment and the Effect of Competition," in Gardiner C. Means et al., *The Roots of Inflation* (New York, 1975), pp. 137ff. Since 1976 the situation in West Germany has changed.

38. In a dictatorship, wages can be fixed so low that they are easily compatible with full employment.

39. The same conclusion is drawn by Karl Schiller; he assumes, however, that "currency dumping" only began after his resignation from the post of West German economics minister in July 1973. Cf. Karl Schiller, "Wie lautet die wirtschaftspolitische Botschaft heute?" (What is the economic message of today?), in *Die Welt*, June 11, 1977.

40. Revaluations of undervalued currencies and devaluations of overvalued currencies are only treatments of symptoms (*Kuren am Symptom*). In a developing world economy, in which new and better products and production processes are always appearing, wage increases differ from country to country, etc., fixed exchange rates continually give rise to imbalances.

41. Cf., however, Richard T. Gill, *Economics and the Public Interest* (Pacific Palisades, Ca., 1968), pp.189 ff. The inadequacy of the division of the causes of inflation into "demand pull" and "cost push" is mentioned by William R. Hosek, *Macroeconomic Theory* (Homewood, Ill., 1975), pp. 272 ff.; cf. also Edward Shapiro, *Macroeconomic Analysis* (New York, 1966), pp. 498 ff., 514ff.

42. Cf. Keynes, *General Theory*, op.cit., p.116.
43. Economic theory tends to overlook the fundamental difference between actions and (mere) reactions (or "instinctive behavior"). Although Arrow talks of "actions" he uses it in the same sense as might be applied to the "actions" of animals. Only people who can think and create new things can act (which does not mean, however, that all human behavior consists of actions based on rational decisions). In a stationary model, human actions are not to be found. Cf. Kenneth J. Arrow, *Aspects of Risk-Bearing* (Helsinki, 1965), p.18.
44. Even Ricardo was aware of exceptions, e.g., in monetary and currency policy, cf. Ricardo, op.cit., Chapter 27 "On Currency and Banks."

Chapter 5

1. Erich Schneider, op.cit., Vol. II, p. 32.
2. Samuelson, *Economics* op.cit., pp. 360, 430, where Samuelson teaches that a firm under conditions of "perfect competition" "faces a (virtually) horizontal *dd* demand curve for its product—its elasticity of demand is infinite"; cf. also Brandt, op.cit., p. 53.
3. In reality, however, it is only *one point on the (real) sales curve:* The so-called "price-sales line" or "sales line" is produced by joining this point to the vertical axis. The real sales curve and the real demand curve, however, are not related to one price, but to different prices. Cf. my book, *Kapitalismus, Sozialismus . . .* , op.cit., p. 43.
4. Samuelson, *Economics* op.cit., p. 457 (text to Figure 25,$_1$). Samuelson understands the "*dd*-curve" to be the "firm's demand curve" which again is wrong, because Samuelson does not mean the demand of a firm, but its sales. Any firm buys and sells products. It is therefore illogical to speak of a firm's demand if its sales are meant. The confusion of demand and sales curves is found in almost all textbooks and the result of neoclassical economists wrongly identifying firms with suppliers and households with demanders or buyers. Even Sweezy does not mean the demand curve of a household but the sales curve of a firm when he misleadingly talks of the "kinky demand curve." In fact, every firm has suppliers from which it demands goods and customers to whom it sells its products. Its sales curves are therefore not identical with its demand curves. Cf. Section 1, Chapter 8, and my paper "Anpassung und Gleichgewicht am Markt" (Adjustment and Equilibrium on the Market), *Jahrbücher für Nationalökonomie und Statistik*, Vol. 170 (1958), pp. 217 ff., especially 245–46, 259–61, 462.
5. On the doctrine that customer preferences are sufficient to justify the existence of a monopoly, which was first made by Wicksell and adopted later by Sraffa, Robinson, and Chamberlin, cf. above §4 of Section 3, Chapter 2.
6. This results from the idea that an increase in production raises a firm's profit, as long as marginal revenue is higher than marginal cost, and that its profit falls, as soon as marginal cost exceeds marginal revenue.
7. Sraffa, op.cit., p. 543.
8. Cf. Chamberlin, op.cit., pp. 84–85.
9. A similar definition is to be found in my book, *Schöpferischer Wettbewerb und klassenlose Gesellschaft* (Creative Competition and a Classless Society) (Berlin, 1952), p. 111; regarding new definitions of competition, cf. also J.M. Clark, "Toward a Concept of Workable Competition," *American Economic Review*, Vol. XXX (1940), pp. 241–56; Fritz Machlup, "Competition, Pliopoly and Profit, *Economica* NS (1942), pp. 1–23, 153–73; Joel B. Dirlam and Alfred E. Kahn, *Fair Competition, The Law and Economics of Antitrust Policy* (Ithaca, N.Y., 1970); Jack

Downie, *The Competitive Process* (London, 1958); Clark, *Competition as a Dynamic Process*, op. cit.; *Wettbewerbstheorie* (Theory of Competition), edited by Klaus Herdzina (Cologne, 1975), with reprints from Schumpeter, Clark, Mason, Bain, Edwards, and others; cf. also my paper "Konkurrenz und Monopol in Wirklichkeit" (Competition and Monopoly in Reality), in *Jahrbuecher fuer Nationaloekonomie und Statistik*, Vol. 161 (1949), pp. 222–96.

10. Cf. Keynes, *General Theory*, op.cit., p. 117. Harrod speaks of the "in fact infinitely elastic . . . supply of capital," cf. Harrod, op. cit., p. 27.

Chapter 6

1. Cf. Francois Perroux, "Esquisse d' une théorie de l 'économie dominante" in *Economie appliquée*, Vol. I (1948), pp. 243 ff. Perroux mainly applied his concept of dominance to dominant countries. On the following comments, cf. my book: *Wirtschaftliche Macht*, op.cit; also my paper, "The Economic Theory of Power," in the symposion *Die Konzentation in der Wirtschaft-On Economic Concentration*, 2nd ed. (Berlin 1971) Vol. I; see also the papers of Perroux, Lord Balogh, Alexander Gerschenkron, Alec Nove, Oskar Morgenstern, Kurt W. Rothschild, Louis Zimmerman et al., in *Macht und ökonomisches Gesetz*, edited by Hans K. Schneider and Christian Watrin (Berlin, 1973), and the contributions of H. Albert, J. Harsanyi, J. Pen, D. Lynch, J.K. Galbraith, and others in *Power in Economics*, edited by K.W. Rothschild (Penguin Books, London, 1971).
2. On the economic significance of voluntary and forced revaluations, cf. my book *Wirtschaftliche Macht*, op.cit., pp. 3–16.
3. Eugen von Böhm-Bawerk, "Macht oder ökonomisches Gesetz?" in *Zeitschrift für Volkswirtschaft, Sozialpolitik und Verwaltung*, Vol. 23 (1914), p. 266.
4. Economic power is always present when a firm or household can create (economic) advantages for itself to the detriment of others. Max Weber's famous concept of power, according to which the powerful achieve their aims against opposition (*Widerstreben*), is to narrow from the economic point of view. If, for example, knowledge gives power, economic power can also be exercised without opposition. A shareholder who does not know that the management is taking something away from him cannot defend himself. The same applies to economic "bondage": anyone who has lost his own free will no longer resists. Cf. Max Weber, *Wirtschaft und Gesellschaft*, (Berlin, 1964), Vol. I, p. 38.
5. Cf. above pp. 97 f.
6. Cf. William J. Baumol, *Business Behavior, Value and Growth*, (New York, 1959).
7. With regard to the demand monopoly, cf. Section 2, Chapter 8.
8. Cf. my book *Wirtschaftliche Macht*, op.cit., pp. 13 ff., 128 ff.
9. Even if the colonies are mentioned, as by Smith, for example.
10. Meilicke even talks of enslavement when referring to affiliates of a corporation, cf. Heinz Meilicke "Korporative Versklavung deutscher Aktiengesellschaften durch Beherrschungs- und Gewinnabführungsverträge gegenüber in- und ausländischen Unternehmen," in *Berliner Festschrift für Ernst E. Hirsch* (Berlin, 1968), pp. 99 ff.
11. The concepts of the power of supply and the power of demand are misleading. It is not supply or demand, but the individual supplier or demander which in this case has the power to give orders to a partner and thereby to force him to make revaluations. Supermarkets in West Germany which force their suppliers to give them price reductions of 30 to 40%, etc., often have a market share of less than 1%. Partner's power and market power are two entirely different things. Cf. my book *Wirtschaftliche Macht*, op.cit., pp. 86 ff.

12. Cf. Ragnar Frisch, "Monopole-Polypole—La notion de force dans l'économie" in *Festschrift für H. Westergaard, Nationaløkonomisk Tidsskrift*, Vol. 71 (1933).
13. The traditional economic theory discusses neither voluntary or forced revaluations. However, the fact that wants can be manipulated is not unknown, cf. George Katona, *Psychological Analysis of Economic Behavior* (New York, 1951).
14. Cf. Myrdal, op.cit., pp. 7 ff.
15. Cf. Perroux, op.cit., who has already dealt with dominance-dependence relationships.
16. Cf. my book *Wirtschaftliche Macht*, op.cit., pp. 86–99.
17. Cf. Heinrich Kronstein, John T. Miller, Jr. and Paul P. Dommer, *Major American Antitrust Laws* (Dobbs Ferry, N.Y., 1965), p. 152; Federal Trade Commission, *Report on Motor Vehicle Industry*, (Washington, D.C., 1939), p. 181.
18. Monopolkommission, *Missbräuche der Nachfragemacht und Möglichkeiten zu ihrer Kontrolle im Rahmen des Gesetzes gegen Wettbewerbsbeschränkungen* (Baden-Baden, 1977).
19. As Alfred P. Sloan, Jr., stated as president of General Motors, cf. Federal Trade Commission, op.cit., p. 174. General Motors did not behave like an option-fixer either. If General Motors has given its dealers the choice of taking thirty additional cars or of receiving no cars at all at the end of the season, the dealers would have enthusiastically decided on the second alternative.
20. Although there were different reasons for the dependence in this case.
21. Monopoly power and partner's power can also be combined into one concept. The public, however, is more opposed to the power of a monopoly than to dominance-dependence relationships, which makes it difficult, and in many cases impossible, for a monopoly to exploit a dominant position.
22. Cf. my book *Wirtschaftliche Macht*, op.cit., pp. 26–27, 30–31.
23. Adolph A. Berle, Jr., and Gardiner C. Means, *The Modern Corporation and Private Property*, 2nd ed. (New York, 1967), who write on p. 293: "It is traditional that a corporation should be run for the benefit of its owners, the stockholders, and that to them should go any profit which are distributed. We know now, however, that a controlling group may hold the power to divert profits into their own pockets."
24. Lenel confuses the power of transnationality and the power of size in classifying as multinational firms only those corporations "which have a turnover of at least DM 500 million, a net product or owner's capital investment of at least DM 250 million and a work force of not less than 50,000." In fact, the dangers of economic power increase, the more types of power are concentrated in one hand. However, this is a completely different problem. Cf. Hans Otto Lenel, "Zur Problematik der multinationalen Unternehmen," *ORDO*, Vol. 27 (1976), p. 184.
25. Cf. von Stackelberg, op.cit., pp. 12–13; Eucken, op.cit., pp. 230–31.
26. Cf. more fully my book *Wirtschaftliche Macht*, op.cit., pp. 99–104, where I use the concept of "dominance" in a narrower sense.
27. Schumpeter, *Capitalism, Socialism and Democracy*, op. cit., Chapter 7. Schumpeter failed to recognize adjustment competition and overlooked the significance of the development of new markets for the regeneration of the concentration process.
28. Adjustment competition and development competition are presented here in simplified form. A more comprehensive analysis is to be found in my book *Kapitalismus, Sozialismus . . .* , op. cit., pp. 19–36, 37–51.

Chapter 7

1. Cf. above §5 Section 3, Chapter 6.
2. France and the United States feared that the inflowing money would cause unemployment as a result of rising domestic prices, which would restrict their exports and stimulate their imports. In today's terms, they feared stagflation as a result of imported inflation.
3. Described by Eucken as a "centrally-administered economy."
4. Views of this kind are still often found today. Thus, Wright writes that the "capitalist system . . . has not been planned in any deliberate, systematic sense." In fact, this system has been the result of state action: abolition of the guilds and of "administered" prices (prices fixed by the guilds), granting of patent rights, antiunion legislation directed against the workers, etc. Cf. F.J. Wright, *An Introduction to the Principles of Economics* (Oxford, 1965), p. 68.
5. Ricardo, op.cit., p. 93.
6. Adam Smith, op.cit., Book I, Chapter 8.
7. Also according to Marx "the sum of the means of subsistence necessary for the production of labour-power must include the means necessary for the labourers's substitutes, i.e., his children, in order that this race of peculiar commodity-owners may perpetuate its appearance in the market." Marx, *Capital*, op.cit., Vol. I, p. 172.
8. Ibid., p. 645.
9. In 1917, the monthly wage of a maid in Berlin was 15–20 Marks and that of a (female) cook 25–30 Marks.
10. On December 8, 1931, for example, the German chancellor Brüning froze the prices of branded goods (*Markenartikel*) after he had lowered their prices by ten percent. A price commissioner had the job of controlling the firms to ensure that they observed the prices fixed by the state. Similar government action is also to be found in a number of other countries.
11. Many current textbooks travel along two lines at once. They adopt the results of state-free models and point afterwards to the "economic role of government" (Samuelson). This induces an error of logic, if the economic role of government is not also analyzed with the help of models. Cf. Samuelson, *Economics*, op.cit., pp. 43–44.
12. Cf. Karl R. Popper, *The Logic of Scientific Discovery*, 2nd ed. (London, 1960), pp. 27–48, 215–50.

Chapter 8

1. Ricardo discusses this trend in connection with agriculture, Ricardo, op.cit., p. 120.
2. Marx, *Capital*, Vol. III (Hamburg, 1894; Moscow, 1971), p. 212.
3. Cf. Eugen vom Böhm-Bawerk, *Kapital und Kapitalzins*, 4th ed. (Jena, 1921), 2. Abt., Vol. I., Book 2.
4. Marx, *Capital*, op.cit., Vol. I, p. 150.
5. Ibid., Vol. III, op.cit. p. 214.
6. Ibid., Vol. I, p. 217.
7. Ibid, Vol. III, p. 819.
8. Ibid. Cf. also Robinson and Eatwell, op.cit., pp. 264–92.
9. This doctrine is to be found in almost all textbooks. Cf., e.g., Stonier and Hague, op.cit., pp. 73–74; but compare Donald Stevenson Watson, *Price Theory and Its Uses* (Boston, 1963), p. 85.
10. Thomas E. Holland, *Microeconomic Theory and Functions* (New York, 1973), pp. 56–57; Stigum and Stigum, *Microeconomics*, op.cit., pp. 45–46.

11. Cf. Marshall, op.cit., pp. 109–10.
12. Jan S. Hogendorn, *Modern Economics* (Cambridge, Mass., 1975), pp. 43–45.
13. Ibid., p. 40.
14. Cf. above §4 Section 3, Chapter 2.
15. Paul M. Sweezy, "Demand under Conditions of Oligopoly," in *Journal of Political Economy*, Vol. 47 (1939), pp. 568 ff.; George J. Stigler, "The Kinky Oligopoly Demand Curve and Rigid Prices," in *Journal of Political Economy*, Vol. 55 (1947), pp. 432 ff. The theory of the "kinky demand curve" is represented without further examination in many textbooks. Cf., e.g., Samuelson, *Economics*, op. cit., pp. 483–84; Woll, op. cit., pp. 157, 162; Henderson and Quandt, op cit., pp. 210–12; Cliff Lloyd, *Microeconomic Analysis* (Homewood, Ill., 1967), pp. 215 ff.; Frank Livesey, *A Modern Approach to Economics* (London, 1977), pp. 103–4; Josef Hadar, *Elementary Theory of Economic Behavior* (Reading, Mass., 1966), pp. 139 ff.; A. Koutsoyiannis, *Modern Microeconomics* (London, 1975), pp. 230 ff.
16. Cf. my book *Mikroökonomische Theorie* (Tuebingen, 1966), Vol. I, pp. 120–23.
17. Cf. above §2 Section 3, Chapter 1.
18. Marx, *Capital*, op.cit., Vol. I, p. 44.
19. This is not intended to dispute the fact that the opposite trend may occur, as current developments in the printing trade show.
20. Ricardo, op.cit., p. 12. The assumption that "competition operates without restraint" is often made even today, e.g., in Samuelson's "multiplier-accelerator mechanism," cf. Section 3, Chapter 4, of this book.
21. With the exception of changes in capacity.
22. This statement does not become any less valid if, disregarding the original starting point, a distinction is made between "narrow" (*enge*) and "broad" (*weite*) oligopolies. The number of competing firms is neither solely or mainly decisive for the quality or the intensity of competition. But cf. Erhard Kantzenbach, *Die Funktionsfähigkeit des Wettbewerbs*, 2nd ed. Goettingen,1967); for a criticism, cf. the papers of Erich Hoppmann and Erich Kaufer, in *Jahrbücher für Nationalökonomie und Statistik*, Vol. 179 (1966) and Vol. 181 (1967/68).
23. Both are wrong. It is not the number of participants in the market which determines the quality of competition, but qualitative aspects such as the ability to compete and the competitive spirit.
24. Eucken, op.cit., pp. 127, 146 ff., especially the table on p. 177; cf. also G.B. Richardson, *Economic Theory*, (London, 1964), pp. 111 ff.
25. Karl Menger, *Dimensionstheorie* (Leipzig, 1928), p. 76. In this context, cf. also the representation of the Keynesian model as a "system of simultaneous linear relationships" in Arthur S. Goldberger, *Econometric Theory* (New York, 1964), pp. 288 ff.
26. Where I_{ind} represents the investment initiated by the rise in consumption, β the acceleration coefficient, and $\frac{dC}{dt}$ the rise in consumption over time. Cf. Samuelson, *Economics*, op. cit., pp. 246–48; Lipsey and Steiner, op.cit., pp. 525 ff.; Ulmer, op.cit., pp. 314 ff.; Gerald Sirkin, *Introduction to Macroeconomic Theory*, 2nd ed. (Homewood, Ill., 1965), pp. 89 ff.; Allport and Stewart, op.cit., pp. 71 ff.; Thomas F. Dernburg and Judith D. Dernburg, *Macroeconomic Analysis*, (Reading, Mass., 1969), p. 169; Klein, op.cit., pp. 12, 165; Erich Schneider states as preconditions "given technology" and full capacity utilization (as well as closed economy). Two decisive preconditions are missing: (1) the operation of competition and (2) the lack of customer preferences. Cf. Erich Schneider, op.cit., Vol. III, 11th ed. (Tuebingen, 1969), p. 245.
27. Samuelson, *Economics*, op. cit., p. 247.
28. Ibid., pp. 246, 247 (Table 14-1). Samuelson also adopts the usual assumption

that demand remains constant after the increase which initiates the accelerator. In addition, he assumes a closed economy.

29. The cartels (and syndicates) in the basic materials industries (coal, iron, steel, cement, etc.), which were mostly established before the turn of the century, served not least to balance out the fluctuations in demand (and investment) initiated by the accelerator.

30. Samuelson, *Economics*, op. cit., p. 216. Cf. in this context also the representation of "dynamic models" in Goldberger, op. cit., pp. 373 ff.; cf. also Edwin G. Dolan, *Basic Economics* (Hinsdale, Ill., 1977), pp. 144 ff.; R.J. Barnes, *Economic Analysis* (London, 1971), pp. 249 ff.; Lorie Tarshis, *Modern Economics* (New York, 1967), pp. 428 ff.

31. Samuelson, *Economics*, op.cit., p. 216.

32. Samuelson, like Kahn or Keynes, does not distinguish between equilibrium income and income during the adjustment process.

33. Samuelson, *Economics*, op.cit., p. 216.

34. Keynes, *General Theory*, op.cit., Chapter 10: ". . . the total employment caused by . . . increased public works will be ten times the primary employment provided by the public works themselves . . ." (if the multiplier is 10). The result is different if the "primary investment spending" is repeated in all succeeding periods. Cf. the paper, "Der Einfluss von Erwartungen und Umwertungen auf Multiplikatorprozesse," in *Theorie und Praxis des finanzpolitischen Interventionismus*, edited by Heinz Haller et al. (Tuebingen, 1970), pp. 581–94.

35. This problem has nothing to do with the "foreign trade multiplier," cf. Samuelson, *Economics*, op.cit., pp. 621–22.

36. Where dY represents a change in (equilibrium) income, $1 - \frac{dC}{dY}$ the marginal savings quota and dI the change in investment.

37. Wicksell, op.cit., Vol. I, p. 127: "However, it is almost a tragedy that *Walras*, who is otherwise so clear and quick-thinking, believed that he had found . . . this strict proof simply by dressing up an idea, which seemed to him to be inadequate when expressed in normal language, in a mathematical formula."

38. The fact that utility is not an "interpersonally uniform unit of measurement," indeed not a unit of measurement at all, is also touched upon by Erich Streissler and Wilhelm Weber. Cf. Wilhelm Weber and Erich Streissler, "Nutzen" (Utility), in *Handwörterbuch der Sozialwissenschaften* Vol. 8, (Stuttgart, 1964), pp. 1 ff.

39. Myrdal, op.cit., pp. 94, 96.

40. Ibid. Literally, Myrdal says: "Efforts are in fact made to create a subjective theory of value with no psychological content. In so doing, those concerned have undoubtely become lost in empty mathematical scholasticism."

41. Renè Descartes, "Discours de la méthode," in *Essais philosophiques* (Leyden, 1637).

42. Adam Smith, op.cit., Book I, Chapter VI.

43. The concept "labour productivity" comes from Marx. As an increase in productivity is not due to labor but to new and better capital goods, it would be more correct to call it "capital goods' productivity."

44. "Whatever measures may be taken to create employment . . . there are essential preconditions for their success: *well ordered public finance, thrift in public and private economy and in the standard of living* . . ." Cf. *Brauns Report* (Gutachten zur Arbeitslosenfrage), (Berlin, 1931), Part II, p. 4.

45. Keynes, *General Theory*, op.cit., p. 63.

46. Cf. e.g. Erich Schneider, op.cit., Vol. III, pp. 141–42 especially 146–47.

47. Keynes, *General Theory*, op.cit., pp. 163–64.

48. The treatment of the concepts of (natural) returns and (economical) revenues is equally confusing, as more than a few authors start out from the bold assumption that the level of revenue corresponds to the amount of output. Cf. Cournot, op.cit., Chapters 5 and 7; *von Stackelberg*, op.cit., Chapter 2; Triffin, op.cit., p. 20: "The analysis leaves the time element entirely aside and proceeds on the assumption that, through costs and revenue, profits are unequivocally related to the firm's output."
49. Cf. Triffin, op.cit., pp. 74–75; see also McConnell, op.cit., p. 580.
50. Cf. John M. Blair, *Economic Concentration* (New York, 1972), pp. 19, 633.
51. The concept of the "price leader" (instead of "market leader") is still used in textbooks. Cf., Richard H. Leftwich, *The Price System and Resource Allocation*, 7th ed. (Hinsdale, Ill., 1979), pp. 305–8; Blair, op.cit., p. 588; cf. also Walter Adams, "The Steel Industry," and Lawrence J. White, "The Automobile Industry," both papers in *The Structure of American Industry*, edited by Walter Adams, 5th ed. (New York, 1977), pp. 106 ff, 187 ff.
52. Cf. Ragnar Frisch, "Propagation Problems and Impulse Problems in Dynamic Economics," in *Economic Essays in Honour of Gustav Cassel* (London, 1933); cf., e.g., also D. R. Croome and J. N. Robinson, *Understanding the Economy: An Introduction to Macroeconomic Theory* (London, 1972), Chapter 7.
53. Erich Schneider, *Statik und Dynamik, Handwörterbuch der Sozialwissenschaften*, Vol. 10, (Stuttgart, 1959), p. 23; cf. Klein, op.cit., pp. 252–59; Dernburg and McDougall, op.cit., pp. 239–47; there is an interesting diversion in Lipsey and Steiner, op.cit., p. 340; cf. also Bernard Schmitt, *Macroeconomic Theory: a Fundamental Revision* (Albeuve, 1972), pp. 15 ff.
54. Chamberlin and Robinson incorporate "quality" into their analyses, but without using diagrams with three dimensions.
55. Cf. Marx, *Capital*, op.cit., Vol. I, pp. 78, 592.
56. Cf. e.g. Samuelson, *Economics*, op.cit., pp. 44, 680–81, 812–13.; John A. Guthrie and Robert F. Wallace, *Economics*, 4th ed. (Homewood, Ill., 1968), pp. 13–14, 22–23, 782 ff.; cf. also H. Speight, *Economics, The Science of Prices and Incomes* (London, 1964),pp. 103 ff.
57. W. Stanley Jevons, *The Theory of Political Economy*, 2nd ed., (London, 1879), p. 112.
58. Cf. Joseph A. Schumpeter, *Theorie der wirtschaftlichen Entwicklung* (Theory of Economic Development), 5th ed. (Berlin, 1952), pp. 334 ff. On the theory of growth, see Domar, op cit.; Solow, op. cit.; Solow, *Growth Theory* (Oxford, 1970); cf. also Nicholas Kaldor, "Capital Accumulation and Economic Growth," in *The Theory of Capital*, edited by F. A. Lutz and D. C. Hague (London, 1963), pp. 177 ff.; R. G. D. Allen, *Macro-Economic Theory. A Mathematical Treatment* (London, 1967), Chapters 13 and 14; William H. Branson, *Macroeconomic Theory and Policy* (New York, 1972), pp. 366 ff., 391 ff.; cf. also the essays of Edward F. Denison, Thomas M. Humphrey, and Robert M. Solow et al. in *Readings in Macroeconomics*, edited by William E. Mitchell et al. (New York, 1974), pp. 219 ff.; and especially Gottfried Bombach, "Wirtschaftswachstum," in *Handwörterbuch der Sozialwissenschaften*, Vol. 12 (Stuttgart, 1965), who speaks of a "natural rate of progress."
59. Von Stackelberg, for example, only considers the "free economy" (*freie Verkehrswirtschaft*) to be conceivable as a "closed system" "if it is composed . . . of markets with perfect competition, with polypolistic competition or with isolated monopolies." Cf. von Stackelberg, op.cit., p. 335.
60. Cf. Eucken, op.cit., pp. 114–15, 122 ff., 126 ff., 146 ff. Like many other authors, Eucken includes under the free economy all the market structures listed in his table, cf. p. 177.

61. Cf. as example of many other authors, Samuelson, *Economics*, op.cit., Chapter 4; Brehm, *Introduction to Economics*, op.cit., pp. 10 ff.; W. Carl Biven, *An Introduction to Economics* (Columbus, Ohio, 1970), pp. 228 ff., 237 ff.; Barnes, op.cit., pp. 40 ff., 110 ff.; Leftwich, op.cit., pp. 87, 145–55, 231–92.

62. Cf. e.g., Erich Schneider, op.cit., Vol. II, p. 73, but see also Samuelson, *Economics*, op.cit., p. 458.

63. Cf. Erich Schneider, op.cit., Vol., II, pp. 142 ff., for whom "uniformity of a good" is compatible with personal, material, and geographical price differentiation.

64. Cf. Woll, op.cit., pp. 149 ff.

65. Cf. Leftwich, op.cit., pp. 29–32. However, the model of perfect competition has nothing to do with real competition. In reality, competition is an adjustment process and a development process. Cf. my book *Schöpferischer Wettbewerb* (Creative Competition), op.cit.; Downie, *The Competitive Process*, op.cit., and many others.

66. The same is true for the cobweb theorem, which applies a result from the model of perfect competition (i.e., $MC = P$) to oscillatory processes which take place within space and time. Oskar Lange and all other economists who adopt his solution have in this case exchanged basic premises without realizing it. Cf., e.g., Samuelson, *Economics*, op.cit., pp. 381–83, whose description also contains an inherent contradiction. On p. 380 (and pp. 58–59) he states that the supply curve shifts under the same conditions as he gives on pp. 381–83 for it remaining constant. Cf. also Barnes, op.cit., pp. 73 ff.; Richard A. Bilas, *Microeconomic Theory. A Graphical Analysis*, (New York, 1967), pp. 31 ff.; Donald S. Watson and Mary A. Holman, *Price Theory and Its Uses*, 4th ed. (Boston, 1977), pp. 242 ff.; Dernburg and Dernburg, op.cit., pp. 100 ff.; Dolan, op.cit., pp. 390 ff., who discusses the cobweb theorem in connection with agricultural markets; Allport and Stewart, op.cit., pp. 366 ff., who speak of "a simple dynamic theory of price."

67. Cf., above §5 Section 4, Chapter 2.

68. Cf., e.g., Lipsey and Steiner, op.cit., pp. 457, 459, 461; Ferguson, op.cit., pp. 349 ff.

69. Cf. Klein, op.cit., pp. 146, 199–200.

70. On the subject of the concept "true," cf. Bertrand Russell, *Einführung in die mathematische Philosophie* (Introduction to Mathematical Philosophy) (Darmstadt, n.d.), pp. 163–64, 204; cf. also Rudolf Carnap, *Der logische Aufbau der Welt. Scheinprobleme in der Philosophie*, 2nd ed. (Hamburg, 1961), pp. 252 ff., especially 253. But cf. Karl R. Popper, *The Poverty of Historicism* (London, 1957), who like Comte and Mill emphasizes "the unity of method" for "theoretical or generalizing sciences, whether they are natural sciences or social sciences," (p. 130) without, however, mentioning the decisive material difference: the theoretical natural sciences examine a (mainly) constant object of analysis, while the theoretical social sciences investigate an object of analysis which is variable as a result of the human ability to create new things—and therefore of human actions and human "policy" and in which experiences, expectations, and valuations change, and learning processes, and innovations are relevant. The method of the natural sciences are therefore not directly applicable to the social sciences.

Chapter 9

1. On the theories of "monopolistic" and "imperfect" competition, cf. Section 3, Chapter 2.

2. Insofar as the authors do not differentiate between "short-run" and "long-run" supply curves, thereby contradicting Jevons's law of indifference.
3. There are certain exceptions in authors such as Sraffa, Chamberlin, Joan Robinson.
4. According to Marx (and many textbook authors of today), equivalents are exchanged, cf. Marx, *Capital*, Vol. I, op.cit., Part I and II.
5. Although he mentions the necessity of net investment in Vol. III, as will be remembered. Cf. Marx, *Capital*, Vol. III, op.cit., p. 819.
6. Cf. my book *Kapitalismus, Sozialismus*, op.cit., pp. 2 ff.
7. Ibid., pp. 182–204.
8. Cf. Jürg Niehans, "Economics: History, Doctrine, Science, Art," in *Kyklos*, Vol. 34 (1981), pp. 165–77, who maintains "that the object of economics is the chain of unique events we call human history" (p. 165). This is a misunderstanding, although Walter Eucken already believed that our object is "economic reality as it is today and as it has ever been" (Eucken, op.cit., p. 104). However, history and theory are two entirely different fields with two different objects of analysis.
9. On the method of varying abstraction which does not operate solely with price and quantity, but gradually incorporates all economic important values into the analysis, cf. my book, *Kapitalismus, Sozialismus*, op.cit., pp. 11 ff.
10. Cf. Joan Robinson, "Time in Economic Theory," in *Kyklos*, Vol. 33 (1980), pp. 219–29: "All this . . . indicates work to be done, provided that we give up the search for grand general laws and are content to try to enquire how things happen" (p. 228).

Index of Names

Abbott, 38, 199
Adams, 204
Albert, 199
Allen, 204
Allport, 190, 202, 205
Amoroso, 126, 129
Arrow, 112, 190, 193, 197
Aston, 196
Attiyeh, 189

Bach, 189
Bacon, 142
Bain, 199
Balassa, 193
Balogh, 199
Barnes, 203, 205
Baumol, 135, 199
Becker, 190
Behrens III cf. Meadows, D.L.
Bentham, 20f., 136
Berle, 143, 200
Bergstrom, 197
Bilas, 205
Biven, 205
Blair, 173, 204
Bodin, 87
Böhm, 47
Böhm-Bawerk, 129, 131, 199, 201
Bombach, 204
Bowley, 41, 44, 189, 190
Brandt, 192, 198
Branson, 204
Brauns, 171, 203
Brehm, 189, 205
Brems, 191
Brüning, 142
Bülow, 193
Büsch, 49
Burrows, 195

Carnap, 205
Cassel, 204
Chamberlin, 26, 42, 45f., 52f., 57, 123f., 157, 189, 190ff., 198, 204, 206
Clark, 191, 198f.
Cochrane, 195, 197
Coddington, 196

Comte, 205
Cournot, 26, 41ff., 126, 129, 135f., 157, 162, 168f., 173, 191, 204
Croome, 204

Dale, 190
Darby, 195, 197
Deane, 188
Denisen, 204
Dernburg, J.D., 202, 205
Dernburg, Th.F., 195, 202, 204f.
Descartes, 203
Dewett, 189
Dewey, 189, 191
Dirlam, 198
Dolan, 203, 205
Domar, 65, 97, 103, 193, 204
Dommet, 200
Downie, 199, 205

Eatwell, 189, 196, 201
Eckstein, 197
Edgeworth, 19, 21f., 25, 34, 114, 156, 159, 188
Edwards, 199
Engels, 175
Erhard, 101
Eucken, 46ff., 162, 173, 177, 190ff., 200ff., 204

Federal Trade Commission, 200
Fellner, 193
Ferguson, 190, 205
Fourier, 150
Friedman, 16ff., 73, 189, 193, 196f.
Frisch, 65, 137f., 174, 200, 204

Galbraith, 199
German Monopolies Commission, 140, 200
Gerschenkron, 199
Giffen, 155f.
Gill, 197
Glahe, 193
Goldberg, 88, 192
Goldberger, 202f.
Gossen, 20ff., 28f., 32, 34, 156, 159

207

Gubins, 195, 197
Gutenberg, 190, 192
Guthrie, 204

Haberler, 64, 68, 110, 193f.
Hadar, 202
Hague, 192, 201, 204
Hahn, 193
Haller, 203
Harrod, 65, 193, 195, 199
Harsanyi, 199
Hayek, 14, 42, 191
Hegel, 37
Hegeland, 196
Helmstädter, 189
Henderson, 91, 189, 196, 202
Herdzina, 199
Hicks, 65, 95ff., 100, 103, 112, 196
Hirsch, 199
Hitiris, 195
Hogendorn, 156, 202
Holland, 155, 201
Holman, 205
Hoppman, 202
Hosek, 197
Howard, 190
Huffnagle, 193
Hume, 85ff., 97, 104ff., 112, 178, 187,
    195
Humphrey, 204
Hyde, 194

Jaffé, 188
Jevons, 20, 22, 28, 37ff., 42f., 46, 49,
    53f., 95, 130, 137, 157, 160, 174f.,
    177, 188, 190ff., 204, 206

Kahn, A.E., 198
Kahn, R.F., 80, 100, 165f., 195, 203
Kaldor, 193, 204
Kant, 19, 39ff., 129, 167, 188, 190
Kantzenbach, 202
Katona, 200
Kaufer, 202
Kehrbach, 188
Kennedy, 150
Keynes, 46, 61ff., 66, 73ff., 83f., 87, 95,
    100f., 104, 106, 110ff., 117, 129, 148,
    151f., 165f., 168, 171f., 176, 178, 184,
    193, 195f., 197, 199, 202f.
Kiker, 195, 197
Kindleberger, 195
Klein, 58, 112, 178, 189, 202, 204f.

Klingaman, 196
Kohler, 188, 190
Koopmans, 16, 188
Koutsoyiannis, 202
Krelle, 192
Kronstein, 200

Lancaster, 47, 197
Lange, 47, 55ff., 192, 197, 205
Lassalle, 194
Leftwich, 204f.
Lenel, 47, 177, 200
Lenin, 74
Leontief, 47, 55ff., 192
Levy, 189f., 194
Lichtenberg, 9f.
Lipsey, 189, 192, 202, 204f.
Livesey, 202
Lloyd, 202
Lumsden, 189
Lundberg, 193
Lutz, 204
Lynch, 199

Machlup, 198
Malthus, 66, 70ff., 194
Mandeville, 171
Mansfield, 197
Marcuse, 70
Marshall, A., 21, 156, 184, 189f., 202
Marshall, H.A., 196
Marx, 18f., 24f., 35f., 66, 68f., 94, 103,
    141, 146, 148, 150f., 153ff., 160, 163,
    170f., 174f., 182, 187f., 193ff., 197,
    201ff., 206
Mason, 199
McConnell, 197
McCormick, 190
McDougall, 195, 204
McIntyre, 197
Meadows, D.L., 66, 70, 72, 194
Meadows, D.H., cf. Meadows, D.L.
Means, 143, 197, 200
Meilicke, 199
Menger, 28, 137, 163, 190, 202
Mill, 194, 205
Miller, J.T., 200
Miller, R.L., 196f.
Mirrlees, 193
Mitchell, 204
Moore, 192, 196f.
More, 22
Morgenstern, 199

Mould, 196
Myrdal, 138, 170, 192, 200, 203

Nelson, 193
Nevin, 189
Niehans, 95, 167, 185, 206
Nichols, 192
Nicholson, 188, 192
Nove, 199

Ott, 41, 162, 190, 192

Pareto, 21f., 28f., 37, 156, 159, 170, 189
Pen, 199
Perlman, 196f.
Perroux, 138, 199f.
Peterson, 188
Phillips, 104f., 110, 197
Plato, 17f., 188
Poindexter, 196f.
Popper, 70, 180, 201, 205
Preiser, 47, 191
Proudhon, 24f., 150

Quandt, 91, 189, 196, 202
Quesnay, 178

Randers cf. Meadows, D.L.
Reynolds, C.W., 192
Reynolds, L.G., 189
Ricardo, 18f., 35f., 61, 66ff., 103, 112,
    146, 148, 150f., 153f., 160f., 163, 168,
    170, 182, 187, 190, 193f., 197, 201f.
Ricci, 192
Richardson, 202
Rickard, 196
Robinson, J., 26, 42, 45f., 153, 157,
    173, 180, 184, 189ff., 196, 198, 201,
    204, 206
Robinson, J.N., 204
Rodenstein-Rodan, 192
Rogers, 189
Rose, 194
Rothschild, 197, 199
Russell, 205

Samuelson, 17, 23, 25, 41, 46ff., 52ff.,
    57f., 65, 68, 95ff., 100, 102ff., 112ff.,
    116, 153, 163f., 166f., 173, 187ff.,
    192, 194ff., 201ff.
Samuels, 11ff.
Say, 61f., 150, 168, 192f.
Schiller, 197

Schmitt, 204
Schmölders, 191
Schneider, E., 26, 41f., 49, 52, 113f.,
    163, 174, 177, 189ff., 198, 202ff.
Schneider, H., 196
Schneider, H.K., 199
Schopenhauer, 173
Schultz, 192, 197
Schumpeter, 176, 186, 190, 193, 199f.,
    204
Schwier, 189
Senior, 171, 195
Schackle, 194
Shapiro, 197
Shaw, 148
Sichel, 197
Sirkin, 202
Sloan, 200
Smith, 18f., 24f., 52, 68, 133, 146,
    148ff., 163, 168, 170f., 183, 187f.,
    194, 201, 203
Sidgewick, 41
Solow, 65, 104, 112, 158, 175, 193,
    204
Speight, 204
Sraffa, 45f., 121, 157, 188, 190ff., 198,
    206
Stackelberg, v., 39ff., 44, 50, 52, 91,
    162, 190ff., 196, 200, 204
Stammer, 193
Steiner, 189, 192, 202, 204f.
Stewart, 190, 202, 205
Stigler, 190, 202
Stigum, B. 192, 200
Stigum, M.L., 192, 200
Stonier, 192, 201
Streissler, 203
Sufrin, 189f., 194
Sweezy, 157f., 202
Swift, 88

Tarshis, 203
Taussig, 68, 194
Thalheim, 193
Tinbergen, 99, 192, 196f.
Tisdell, 190
Tobin, 65, 193
Toynbee, 85
Triffin, 44, 173, 191, 204
Trotsky, 74
Turgot, 23, 194

Ulmer, 192, 202

Veblen, 156
Viner, 194
Voltaire, 130

Wallace, 204
Walras, 21, 28, 137, 188, 203
Watrin, 199
Watson, 201, 205
Weber, M., 199
Weber, W., 203
Weidenaar, 188
Weiler, 188
Westergaard, 200
White, 204

Wicksell, 45ff., 168, 188, 191, 193, 198, 203
Williams, 193
Wöhe, 190
Woll, 49, 91, 177, 192, 205
Wolozin, 197
Wright, 201
Wykoff, 196f.
Wykstra, 196f.

Yntema, 197

Zeno, 116
Zimmermann, 199